Broken Harmone:

My House Series, Book 2

By

M. Marie Walker

This book is not a standalone.

This is a work of fiction. Names, characters, places, brands, media, and incidents are the products of the author's imagination or are used fictitiously. Any resemblance to actual events, or persons, living or dead, is entirely coincidental.

No part of this book may be reproduced, stored in a retrieval system, scanned, photographed, transmitted, or distributed in any printed or electronic form without explicit written permission from the author.

**Trigger Warning: Abduction, Abuse, Violent behavior, Strong language, Moderate graphic scenes. Sexual Assault.

Disclaimer: The book cover uses a model image. There is no connection between the models in the image and the characters in the novel. The individuals depicted are models and used only for illustrative purposes.

I dedicate this book to everyone who believes in love. Who believes that life is full of second chances. For the ones who know that even though obstacles may get in the way, real love always finds its way back to one another. This is for you. Keep believing.

TABLE OF CONTENTS

PROLOGUE

Late May

Fifteen Years Ago

"Where the hell is she?" I glance at my watch for the sixth time, pacing back and forth across the patchy grass of the park. We've met here every day for the past five years, so I know the area well. As I push my freshly twisted hair out of my face for the third time; I run my tongue over my stupid braces. I'm glad I only have another year to wear them. After stopping in front of our bench, I remove the ring from my pants pocket. As if it were a national treasure, I hold it securely in my damp palm.

Today, I'll tell her how I feel about her. No turning back… not that I want to. Even when we'd first met at eleven years old—me, the skinny annoying little boy with braces, and her, the fiery little girl with sandy brown hair, glasses, and the butterfly birthmark—I knew she was special from that moment.

I put the ring back into my pocket and continued to pace. What if she doesn't take me seriously? What if I make a fool of myself? I exhale a shaky breath, releasing the sudden onslaught of unease I'm experiencing. She's the secret I've kept hidden from everyone; Marlon being the only exception. He swears he won't tell anyone because you know, bro code and all.

Call me selfish, but I want what we have to stay between us. She and I are just friends though. *I* want us to be more than that, but I don't know if she feels the same. I mean, if she gets tongue-tied, a racing heart, and tingly all over every time we see each other, then maybe she *does* feel like I do... or it could be a sign of a medical condition. I don't know, shit. I smile, knowing that's so far-fetched. Bee gets me though; knows the *real* me and still sticks around.

I appreciate the hell out of her... love her, and whenever she gets here, I'm gonna tell her that— I catch the distinct fragrance of vanilla and cocoa as the wind whistles by me. I know it's *her*. When I turn, she's standing a few inches from me, her eyes widening as if she was getting scolded for something.

It's beautiful here. The trees surround us. They're covered with vibrant leaves; the sun spying on us with its warm rays of light. Squirrels dart through the grass, and birds chirp in the branches as they sway. Joggers pass by on the hiker's trail, kicking up the dirt, but I only see *her*. Perfect almond shaped eyes, full lips, and a figure that would put Ryan Destiny to shame. I am absolutely captivated by her beauty.

She fidgets in front of me, as her words come out in a breathless rush. "So sorry I'm late. My mom wouldn't let me leave until I opened the gifts my granny sent."

Some might argue that a sixteen-year-old doesn't know what

love is, but *this* sixteen-year-old has no doubt about it. I know that if it hadn't been for Bee these past five years, I would have lost my mind. She's been a lifeline to me.

I can't look away. It's as if I'm in a trance, dazed by the sheer vision of her. She's not dressed in her usual jeans and T-shirt. No, she's wearing a yellow and white flowered sundress that fit every curve of her perfect body.

She creases her brows. "What's wrong? Is it too much? I knew I should've come in jeans and a T-shirt. I look stupid, right? I don't know what—"

"You look beautiful, Brooklyn Avery. You're… perfect." I confess, moving to stand in front of her. Her hair isn't in its usual ponytail, but thick, sandy brown locks flow over her shoulders, waving softly with the breeze. "Sorry I didn't say anything at first. Honestly, you took my breath away and I couldn't form words." I move closer. "I-Is this, okay?" I ask, gently brushing the hair away from her eyes.

She jumps at the sudden gesture, her brows raised to her hairline but then her expression relaxes a bit as she nods and smiles that infectious smile that always warms my heart and gets my blood pumping. "Happy sweet 16th birthday, Brooklyn." I kiss her cheek. . As the sun kisses her skin, the shimmering of her favorite strawberry lip gloss attracts my attention. Her entire transformation has me gawking at her.

I can't remember how we decided not to tell each other our

real first names— well, we used our real *middle* names— but instead, made-up nicknames. I came up with the idea when we were eleven years old— even though it's not the first time I've pretended to be somebody else. It's funny, even though Bee and I are as tight as a knotted rope, we've never gone to the same schools; never had an encounter where someone used our real names in front of one another, but the nicknames just stuck. It feels… natural for us.

"Thank you, Harmone Julian." Her voice just above a whisper, as she grazes my jaw with her knuckle. Slowly, her hand descends until she reaches my bottom lip, brushing the pad of her thumb against it. I swallow hard. All the blood in my sixteen-year-old body rushes southward in a split second.

I peek over Brooklyn's shoulder as another jogger breezes past, getting an eye full of the PDA show we're putting on in the semi-secluded area of the park. "Why did you dress differently today?" I ask, my attention drawn to her sparkling bronze eyes. She's not wearing her glasses, so the light dusting of toffee eyeshadow reminds me of brown sugar dipped in gold. "Are you tryin' something new?" I refocus my eyes on her lips.

"For you. I… wanted you to finally see me… that I'm not *just* your friend but a… woman." Her eyes find mine; my breath catching as she explores my chest with her other hand feeling through my shirt, a fire in her eyes that I've never seen before.

Holding onto Brooklyn's hand, I stop her movements. I need

to use my words right now, and I can't do that with her fingers roaming my body. "I *see* you. I've always seen you, Brooklyn. You're the highlight of my day. For the last five years, you've been an anchor for me; my calm, and one day when we're old enough, I'm gonna marry you." I take the promise ring from my pants pocket. My hand trembles as I hold it out to her. It took me an entire year to save up for it but I was determined to get her a gift that's real, not some knock-off.

She glances down at the emerald promise ring—her birthstone—and back to me again, her eyes shimmering with unshed tears. "Promise?"

With unyielding love, I say, "I promise." My hand quivers, as I take her soft one in mine and place the ring on her finger. I kiss her hand afterwards as if it's the most coveted jewel in the world.

Brooklyn rises on her toes, brushing her lips against mine. Embers of kinetic flames explode inside of my body, as I reach for Bee's waist, pulling her closer. My hand travels the length of her back as she wraps her arms around my neck. I know from this point on, she's it for me…. She's my forever.

Later that evening……..

I sit on our park bench, wincing in pain from the body shots my dad rained down on me an hour ago. What a difference six hours make; from absolute excitement to extreme hate. From past beatings and broken arms, to fractured ribs and the various cigarette burns to my chest— resentment for Don is rooted in my DNA.

I made the mistake of stepping in between him and my mom fighting— well, him beatin' on my mom— and paid the price for it.… again. Of course, I would go through hell and back for her, but I don't get why she just doesn't leave him. He will end up killing her one day, and that's the day I'm gonna take *his* life.

When shit like this happens, I need to vent and Bee's listened to plenty of my angry rages in the past— like when I go on rants because I can't run away and leave my siblings and mom behind. She's been there to center me through all my constant struggles.

I hold onto my pulsing side while checking my phone. Over an hour now. My gut clenches as tight as a bow string. She at least texts if she's running late— and that's rare.

Worry spreads over me like hot tar on a weathered roof. I inhale a ragged breath, causing the pain to radiate. I lift my t-shirt: deep purplish bruising and swelling. Pulling my shirt back down, I exhale carefully. "Shit." It's been about a year since the last time this happened, but how my ribs throb is nothing compared to the feeling of dread that's ever-present in my gut.

I try calling. Straight to voicemail. Damn it. Something has to be wrong. "Hey Brooklyn, is everything alright? Call me when you get a chance, I'm worried. I just… I need you. Okay, bye." I end the message on a jagged exhale. I lean back against the park bench; frustration, disappointment and unease invading me all at once. I wait another hour. Nothing. I'm officially freaking out now. She's never— my phone buzzes in my lap. I fumble with it then answer. "Brooklyn! Are you alright—"

"Not her, bro, sorry. She didn't show?" I hear the concern in my brother's voice.

I sigh; shoulders slump as I tilt forward. It feels as if I'm being buried under the snow of an avalanche. "No, and it's unlike her. I'm worried, Marlon."

My younger brother is the backbone of our family. Even though he's a couple of years younger, he's protective of me and our younger sister, MyIesha.

Marlon and Iesha are like night and day. In the midst of chaos, my brother is usually level-headed. He wears his heart on his sleeve; he's one in a million. MyIesha, on the other hand, is a bit of a firecracker. She's outspoken, over-exaggerates and whatever flows through her mind, comes out of her mouth. She's gotten into more than a few fights because of her smart-ass mouth. She's a handful, even at age twelve. Marlon has a way of keeping us in line though. It's a trait he inherited from our mom.

"I know, but you need to get home. Dad found out you were gone, and he's pissed." He whispers through the other end of the line. Don must be close.

I hurt as I stand, starting to walk toward the trail that leads out of the park. "I'm on my way." I take off in a sprint. My ribs feel every vibration against the hard pavement. "Thanks, bro." I pant before ending the call and race down the near empty street. Don's gonna beat the hell out of me.

As I hobble into the house, the pounding in my side is so bad, it made it difficult to breathe.

"Where the hell were you?!" Don bellows, meeting me at the front door. I straighten a bit, refusing to let him see me suffer.

He reminds me of a bear protecting its territory— Don's territory being this house, and everything attached to it. That meant *us*. His eyes are wild, dangerous, and glow with hellish intent. He weighs twice as much as me— all muscle— overshadowing me like a lion that's captured its prey.

"I had to meet up with a friend."

"Yeah? What friend? I know all of them. And I told your ass not to go out after nine o'clock, didn't I?!" He roars, jabbing his finger into my chest.

"I have friends you don't know about. And it was important, sorry." I grunt, justified anger flowing through me. I know I'm asking for it, but I don't care. I need to find—

"Who?!" He demands, his nostrils flaring like a raging bull.

"None of your business." I shove past him. "You *wanted* me home. I'm home. Leave me alone."

He catches my arm and swings me around like a rag doll. With the force of him swinging my body back toward him, an intense jolt of pain shoots from my ribs to my chest. I clutch at my side, gasping.

Don grins at my discomfort, then with a demanding growl, he says, "Give me your cell." He grabs my t-shirt, jerking me toward him.

"You're not gettin' my phone!"

"Give me the goddamn phone, Mike!" Don snatches my cell from me, pushing me so hard, I slam against the front door, doubling the burning agony shooting through me. I crumble to the floor as I begin to feel beads of sweat form on my forehead.

He backs away as he scrolls down my messages. The look that travels across Don's face is as cold as his frigid heart; I know without a doubt, he found the texts between me and Brooklyn. With a snarl, the bastard throws my phone against the wall, shattering any hopes of contacting her. I feel sick to my stomach.

"You son of a bitch!" I yell through the agony. I try to stand, but slide back to the floor, and scream as sweat drenches my face.

Don takes his time walking the short distance over to me, then kneels until he's eye-level. "You need to get that checked out, son. You don't look so good." He says with the most menacing grin I've ever seen. Then, leaning forward, he kisses my forehead with the gentleness of a loving parent before standing again. I lean my head against the wall, closing my eyes to stop tears from falling; Brooklyn's face is the last thing I see before darkness blurs my vision.

CHAPTER 1

Present Day

Thanksgiving

I stand in the center of my living room, speechless, as if I'm in the middle of a horror movie. My brother, his girlfriend, Koko, and their newborn baby girl that she cradled in her arms, sit on the oversized sofa. Her brother, George is beside her, as Jermaine leans against the arm of the sofa; all of them gaping at the circus that's happening before their eyes.

Searching every face in the room, I catch glimpses of shock, guilt, sorrow, or ruin carved into each of their expressions.

MyIesha, my baby sister, is standing between the sofa and Christmas tree, having an ear-piercing, one-sided argument with her cheating boyfriend, Jason. He stands there with drooped shoulders, taking every bit of fury coming from my sister, that he so rightly deserved.

Jakyra— who's supposed to be my damn wife— stands guilty before me, shaking her head. I don't understand why she's acting like she's done nothing— she thinks she can erase the countless bouts of infidelity she's committed— the latest one resulting in pregnancy.

Everything looks the same, but it isn't. I can see the festive décor throughout the house, and half-eaten pie remains on the table. The family's still gathered together, but from the moment I discovered Jakyra wasn't carrying my baby, my entire world changed. The pounding in my chest is so loud, I can barely make out what Jakyra's saying— it sounds more like begging than anything else. I can't believe she did this *again*.

I changed myself for her, inside and out. I've gone to AA, I sat through anger management sessions, I cut my damn French braids, and switched out my jeans and tees for a suit and tie. It's not a complete change; but I've come a long way. With a bad attitude and drinking binges, I wasn't exactly a joy to be around. I was a mess, but did she have to do this?

I jerk my head in Jason's direction. "What happened to family, *brothers*?" I tighten my jaw, fury burning in my gut the longer I glare at him. "I trusted you, goddamn it!" I yell. Jason finally tears his gaze away from the floor, peering over at me before averting his guilty eyes again. I clench and unclench my fists. When I get a hold of him, I swear on all that's unholy, I'm gonna—

"Please, Mike!" Jakyra begs with desperation as she reaches

for me.

I step back. My chest feels so tight, I can barely breathe. It's as if my lungs refuse to fill with oxygen. "Don't fuckin' touch me, Jakyra!" I snap. The hurt I feel in my chest is so agonizing, I can barely keep myself upright. I clench my fists even tighter to channel my anger there but fail.

Backing away a little more, I take in Jakyra's current state: her tired, puffy red eyes, slouched stature, and the now noticeable bulge in her belly; a tiny life growing inside that I'll never get the chance to experience with her. How the hell did I *not* notice that her belly is bigger than it's supposed to be at two months. Well, I guess thinking that your wife is carrying *your* child, not someone else's, is a valid fuckin' reason.

I chance another glance at her. She seems exhausted. Before our separation, she suffered almost two years of abuse and neglect— not to mention the shit I put her through these last few months alone. *I* did this to her; forced her to the edge of the cliff and pushed her right over. My heart aches for a whole different reason now.

I still love her, but the wounds that she inflicted on me with her continuous unfaithfulness are too deep to repair now. This isn't anything new though. Jakyra's been doin' this shit before we even separated over a year ago. Even though her cheating in the past is my damn fault too, when we got back together these past eight months, I thought things had changed. I was wrong.

My eyes begin to mist over; I can't continue to hurt her, or myself. Now, she's having another man's baby… someone I considered a brother. This is the last straw. "I want a divorce." I push the words out, barely completing the sentence. Four little words that will change my life from this point on.

I turn away, heading for the door. I need to get out of here as soon as possible. The walls seem like they're closing in on me, as the reality of what I just said began to sink in. My heart tears a thousand different ways. From behind me, I hear her call out to me in anguish, pleading for me not to leave. I can't. I might damn well change my mind if I look back, so I storm out the door.

As I step into the crisp night air, I exhale, long and deep, closing my eyes as the tears begin to fall. "Fuck. I need a drink." I breathe out, wiping the tears off of my face. I Google the nearest bar, hell, looking for *anywhere* that serves alcohol, so I can dull this pain I'm feeling right now. I'm angry at myself for still caring. I want to hold her in my arms, but guilt is outweighing anger at this point. After everything I did to Jakyra, all that I put her through, she still loves me. Still stayed. And me? The first opportunity I get, I bolt.

Then I think about MyIesha's boyfriend, one of my supposed best friends. Heaviness presses down on me even more as I scroll until I find what I'm searching for… because right now, I really need that damn drink. Shoving my phone back into my pocket, I rush to my SUV, and head to my destination. I wanna forget this night ever happened.

CHAPTER 2

Jakyra

"Michael no! Please come back! I'm so sorry!" I beg, as I watch him walk out the door and out of my life. The slam of the door echoes throughout the house, and my knees buckle under me as I collapse to the floor, devastated.

I hear talking or… arguing? I don't know, but the sound of voices surrounds me. I don't bother to make out what's being said because my mind is a jumbled mess at this point. My worst fear happened today. What I dreaded unraveled right before my eyes.

My heart clenches in my chest, smashing the hope inside of me, to tiny pieces. I lost him for good this time. My marriage with Mike is in ruins, and it's all my fault. I pushed him too far; shattered this little world we created for ourselves, and now…now…. he's left me.

I cheated on him… again. I'm pregnant with another man's

child. Not just *any* man, someone I *knew* was off limits; who Mike considered family. Damn it, why did I think it was a good idea to sleep with Jason in the first place. Why did I—

"I agree. I'll take her with me. You can let Mike know where she is if he wants to talk." My brother, Jermaine, responds to Marlon; his tone even, but laced with concern. His voice helps to drag me out of my thoughts. I'm sure Jermaine knows there's little chance of Mike coming to find me, but I appreciate him trying to lift my spirits.

I feel the warmth of his arm as he wraps them securely around my waist, guiding me toward the door.

When was I even lifted from the floor?

As we exit the house, Jermaine stops in front of me, pulling me into a tight embrace. "I'm so sorry this happened to you. I hate to see you hurting like this." My wonderful brother consoles, as he gently strokes my back in soothing circles. I bury my face into his chest releasing every ounce of loss and distress, sobbing so intensely that I can barely catch my breath.

I'm so glad he's here. Jermaine is laid-back and supportive of both me and our eldest brother. Johnee, not so much. He's a bit rough around the edges, stubborn and an asshole at times, but he loves us and would protect us with his life.

I grip Jermaine a little tighter, as tears splatter my cheeks, soaking the middle of his shirt. "It- it's all my fault. *I* did this. I deserve everything that comes my way." I choke out, voice gravelly from crying. I try to control my sobs, but it's no use.

Jermaine pulls back slightly so that his intent stare bore into my dismal one. "No Kyra, you *don't* deserve this. Yes, you fucked up, but all the shit that's happened up to this point wasn't all you." He wraps his arm around my slumped shoulders and leads me to the car, helps me inside, even secures me in the seat belt—*bless his heart*— then closes my door. As he hops in the driver seat and starts the engine, he says, "Who knows, maybe after Mike calms down, he'll—"

"That's not gonna happen."

"You don't know that Kyra. He might—"

"He won't."

"But—"

"Jermaine, I appreciate your optimism, but I *know* Mike. He's done. I saw it the moment his eyes met mine. So please, just let me drown in my sorrow. I deserve this." I murmur, cutting him off, wishing I could disappear into the warmed leather seat.

I turn my face toward the window, as I watch the trees go by in a blur; my tears like an overflowing dam.

CHAPTER 3

Mike

I pull into the well-lit parking lot of Hartley's Bar and Grille, which looks nothing like the usual hole in the wall bars that I'm accustomed to. This place looks more like an upscale lounge from the outside, with the fancy lights, warm colors, and artistry on the building with crisp landscaping. I have to recheck my phone to make sure I'm at the right address.

After confirming the address is correct, I park horizontally across three parking lanes, but keep the engine running. I chose a different location than the usual because I know there's less chance of seeing anybody that would recognize me. That, and the fact that I'm sure Marlon will come looking for me and right now, I don't wanna be found.

I sit back in my seat and scan the parking lot. There are a few cars, but not enough to pack the place out. Good, I don't want a crowd. I just want to wallow in my misery with a shot… or six.

I pull the visor mirror down to check and see if there are any more dried tear stains on my face, when I see the scar above my right eyebrow, and the painful memory of how I got it. My stomach churns. It's the first time I hit her, and of course she fought back. Why wouldn't she? I have three stitches and a scar to prove it. I close my eyes as the intruding memory surfaces once more.

I'm not up for this shit with Jakyra right now. I mean, I know she's upset because I missed our reservations for dinner tonight, but damn. I just lost my job, for no fuckin' valid reason, car note is due the end of the month, rent for this overpriced goddamn town home is due in a couple of weeks, not to mention car insurance.

We were already struggling before, but we made it work somehow. Now, I had no job and bills that I couldn't afford to pay... this month alone. Shit. How did I even get this far behind? I swear on all things holy, one day I'll have my own business, then shit like this won't—

"Are you even listening to me, Mike! I can't believe you didn't remember! I went through hell getting those reservations. It's one of the best restaurants in Jersey! You could have at least—"

"Jakyra! I'm sorry. I forgot, shit! Now, would you please be quiet?! I have a fuckin' headache!" I bellowed, interrupting her mid-sentence.

She glared at me. Hurt flashed in her honey hazel eyes as she stalked over to me, pointing her manicured finger in my face. She knew I hated that shit. "Sorry doesn't cut it, Mike! You should've called and let me know you were going to ruin our night instead of having me sit here and wait for you like a fuckin' idiot!" She yelled.

I let out a frustrated breath. I get she's angry, but she's goin' way overboard and it's starting to piss me the fuck off. My jaw clenched as I frowned, pushing her finger away from my face. "I get it goddamn it! You're pissed off, but if you haven't caught on yet, I've had a horrible fuckin' day. I needed to chill out for a while before I came home, so I went to the bar for a few drinks and lost track of time." I explained, trying to rein in my temper, but it wasn't working. I was still all kinds of tense. "We can go to dinner another time. I just wanna take a shower and sleep until next week." I moved past her.

As I passed by, she grabbed my arm and swung me back around to face her. Her eyes were misty, her lips pressed together, and body tensed. What the hell is wrong with her? She's takin' this too damn far!

"You went to a bar! That's your excuse?! You had a crappy fuckin' day! That's why you stood me up!" She shouted, as her chest heaved. "You're the most inconsiderate bastard I've ever known!" She roared, shoving me with every ounce of strength she had.

My eyes narrowed as I glowered at her, and in a knee jerk reaction, came across her face with my hand, hearing the echo of impact throughout the living room. It fell eerily silent as my eyes *widened in shock of my actions. At once my arms rose, reaching out to her— all anger dissolved like sugar in water. My heart pumped wildly as I realized what the hell I just did; instant regret and guilt settling in my stomach like lead. "Kyra, I'm sorry! I didn't mean to hit you!" I rushed to say. Tears escaped her eyes, and it damn near brought me to my knees. As I tried to wipe them away, she drew her hand into a fist and swung wildly. I stepped back, turning my head a bit so she didn't hit me, but her $4000 diamond and platinum wedding ring—that I spent a year and a half saving for— caught me right above my eyebrow. The blood immediately began seeping from the wound.*

Damn it.

I quickly covered the gash as I took my shirt off in one fluent motion and placed it over my eyebrow, removing my bloody hand. I glanced over at Jakyra, as she took wobbly steps away from me. I can't believe I hit her. Shit.

"Way to ruin our two-year anniversary, asshole." Jakyra stifled out.

I gave her a once over, just noticing the beautiful deep violet knee length one sleeve dress that clung to her body. My favorite color.

Damn.

She had on black stilettos with a matching clutch and the diamond earrings and necklace that I bought last year as an anniversary gift.

Shit.

*She looked beautiful. She was waiting for me, and I forgot our damn anniversary. She was right, I **did** ruin everything. I closed my eyes, sighing. "Fuck."*

The sound of a honking horn next to my SUV drags me out of my thoughts. I glance out of my window to see a security guard leaning over in his vehicle, looking on in concern. "Everything alright sir?"

"Uh, yeah, I'm good. Just deep in thought. Thanks for asking." I assure him, pushing the visor mirror back up.

"Okay. Just checking. And sir?" He continues, pointing to my SUV. "Would you mind parking in one spot instead of three?"

"No problem." I answer, not realizing I'm still parked wrong. The security guard nods his head then pulls off. I put the SUV in drive, parking closer to the entrance, then shut off my car, get out, and press the alarm. *Time to get shitfaced.*

I step into the bar, and it's just as sophisticated as the outside. I don't know what else I expected though. It has a huge, sculpted glass circular bar in the center of the room with colorful display lights in place, and five bartenders working the bar.

There's tables for dining, booths and lounge chairs, a VIP section, and a moderate sized stage for karaoke, with two huge flat screen karaoke monitors suspended in midair. I don't know how they did it, but it looks cool as hell the way they had the stage set up—flashing strobe lights, cordless mics, and an epic video wall.

The lighting is perfect inside the lounge— not too bright, not too dim— and the soothing sound of 90's R&B filters through the large space. It even has a dance floor close to the karaoke stage. *Damn, I'm impressed.* It's a step up from the bars I've been to, and Chris, my personal assistant/friend/pain in my right ass cheek, would love it.

I make my way over to the far end of the bar where there's fewer people and take a seat on the black highchair bar stool, genuine leather no doubt. I wave the bartender over and he makes his way to me quickly.

"Good evening, sir. Happy Thanksgiving! My name's Tony, what can I get for ya?" He asks, a little too eager for my taste.

"It's Mike, and it hasn't been an incredibly *happy* Thanksgiving. Hence me sitting in a bar ordering a drink." I respond, a little less than friendly.

"Oh, I'm sorry to hear that. Wanna talk about it?"

I lean my elbows on the bar, making deliberate eye contact. "Not really. That drink?" I press, trying to get the ambitious, blond-haired guy to focus on the task at hand.

He clears his throat, taking his small notepad in hand. "Sure. What'll ya have?"

"Two double shots of your best top shelf whiskey. It doesn't matter what it is, just keep'em comin'. Got it?"

"Not a problem, Mike. I'll be back in a sec with those drinks!" He takes my credit card and starts on my drinks.

The guy's a little too enthusiastic for me, but I guess he's just doin' his job.

No sooner than me taking my phone out of the inside of my suit jacket, Mr. happy- go- lucky, tattooed bartender places the shot glasses in front of me, along with my credit card.

Dude's efficient, I'll give him that.

"Here you go, Mike. If you need anything else, just give me a holler." He slides a few napkins beside my drinks. "And I hope your night gets better for you."

"I doubt it, but thanks anyway." I answer in earnest. He gives a quick nod and moves along to the next customer.

I exhale, taking one of the shot glasses in hand, frustrated at the fact that for months I've made progress in my sobriety journey, and with this one drink, I'm about to fuck it all up.

CHAPTER 4

Erin

I notice him when he first walks in. He seems… distracted, unhappy. Yeah, I can spot misery from a mile away but even in his saddened state, I can't help but take in his appearance. "Wow." He is *fine*. Like, Lance Gross fine. My fingers twitch with eagerness to trace the outline of his strong jaw and— sexy as sin— 5 o'clock shadow.

From the burnt orange suit jacket, with black shirt and pants, to his shiny black shoes. He's well put together, and by the looks of the muscles that stretch the arms of his suit jacket, I'm fairly sure he works out. I shake my head, embarrassed for gawking at this man, but it's like I sensed his presence when he entered the bar. *Weird*.

My eyes travel up the length of his muscular frame to his face, and hot damn. I lose my breath at the sight of him. He looks to be about six feet and his creamy caramel complexion has me wanting to lick him like melting ice cream. "Simply gorgeous." I whisper to myself as I imagine running my fingers through his short, curly black hair.

From where I'm sitting, his eyes look like a glassy mocha brown that seems to change with his declining mood. I take a sip of wine—practically salivating—disregarding the presentation I'm supposed to be finishing for tomorrow. The presentation! "Damn it!" I scold myself, tearing my gaze away from the deliciously edible man that's currently sitting at the bar, staring at a drink he hasn't touched for almost an hour. *I wonder what that's about?*

I glance down at my work and let out an aggravated huff. "I can finish this at home tonight. It'll only take half an hour at the most." I decide, finally giving in to this sudden infatuation with Mr. GQ.

I begin packing my things up. After I'm situated, I move to pick up my purse and over the shoulder briefcase and spill wine all over the table. "Shit. Shit!" I whisper-yell, quickly grabbing napkins to clean the mess up. My hands tremble, and breaths come in short pants, as I wipe across the table until it's spotless. "Calm down, Erin. It's *just* wine. You're fine. Everything's fine." I murmur, as if I were giving someone a pep talk.

I take in a deep breath, then exhale, until the tremors are gone, and my breathing returns to normal. Standing, I smooth the non-existent creases out of my skirt, glancing toward the bar. Then, with a smile on my face and a pep in my step, I stride forward. "Okay, let's go meet Mr. GQ."

CHAPTER 5

Mike

"I can't keep'em comin' if you don't take your first two down, Mike." Tony the bartender jokes. I peer over at him, unimpressed. He throws his hands up in surrender, then saunters over to the customer a few bar stools from me.

As I stare back down at my perfectly untouched shot glasses, I glance over to my phone for the fourth time as it vibrates, showing Jakyra's face on the screen. Declining the call, I take the shot glass in my hand once more. "Take the goddamn drink." I mumble, raising the glass slowly. I inhale deeply and a mixture of coconut and cucumber melon fragrances invades my senses. Before I can figure out where it's coming from, someone taps my shoulder. I turn to give them an annoyed, "don't bother me" glare, but the sight before me, knocks the air out of my lungs, rendering me speechless.

"Hey! I noticed the dilemma with the drinks. I came over to intervene. If it's taking you this long to decide, then you *probably* shouldn't." She advises, in an energetic, vibrant voice.

A faint smile finds its way to my lips. "Is that right?" I give her a once-over. "Well, thank you. You just made my decision a lot easier." Placing the shot glass back on the bar, I turn fully toward this stunning human being.

If I had to guess, I'd say she's about five foot nine , but it's hard to pinpoint when she has on dark orange six-inch heels. The fitted navy-blue pencil skirt, clings to her body for dear life. The swell of her breasts grace me with their presence in the long sleeve wrap around navy blue blouse with soft green floral print. *Yeah, I'm a perv, I know*, but her body is fit and she's Nia Long caliber beautiful.

Damn.

I'm finding it difficult to concentrate when I look at her. It seems as if she can see right through to the core of my soul; like she can see… *me.* It feels oddly familiar.

She smiles brightly at me, revealing a dimple in the right side of her cheek, that peeks through like the sun on a cloudy day. Her lips are full, and fuckin' kissable. I instantly begin to imagine the way her lips would feel against mine. I groan inwardly at the thought.

Goddamn it, get it together. You just ended your marriage.

As I continue to ogle her like a mindless idiot, I notice the color of her eyes; a sparkling bronze, so full of innocence.

I wouldn't mind corrupting… Stop it, Mike.

Her eyes can melt the coldest of hearts. Her skin though, reminds me of a smoky topaz crystal in all its glory; smooth, almost flawless. Her hair is in a low bun— not a hair out of place. I can tell that it's thick; as shiny as a beautiful onyx.

Overall… perfection. She's perfect and the shit I wanna do to her right—

"Are you done checking me out?" She interrupts my dirty thoughts, giving me another seductive smile.

I clear my throat, licking my lips with sudden desirous fixation. "Uh, what's your name, Dimples?" I change the subject, hoping she takes the bait.

She places her hands on her hips, tilting her head to the side. "You're deflecting, Mr. GQ. I asked you a question. Are you done checking me out?" She repeats, twirling around to give me a full view. I jump at the opportunity, scanning her from head to toe, taking in her full beauty and I swear my heart skips a beat.

What the hell was that?

I swallow, trying to regain some moisture into my now dry throat, gazing into her warm eyes once more. "I am. I gotta say though, it's hard *not* to check you out." I admit, trying to slow my stammering heart.

What the fuck is goin' on here?

"And where did GQ come from?" I move a little closer, as if there's an invisible thread pulling me toward her.

"It's the nickname I decided to give you when I was checking *you* out earlier. I'm Erin, by the way. Erin Brooks." She holds out her hand for me to shake.

Her energy is contagious. Damn, that's sexy as hell.

I take her soft hand in mine, never breaking eye contact. "It's nice to meet you, Erin. I'm Mike—" Lifting her hand, I brush my lips lightly against her knuckles. She shivers at the contact. "–Harmon." I finish, still holding onto her hand.

I announced my divorce, walked away from my wife, and had a minor breakdown. Why am I already flirting with a random woman I just met?

What the hell am I doin'?

"Well, it's an absolute pleasure to meet you, GQ… I mean, Mike." Erin gives me a toothy grin, as she tightens her grip on my hand. "Shall we sit at one of the booths and continue our conversation?"

Hell yeah! I wanted to yell.

"Lead the way." Erin releases my hand, grabs the two shot glasses— that I'd completely forgotten about— and starts for one of the booths in the back near the karaoke stage.

I grab my phone from off the bar, and right on cue, it vibrates in my hand. I don't have to look at it to know who it is… my wife. My finger hovers over the answer button, debating whether to pick up. In the end, I decline the call. I stand there staring at the blank screen, when I feel a gentle hand, almost calming, on my back.

"Is everything okay?" Erin asks.

I exhale, turning toward her as I switch my phone off, putting it back into my suit jacket. "Everything's great." I lie. "You found us a booth?"

"Yup, and I took the liberty of ordering water, pop, and juice for you. Didn't really know which you'd prefer." She shrugs, backing away from me, swaying her hips to the upbeat tempo of the current song that's playing. "I know for a fact that alcohol is off the table, and I knew you'd probably be thirsty."

"You have no fuckin' clue." I murmur, walking toward the booth.

###

It's been about two hours and Dimples and I have been talking nonstop. It's like we've known each other our whole lives… *shit is almost scary.* I've come out of my suit jacket and rolled the arms of my sleeves up. Erin's kicked off her shoes. We've done everything from Karaoke to darts and now we've just come back to our booth from the dance floor.

I gotta say, the enthusiastic bartender Tony was right. My

night *did* get better. Much better than I would have ever expected.

"So, Ms. Brooks, what do you do for a living?"

"I'm an Exec PA for an international software company. What about you?" She downs the second shot glass that was formerly my comfort.

I sit back, taking a swig from the bottled water in front of me. "I own an Interior Design company."

"Wow, that doesn't—"

"— Seem like something I'd be interested in? I get that a lot." I put the half empty bottle on the table. "It wasn't my first choice, in the beginning. I'm honoring my mom's memory. I started the company because of her. It was her dream to become an interior designer, but she never got the chance because of that—" I catch myself before I can finish. I don't wanna get into that shit right now— not when I'm enjoying myself so much.

Drawing in an uneven breath, I exhale, reining in my anger. I force my shoulders and face to relax, sensing the tension in my body.

Erin slides closer to me; her eyes full of an emotion that I can't quite place. "I'm sorry. You don't have to talk about it, but it's amazing what you're doing for your mom. I admire that." She touches my hand, lightly brushing her fingertips along my knuckles, and I feel a tingling spark at the contact.

I glance up, meeting her beautiful eyes, and she offers me a mind-numbing smile, that makes *me* smile. "Thank you." The intense pull to this heavenly soul increases the more time I spend with her. Gratitude suddenly hits me like a ton of bricks. "Not just for the compliment, but for tonight. I was in a bad place when I came in here, but you— changed that." I instinctively lean in, as if being magnetically pulled toward her.

"No need to thank me, Mike. I'm glad I was able to… distract you." She scoots even closer.

The atmosphere crackles around us with rising heat. It's as if there's a five-alarm fire…. and we're the flames.

I have never experienced this kind of chemistry with a woman before, not even Jakyra… well, I have with one other girl, but that was a long time ago.

Our lips are inches apart. My gaze drops from her mesmerizing eyes to her lips and back again. I can feel the warmth of her breath against my face. She doesn't know it, but I'm seconds away from spreadin' her ass out on this damn table and—

"Mike! What the hell bro! You don't know how to answer your damn phone? I've been goin' fuckin' crazy not knowing if — Oh, my bad." My irritating ass brother interrupts, as Dimples and I jump back from one another like we got caught by the principal.

Marlon glances back and forth between the two of us, his eyebrow rising in suspicion. "Am I…interrupting something?"

Yes, you are! Damn his nosey, cockblockin' ass.

I clear my throat, snatching my suit jacket while sliding out of the leather seated booth, Erin following seconds after. She slips on her heels and sidles up next to me where the three of us stand in awkward silence.

After a few more uncomfortable seconds, I come out of my stupor and finally try to form words. "Uh, what the hell are you doing here, Marlon? I thought you would have gotten the hint when I sent you to voicemail or when I turned my damn phone off." I pull my suit jacket on and button it.

Marlon steps closer to me, placing his hand on my shoulder. "I'm worried about you, bro. I mean, with everything that happened today. You scared the shit outta me. The only reason I didn't come after you sooner is because Koko threatened my ass with bodily harm." He explains. "*She* said give you some time, but when you didn't come back home, my mind started racing. I thought you…" Marlon's voice trails off. He peeks over at the table covered with empty shot glasses and a couple of half-filled glasses with amber liquid swirling in them, then glances back towards me. "Did you—"

"No." I snap. "And it's none of your fuckin' business *what* I do!" I whisper-yell, shrugging his hand off my shoulder. I know I'm being an asshole, but my intuitive brother knows me too goddamn well. It gets a bit irritating.

Marlon steps back, brows furrowing deep, as if somebody just hit on his girlfriend. "Since when, Mike? We've *always* been there for each other. *Always* talked things out. Now, it's *none of my business?!"* Marlon's voice booms throughout the semi-crowded lounge, causing the heads of some to turn in our direction. The hurt in his strained voice doesn't go unnoticed.

I do a quick side glance over to Dimples, who stands quietly by my side, wide eyed and— most likely— uncomfortable by now. I notice her hands shaking a bit as she fiddles with her fingers. I open my mouth to ask if she's alright, when Marlon takes hold of my arm, bringing my attention back to him.

"You *are* my goddamn business; you *and* Iesha. I care what happens to you, and right now I'm worried about your ass. I don't want you to—"

"I won't." I reassure him, coming to the realization of what he must have been thinking while I was gone all this time. He has a right to be concerned… I *did* almost fuck up, and it *has* been what, over four hours now?

Shit. I really *am* an asshole.

I put my hand on the side of his face. "Marlon, I'm fine now, I promise. I had a moment earlier, but…" I peer over at Erin, offering a slight smile, in which she returns a knee-buckling one of her own, making my heartbeat pick up just a little. She seems much calmer now that the yelling has stopped.

What happened to her?

I return my focus back to Marlon, whose features has softened as he realizes that I'm alright. Moving my hand from his face to his shoulder, I squeeze gently. "That moment is over now. I *was* struggling at first, but I had a hell of a distraction." I hint and hear a soft giggle beside me.

Erin covers her mouth. "I'm sorry, I didn't mean to laugh." She apologizes, reaching for her coat. "I uh, I should, get going anyway."

"No, you don't have to—"

"It's fine, really. It's getting late, and I have to finish up a presentation for tomorrow anyway. I *did* enjoy your company tonight, Mike." Erin grazes her nails across my chest lightly, as she turns to grab her briefcase and purse.

My breath seizes at her touch, and I silently curse at myself, knowing that she saw it, her cocky grin, all-telling.

With a sharp inhale, she turns, "Oh, I apologize, I didn't introduce myself." Erin smiles wildly at Marlon, who sees our entire interaction, completely amused at the fact that she has me squirming in place. *Me* squirm? I don't squirm, goddamn it!

I glower at Marlon as he does everything in his power to keep from doubling over in laughter. Asshole.

"My name's Erin! It's nice to meet you!" She introduces, bright-eyed, and back to her energy-induced self. She extends a hand.

Marlon takes hold of it, reining in his laughter. "It's nice to meet you too, Erin. I'm Marlon, Mike's younger brother. Since my brother is being so fuckin' rude, I thought I'd just put that out there." Marlon smirks, shaking her hand.

"Marlon." I warn.

"Damn, I'm joking, Mike. Stop bein' so serious." He releases Erin's hand, jerking his thumb in her direction. "She knows I was joking, right?"

"Of course, it's not a big deal, GQ."Erin rubs my back in small circles, causing an unexpected shiver to take root from the base of my spine to the tips of my fingers.

Stop touching me, damn it!

With a sigh, she says, "Okay, I *really* should be going."

"I can walk you out Dimples, just hold on a sec—"

"GQ, trust me, I'm okay. I'm parked right next to the entrance. I should be fine."

"You sure?"

"Positive." Erin begins her trek toward the exit, sashaying, deliberately swaying her hips back and forth, knowing that I'm watching like the lustful creep I am. She turns back before exiting the door, waving her alluring hand, giving me the most hypnotizing smile that I've ever had the pleasure of witnessing, before finally disappearing out of my line of view.

Damn.

I'm two seconds away from draggin' Erin to my SUV, throwing her inside, stripping her naked and—

"Hey!" Marlon shoves my arm, interrupting my pervish thoughts. "What the fuck, bro? Erin got you *that* wound up?"

"What?" I turn my attention back to my brother.

"I don't even wanna know what the hell you were thinkin' about just now." Marlon chuckles, shaking his head. "By the way y'all were interacting, I thought you already knew her."

"Nope, never met before tonight. Now it feels like we've known each other forever. Weird right?" I ask, hoping he'd agree how weird it is so I wouldn't feel like I was crazy.

Marlon shakes his head. "Not weird at all. It's like that sometimes. I mean, I could sense the sexual tension between y'all from across the bar." We make our way to the exit. "I haven't felt chemistry like that since me and Koko. You can't fake that shit, Mike." He continues, as we stop in front of his car. "Maybe you and Jakyra weren't meant to—"

"Don't, Marlon. Conversations about Jakyra is off limits for now, and don't fuckin' *compare* the two of them."

"I'm not comparing them! I'm just saying that— Fine, I'm sorry. I don't wanna ruin your night. It *did* look like you had a pretty damn good night." Marlon smirks, purposely changing the subject, which I'm grateful for.

My body instantly relaxes as I remember my evening with

Dimples. I smile. "I did, but it's one night. I have no clue how to get in touch with her. I didn't even think to get Erin's number."

"You serious??" He utters, genuinely surprised. "You let her go without any damn way to *contact* her? What the hell did you do with my brother?"

"I know." I shake my head at my own stupidity. "But it is what it is. She was my guardian angel for tonight, but what a hell of a night it was."

"I can imagine." He chuckles, then scans my eyes as if searching for something. "You sure you're alright?"

"I'm good, Marlon. Stop worryin'."

He pulls me into a tight embrace, exhales deeply then releases me, hopping into his car. "You goin' home?"

"Yeah, I'll be leaving after I make a phone call." I roll my eyes at his protectiveness but I'm grateful all the same. He's always been the best of us three and I honestly don't know what I'd do without him. "Damn, I thought *I* was the older brother here." I yell, walking backward toward my SUV.

He put his car in reverse. "Well shit, you don't *act* like it."

"Fuck you." I laugh as he drives away, sticking his hand out of the window to give me the middle finger. I smile, hitting the alarm button of my SUV, get in, start the car, and blast the heat. It should warm up soon, it's cold as hell.

I pull out my phone, powering it back on, waiting a minute for my home screen to pop up. That's when I see the amount of voicemail and texts waiting for me. Twenty-five voicemails, and seventy-two text messages. *Seventy-two* damn text messages!

What. The. Fuck?!

A few are from Marlon and MyIesha, but most of them are from *her*. I exhale a shaky breath as I skim through the texts…

Wifey- "*Michael, please answer your phone. I'm so sorry…*

Wifey- *I need to talk to you, just give me that…*

Wifey- *I know I don't deserve it, but please just hear me out…*

Wifey- *Talk to me, please…I need you, please Mike. I'm lost right now, and I don't know how to get back…*

Wifey- *I'm so sorry Mike, I love you. Please don't leave me…*"

The texts go on and on. My mind's going a million miles a minute. I can feel the sting of hurt settle deep within me like solid cement, as I cut the heat off and raise the window down. Suddenly, it seems as if someone's squeezing the air out of my lungs. My chest is tight, and my heart is in my throat.

I take a few deep breaths to regain control, but it does little. My eyes glaze over, and my hands are clammy as I delete every text. Just as I'm done, my screen lights up.

Jakyra.

I swipe the answer button forcefully and put it on

speakerphone. "What the fuck do you want Jakyra! It should be obvious I don't wanna talk, goddamn it!" I roar, my control teetering on the edge.

"Mike! I know you're mad, and I deserve every bit of your anger, but please, can we just talk in person? I need to see—"

"No."

"But I—"

"No. I don't wanna see you. I don't wanna talk to you. I don't even wanna remember your goddamn name. Stop callin' me and lose my fuckin' number!" I bellow, finally falling into the abyss.

"Please Mike, no!" Jakyra begs, sobbing uncontrollably. The desperation in her voice and sharp shallow intakes of breath coming from her makes me think she's having an anxiety attack, but I'm too far gone to care at this point.

"D-don't leave me Mike, please don't—"

"Fuck you!" I end the call, hurling my phone over to the passenger seat. I slam my fists on the steering wheel several times, so hard that my hands begin to feel numb. "Fuck you, Jakyra! Fuck you!" I clutch the dashboard so tight, I thought I'd rip the damn thing right off.

My heart gallops like a racing horse as I put my head on the steering wheel with my eyes shut tight. I release every bit of pain, hurt, and frustration that overwhelmed me in this moment, with a long, deep, thunderous roar that sounds foreign to my ears.

The one thing that remains is the guilt. It takes up permanent residence in my lungs and is now threatening to drown me. I can't breathe.

Why am I devastated over this?! Why do I even give a shit?! I shouldn't be fuckin' *concerned* if she's hurting! I shouldn't *care* if she needs me! Why do I care!

Because you still love her.

I shake my head at the intruding thought, as I lift up from the steering wheel, refusing to believe what I already know to be true. I still love the woman who slept with my sister's boyfriend. The woman who was one of my best friends. The woman who lied about her pregnancy and was going to let me think she was carrying my child.

I take a few minutes to regain my composure before I grab my phone from the passenger seat and call Chris.

He picks up on the second ring. "Hey Mike, everything alright? You excited about the big day tomorrow?" He asks, unaware of today's blow up.

"Hey Chris, no, that's not why I called. There's been an, uh, change of plans, and I need you to do me a huge favor."

"Sure thing. Whatdaya need?"

"I need you to send an email out to Nate and let him know that I'll be attending the meeting tomorrow, along with you and D. Make sure to apologize on my behalf for the sudden change, okay?" I pull the visor mirror down and wipe the remaining tears that I unwillingly shed.

"Not a problem, but what happened to renewing your vows tomorrow, if you don't mind me asking? I thought you were—"

"I *do* mind, so don't finish that sentence. Just know it's not happening now, alright?"

"Message received. I won't bring it up again." He responds without hesitation.

Christopher Daniels— the glue that holds my company together. Chris has been with me since the beginning of my journey building this company.

I started this business because of my mom, although my performance has been lacking. Being CEO should have given me incentive to act professionally, but that wasn't the case.

The company wouldn't have survived without Chris. He's saved my ass these past eight months, for which I'm grateful.

Although I offered him a higher position within the company, he refused. He said he would rather work personally with me and use his God-given talent, annoying the hell outta me—his words, not mine—so I gave him the next best thing, working as my personal assistant.

He's not only my PA, but one of my closest friends; best friend if I had to give him a title.

"You... okay? You sound off. What aren't you telling me,

Mike?" He always knows when something is going on with me. He and Marlon share that annoying quality. He's a genuinely nice person… *just don't piss him off.*

Don't let Chris's brooding appearance fool you, with his short, dark hair, mysterious eyes, and stubble-covered jawline. Underneath the hard exterior is a man with a heart of gold.

I push the visor back into place. "I'm fine, Chris. It's not a big deal." I don't want to face this right now.

"You sound like you lost in a shouting match with Steven Tyler." I huff at his analogy. I guess I *do* sound a little rough.

"I'll tell you later. I don't wanna talk about it right now, okay?" Please don't push the issue.

"Fine, I'll drop it… for now."

"Thank you." I'm surprised he let it go this easily. Him and I are alike in a lot of ways when it comes to protecting those we care about.

He's about the same height and build as me, a little bulkier though, and definitely more level headed. With tanned skin, a straight nose, and pecan brown eyes; he can easily land a job as a fitness model. I don't know why he's still settling, but I'm glad to have him with me regardless.

We went to high school and college together. We partied together, got drunk together, got in trouble together— hell, we even got dumped on the same day.

Yeah, not my finest moment. The groveling was real that day.

He knows about my past, my drinking and anger issues, and Jakyra—except for what happened today. I'll tell him eventually, just not now. It's still too raw.

"Thank you for this; for even answering in the first place. I know it's kinda late."

"No worries, Mike. It's my job, and more importantly, you're my friend. Now, is there anything else you need me to do for you?"

"No, that's it. Hey, I'm even gettin' my own coffee tomorrow." I joke, feeling a little better after my second breakdown of the night.

"Look at you being all independent. I taught you well."

"That you did." I genuinely laugh. "Thanks again Chris, I'll see you in the morning."

"No problem. Goodnight, Mike."

"Goodnight." I end the call, roll the window back up, throw my phone in the center console, and turn the heat back on. I exhale deeply.

Tomorrow will be better.

I click my seat belt in place, put the car in reverse, then drive out of the parking lot, toward the house I once shared with the woman who still holds my heart in her hand. It's time to find a new place to call home because my current living situation feels like a prison now.

Man, this shit sucks.

CHAPTER 6

Erin

Refreshments? Check.

Projector screen in place? Check.

Laptop charged and connected? Check.

Mr. Leeman's coffee? Check.

I scan through my notes one last time, in final preparation for my presentation. The conference room is empty, but I expect Mr. Leeman any moment. He's *never* late.

"Good afternoon Ms. Brooks! You all set for the presentation?" Like I said, never late. He smiles brightly at me as he sets his belongings on the conference table.

The space we're in is a typical conference room, with a twelve-seat burnt sienna conference table, and bright lilac and ivory walls. Portraits of abstract paintings are displayed throughout the room, with a large projector screen in the center of the wall.

Off to the side, there's a table for refreshments— equipped with every type of snack you could ask for— a Keurig, and a water dispenser.

There's floor to ceiling windows that give the large room natural light, and four large floor plants in each corner… Mr. Leeman likes to make sure all bases are covered.

"Of course, sir. When am I *not* ready?"

"I don't doubt it." He chuckles. "Your work ethic and organizational skills are exceptional." He compliments. "I don't know how we crossed paths, but I'm grateful for all of your demanding work and dedication. Believe me, it hasn't gone unnoticed." He finishes, taking his seat at the head of the table.

I beam with pride, placing his coffee in front of him. "Why thank you, Mr. Leeman! I appreciate your high esteem, I'm honored."

Mr. Nathan Leeman. Owner and CEO of one of the most successful black-owned International Software companies in the business world, and a hell of a boss. I've been his executive personal assistant for a few years now, and let me say, it's never a dull moment working with him.

Nathan is nearing his mid-sixties, with short, graying hair— although, you couldn't tell his age by appearance. He's in excellent shape and health, with really, no signs of aging except for the graying hair on his head and face.

He's so down to earth and despite our age difference, we have an excellent working relationship. He has become my mentor, and a great friend.

"Just giving credit where credit is due." He counters. "Oh, and I really do apologize for the last-minute change in the meeting. It was quite unexpected."

"No problem. I'm looking forward to meeting the actual owner of Adira Interior Designs. I've heard their work is excellent. They go beyond their clients' expectations!" I share, my words oozing with excitement, as I amble along back to my laptop to open the correct program.

"You heard correctly." I listen to the familiar, deep voice say, and I freeze. My heart races, and my mouth instantly becomes dry, as I try to regain control of my stupid body.

I mean, who reacts to the sound of a person's voice like this anyway?

I peek at him through my lashes, and if I wasn't leaning on the table already, I would've fallen flat on my damn face, because on cue, my knees buckle at the sight of him.

He stands there, in all his captivating glory, wearing a rich, deep burgundy three-piece suit, black shirt and tie, with black cap toe designer shoes. The suit hugs his defined physique. Mmm, and his hair… and lips… and I just want to… lick him?

Is it weird to have a deep-rooted desire to lick someone?

Yeah, that's weird. What the hell is wrong with me? That is fuckin' freaky weird, creepy creeper type shit. I need to regain my control— But he *does* look like a whole damn snacc, and I *am* kinda starving for a taste of— No, stop it. That's enough Erin. Concentrate.

I exhale a deep breath to calm my galloping heart. My hands are suddenly sweaty, face flushed, and I'm noticeably hot and bothered.

Shit.

I need to calm the hell down. I have a damn job to do.

"Ah, Mike, glad you could make it!" Mr. Leeman rises from his seat to greet his guests. "We weren't expecting you today, so this *is* a pleasant surprise."

"Good to see you too Nate, and again, I apologize for the sudden change in plans." He shakes Mr. Leeman's hand firmly. "You remember Chris and Dante, don't you?"

"It's not a problem Mike, and yes, of course! It's good to see you again." My cheerful boss greets, shaking their hands as well. "We'll be starting soon, so in the meantime, help yourself to some refreshments." My welcoming boss offers. "Ah, Mike." He calls. "I'd like to introduce you to someone." Mr. Leeman and GQ make their way over to me.

Oh shit. Shit!

Okay, play it cool. Play. It. Cool.

"Mike, I'd like you to meet Erin Brooks, the best damn PA in the world." He boasts, causing me to blush. "Erin, this is Mike Harmon, owner and CEO of Adira Interior Designs." Mr. Leeman introduces, completely oblivious to the electric heat that's swirling between GQ and me.

"I don't doubt it." Mike responds, his eyes roaming my body with molten desire. "Ms..... Brooks." My name rolls off his tongue with thick, hot seductive intent. He extends his hand, amusement dancing in his dreamy eyes.

"It's a pleasure to finally meet you Mr. Harmon. Thanks for coming." I place my hand in his, and sparks of electricity shoot down my arm and through my body.

"No, the pleasure is *definitely* all mine. If you need me to *come* again, I wouldn't hesitate." He smirks, subtly stroking the back of my hand with his thumb. "Who knows, after the meeting, I may need you to *come* with me."

My breath hitches, body tingling with barely contained desire, as I slip my hand from his. "Ex-Excuse me?" I squeak, not recognizing the high-pitched sound coming from my own traitorous voice.

"*To my office.* You may want to come to my office to familiarize yourself with my company and staff if we're going to be working together, right?" He clarifies, all the while giving me the most delicious grin.

I lick my dry lips, trying to stamp down the rising heat from his torturous seductive game. He knows exactly what he's doing… and it's working.

Damn it.

"R-right, yes, of course." I stutter like an absolute idiot.

I can't believe I'm allowing him to fluster me!

I clear my throat, glancing over at Mr. Leeman, texting away on his phone, in a blissfully ignorant state. "We should get started." My boss gives me a quick nod before returning to his seat. As I turn to grab my notepad, Mike gently holds on to my wrist, his touch setting my body on fire—*in all the right places.*

"Where's your office?" He asks quietly.

"Down the hall, three doors away. Why?"

"After this meeting, I'll wait for you there. Is your office door unlocked?"

"Yes."

"Good. Don't keep me waitin'." He orders, his voice deep and inviting. The conversation takes all of ten seconds, but the weight of it is almost suffocating.

I blow out a shaky breath as Mike ambles over to his seat, unbuttons his suit jacket, and joins his two associates, Dante, and

Chris.

Damn, I need to get my shit together. He's really throwing me off my game.

The bastard.

I steel myself, inhaling a breath before releasing it, then take my position to the left of Mr. Leeman, and begin.

CHAPTER 7

Mike

After the meeting I politely excuse myself, allowing Chris and Dante to iron out the last-minute details with Nate. Honestly, my mind is solely on Erin and that damn dress that clung to her body like saran wrap.

A black and yellow printed three-quarter sleeve mesh dress, cut just above the knee. Sheer arms, fitted at the waist and all woman. She's wearing at least 5-inch heels and yellow teardrop earrings.

Hey, I blame Jakyra for my keen sense of fashion, well, and Chris. Sometimes he has me questioning his career choice, but that's a story for another day.

Her makeup is flawless, natural tones and highlights, with her lustrous hair pulled back into a high bun. I knew it was her when I first entered the conference room. I'd recognize that ass from anywhere.

As I walk into her office, I instantly notice the vibrant hues of blues, greens, and whites, with a beautiful view of the downtown skyline. The office is spotless, nothing out of place, much like herself. Not even the Afrocentric artwork on the walls are crooked.

She's a perfectionist or a neat freak. Both would drive me crazy, but I'd suck it up just to grip the curve of her ass while I'm— No, focus. You're here to have a conversation with her.

A Con. Ver. Sa. Tion. That's it.

Settle. The Fuck. Down.

I close the door behind me and take a seat on one of the navy-blue leather chairs in front of her desk, contemplating what I want to say to her once she's here. I can't believe I ran into Dimples again. *Here* outta all damn places.

This shit is crazy.

The click of the door has me twisting in my seat to see the beauty before me.

Erin.

My lifeline last night.

I stand as she closes the door behind her. All that conversation shit I was just talking about, flew right out the window, along with my common sense, as I drank in her natural curves.

"Mike? What did you wanna talk about?" She whispers in a

dangerously seductive tone. I'm not sure if she's doin' this purposely, but hearing my name roll off of her tongue has my body doin' all kinds of shit.

"Erin." I growl, low and thick with lust. I don't know what the fuck is happening to me. All I know is I want her… now.

In a few quick strides, I'm in her personal space where she stands, wide-eyed and wanton. I cradle her face in my hands, my lips hovering just above her own. "I didn't think I would see you again." I brush my lips against hers. Erin's breathing quickens; rapid and shallow, her lips parted. "Must be fate." I murmur against the line of her jaw, ghosting light kisses along its trail.

Her eyes flutter shut, and her hands reach for the nape of my neck, pulling me down to her soft lips, and when our mouths connect, I lose what little control I have left. The flames that ignite between us are like wildfire.

My hands have a mind of their own as I explore her body, tracing the curve of her hips, traveling the arch of her back to her firm peach-shaped ass.

When we finally come up for air, I slowly remove my suit jacket, tossing it on the floor. I ogle her with hooded eyes, as she returns my gaze with a desirous one of her own. Erin gives me a once over, licking her plump lips alluringly, and agonizingly slow.

God…. damn.

Yeah, it's settled. I need to be inside of her. No doubt about it.

Gripping her waist, I press her firmly against me so she can *feel* just how much I want her.

A small gasp escapes her lips before she lifts her hand, to trace the length of my bottom lip with her thumb.

I'm so damn turned on right now, my body is moving before I even have a chance to think about it. I hoist her up, the snug dress automatically rising, as she wraps her legs around my waist, while I dash to the nearest wall.

I press Erin between the cool white wall and my very willing erection. I kiss along her jawline, her soft moans like music to my ears. "I'm gonna fuck you hard against this wall." I say in a husky voice against her ear, nibbling as I speak. "Then I'm gonna fuck you rough on your desk." I continue, placing her back on her feet. "And when I'm done, you're not gonna be able to stand."

"Don't make promises you can't keep." She says, a challenging undertone ringing through. She devours me with her eyes, as she watches me unbutton my vest, and drop it to the floor.

"It's not a promise. It's fact. Take off your panties." I order, unbuckling my belt.

Erin raises her dress, sliding down her underwear, painfully slow. Black, sheer thongs....

Fuck, that's hot as hell.

"Come here." I motion with my finger to her as she yields, sashaying the short distance between us. I quickly unbutton my slacks, lift her up once more, and slam my lips onto hers. Walking us back until we hit the wall, I reach for the condom in my wallet.

Never leave home without it... hey, you never know.

I trail kisses down her neck, savoring her cucumber melon fragrance, mixed with the wonderful scent of her arousal.

Fuckin' beautiful.

As I tear the condom packet open with my teeth, there's a loud knock at the door and we both still.

"Erin, it's Liz." The unfamiliar voice whisper-yells through the door. "Can I come in for a second?" Pressing our foreheads together, we let out a frustrated breath. I put Erin down, as we scramble to get ourselves together, my body protesting the sudden loss of contact with Erin's soft lips and curvy, supple body.

"Uh, yeah Liz. Just give me a second." She answers, breathless, pulling her underwear back on, as I speedily button up my slacks and vest.

Erin rushes to the door, swinging it open. "Hey Liz, what's up?" Liz walks in, closing the door behind her. She immediately notices me buttoning my suit jacket.

I'm turned far enough away that Liz can't see the raging erection I'm sporting, but still able to see her enough to note the huge grin on her face.

She glances over to Erin, who's flustered, blushing, and fidgeting in place, and tries to suppress the giggle that bubbles up on the inside but fails miserably.

Liz is a pale skinned ginger with hunter green eyes. She looks to be in her mid-forties but dresses like she's in her twenties. She's a fraction shorter than Dimples, just as energetic and bubbly, but with a hint of an accent I can't quite decipher. Liz seems every bit the nosey gossiping neighbor type, but I could be wrong.

"Sorry for… interrupting, but Mr. Leeman is looking for you. I told him you were down on the fourth floor talking with the Finance Department. You have about ten minutes, tops, before he comes to your office." She glances at me, then Dimples. "Just wanted to give you a heads up because I can see you were a little…busy." She smirks.

Erin clears her throat. "Liz, it's not what it looks like. We were just—"

"It's *exactly* what it looks like, Liz." I interrupt, turning to face them fully, only after I'm able to readjust myself in my slacks. "Thank you for the heads up." I smile, and Dimples shoots me an icy death glare.

"No problem Mr. Harmon. I guess I'll… leave you to it." Liz gives a quick wave and hums her way out of the office.

Erin closes her eyes, releasing a deep breath. "Oh god. That was so fuckin' embarrassing."

"I don't know. It was pretty damn sexy to me. Seeing you all flustered, hot and bothered, with your dress crumpled and hair, less than perfect. Shit was awesome to watch." I tease, as I take the misplaced strands of hair and smooth them back into place.

There. Perfect.

She stalks over to me, gripping my arm, pulling me toward the door. "Out. Now. Mr. Leeman is gonna be here soon and I don't want him to see you here."

"Not without your number. I will *not* make that damn mistake a second time." She blows out a rough breath, goes to grab her phone from the inside of one of her desk drawers, then rushes back over. I hold out my hand. "Give me your phone." She gives it to me without question, peeking over at the door, ever so often. I type my number into her phone, then call myself so I'd have hers too. "Now, I can sleep at night." I joke, earning an eye roll from her. I lean in, ghosting a light kiss across her lips, then hand the phone to her. "Call me."

She smiles that beautiful smile of hers, looking at the number in her phone, then glances up at me again, eyes dancing with pleasure. "Really? Mr. GQ?" She laughs, and my heart does a backflip.

Man, what the hell is this shit all about?

"You started it, so now you'll have to deal with it." I defend, loving the way I make her blush. I turn to open the door.

"I'll call you, Mr. GQ." She calls out, her voice a playful delight.

"I'm counting on it, Dimples." I answer, closing the door behind me.

As I make my way back to the reception area, I glance over to see Liz smiling at me. "Thank you again, Liz."

"Not a problem, Mr. Harmon."

"Please, call me Mike." I offer, standing directly in front of her desk now.

"Mike." She smiles again. "I think you'll be good for Erin. She deserves to be happy."

I raise an eyebrow, my interest piqued. "Why would you believe she *wasn't* happy?"

"She wasn't." Liz hesitates. "I don't even know if I should be—"

"No, please, tell me. It goes no further than here, I promise."

With a sigh and quick nod, she continues. "It's rare she allows anyone to get close to her like this. Her last relationship nearly destroyed her." She leans in, speaking in hushed tones. "Erin… her ex treated her horribly." Liz pauses a second before continuing. "She hid it well for a while, but one day she finally broke, here at the office. Luckily, only Mr. Leeman and I witnessed it, but she told us everything. She needed therapy for a year and a half. It was awful seeing her so lost."

Liz goes on, but my mind shuts down. I can read between the goddamn lines.

She's been abused.

She had a breakdown.

She made it out of one abusive relationship and I'm trying to drag her into another. What if I become what she was trying to escape? What if I turn into her ex?

Hell, I *was* her ex.

What if I go back to the way I used to be? No, I'm not gonna place anyone else in the position that I put Jakyra in.

Never again.

I need to stay away from Erin. Do my job and move on. I mean, I'm just freshly separated. Why am I even thinking about getting into a relationship this damn soon anyway? I sigh.

"Mike? Are you alright?" Liz asks in concern. "Maybe I shouldn't have said anything. I just thought—"

"No, I'm fine. I'm glad you told me. You're right, she *does* deserve to be happy."

Just not with me.

I was right. Liz *is* a gossip, and I played right into her hands. I asked, now I wish I hadn't. This changes everything. I briefly glance down at my watch. "Look, I need to get going. Please, don't let Erin know that you told me this. I don't want her to feel uncomfortable around me."

"I won't, don't worry. You're a good man. I can tell."

If she only knew.

I force a smile. "Thanks. I gotta run, but nice meeting you." I walk to the elevator so fast; I probably left a trail of blazing fire behind me. Once inside the lift, I lean my head against the back wall. "It won't work between Erin and me."

Fuck.

But our chemistry, our connection. It *feels* right. I blow out a defeated breath.

"I already hurt Jakyra. I won't hurt her, too." I lift my head as I hear the ding of the elevator.

I have to stay away from her.

Shit.

Easier said than done.

CHAPTER 8

Two weeks.

It's been two weeks since I made the decision to avoid Erin, and it's been hard as hell. I mean, I got away with sending Dante to the last couple of meetings, but the damn calls and texts from her are killin' me.

I've known her for what, all of two minutes?

I almost answered my cell phone more than a few times. She hasn't called or text me in the past couple days, so maybe she's finally gettin' the hint. Good.

Then why does my heart feel so heavy? Why does this feel all wrong?

Damn. What is it about Erin that has me second guessing myself? Ugh, this is for her own fuckin' good, and I need to stick to my decision.

"Harmon!" The barista calls out into the crowded café. "Your order's up!"

Zelle's is the most popular café in the city: small, super busy, but has some of the best coffee and sandwiches around.

The ceiling is decorated in splashes of black and burnt orange with hanging decorative lights. The walls are stark white with splashes of burnt orange throughout, and artistry of all thing's coffee across the expanse of the walls.

The tables are small two and three seaters, white and round. The smell of fresh coffee and muffins lingers in the air as the customers crowd around, awaiting their orders.

I make my way to the register, an irritated scowl on my face. I'm not in the best of moods. I, not only, had to avoid Erin, but also Jakyra. I know it's only a matter of time before I'll have to face her wrath.

I had divorce papers served to her last week. I know I should have delivered them to her myself but honestly, I'm not ready to face her yet. I haven't seen her since Thanksgiving and I'm afraid I might cave when I *do* look at her. So yeah, that's what the fuck I'm dealin' with right now.

"Thanks." I grab my breakfast— not giving a damn about what else the barista's saying— head for the exit and into my SUV. As I start the engine, my phone rings. I check to see who's calling before pulling off, heading to work.

Chris.

He doesn't call unless it's an emergency or something is wrong. I answer quickly, merging into traffic and onto the freeway ahead. "What's wrong?"

"Uh, your wife's here, and she won't leave. What do you want me to do?"

Fuck.

I do *not* wanna do this shit with her today.

With a sigh, I say, "Where is she now?" My stomach twists in knots as I await Chris's answer. I increase my current speed on the freeway. I need to handle this and be done with it.

"Waiting outside of your office. Should I call security, Mike? I'm not sure what's going on, but by the way her arms are folded across her chest, the scowl on her face, and the death stare she's currently giving me, I'd say she's pretty damn upset about something." Chris describes, painting a detailed picture of the shit show that's about to take place. "She says she's not leaving until she has words with you."

Of course, she's not.

"Should I—"

"No, don't do anything. Just unlock my door and tell her to wait for me in my office. I'll be there in ten minutes."

"Will do. I'll see you soon."

"Yeah." Ending the call, I toss my phone on the passenger seat. I exhale a long, frustrated breath. "Shit!" I already feel the twinge of a headache developing.

Perfect.

I shake my head, knowing how this will end: yelling, cussing, crying and acts of violence— *aimed toward me.* I have no choice but to deal with it now. Whether I like it or not, it's happening.

CHAPTER 9

Jakyra

I don't wanna cause a scene— that's *not* my intention— but this callous jerk won't answer my calls or texts. He didn't even have the common courtesy to deliver the damn divorce papers— that I'm currently staring blankly at in my hands— himself!

I mean, it's not like I'm some random bitch off the street. We've known each other since childhood. We were friends before we even *thought* about being lovers, and he didn't even have enough respect for me to deliver this shit to me personally! Yes, I'm pissed the fuck off! And he's gonna know just how much when his ass gets here.

I lean against my husband's office door, so ready for this confrontation, when my cell goes off to a familiar ringtone. Digging my phone out of my purse, I answer. "Hey Jermaine, what's up? I thought you were in your therapy session already?"

"We'll be startin' soon. Where are you?"

I push off of the door, walking toward one of the other offices. I don't particularly want to tell my brother where I am because I know he's not gonna like it. "I'm… at Mike's office. He needs to understand that what he did was wrong."

"*Kyra.*" His tone alone tells me I should've kept my damn mouth shut. "We already talked about this shit. He made it clear that he's done. Stop forcin' the fuckin' issue. Give him the goddamn divorce and move on. You're doing nothing but hurting yourself."

I roll my eyes. The one time I need him to be supportive, he does the complete opposite. "I'm not here to argue with him." I lie. "Mike and I just need to work some things out before I sign these papers." I continue my blatant fabrication. There is no way in hell I'm giving up on our marriage. Mike is confused… and hurt at the moment. He'll come around.

"Why don't you—" He's silent for a minute, then he sighs. "No arguing. Just talk, okay? I worry about the stress you put on yourself. Think about my niece, Kyra."

"I do. Every single day. I want my daughter to grow up in an environment where she'll be loved, protected, and taken care of." That's not a lie, but I don't want that with anybody else. Just Mike. "How's therapy been going?" I need to steer this conversation away from me.

"Man, I should have been goin' a long time ago. I don't know why I was ashamed to tell y'all. Ari has helped me in ways I can't even explain. She's young, but the amount of knowledge that's packed into this woman is… wow."

I hear the smile in his voice as he talks about her. "Ari? You're on a first name basis with her, huh?"

"I mean, Dr. Cox." He corrects himself, but it's too late. I already peeped his little slip up. "I didn't call to talk about *me* though." I hear shuffling on the other end of the line then, "I gotta go in, but I wanted to let you know that Johnee has seriously been talkin' about willingly going to the police to turn himself in. He hasn't been the same since…. that night."

Making my way back to Mike's office, I resume leaning against the door. I know exactly what night Jermaine is referring to. I still can't believe he would do something like that…then again, no one knew he was addicted to pills and who knows what else he was using back then. "The guilt is eatin' him up. Maybe this is what he needs for the sake of his mental health. When is he—"

"Jakyra?" Chris calls out, interrupting my conversation like the undercover asshole he is.

"Hey bro, I'll call you back a little later, okay?"

"Alright. Talk soon, love you."

"Love you too, Jay." I end the call, pinning Chris with a frigid glare, which he ignores.

Jerk.

Unlocking Mike's door, he gives me a fake smile. "Mike will be here in about ten minutes, and he said to go into his office and wait for him until he arrives." Opening the door for me, he moves aside so that I can enter, then types something into his tablet. "Would you like anything before I go?" Chris asks, with all the kindness of a saint on a Friday night…. but he's *no* saint.

Yeah, I'd like you to knock some since into Mike's ass so he can come back home, to me, where he belongs.

"No, thanks, I'm fine." I decide on. It's the best answer to give at the moment. I'm reserving my resting bitch face for Mike when he gets here. Well, that and I don't want Chris to think I'm some lunatic bitch.

Too late for that though. Oh well.

As I glance around the office, not much has changed except the wall color. Where it was a dull beige, it's now a fresh powder white with splashes of various browns throughout the office. The chocolate and white carpet matches his brown leather sofa that sits off to the side.

His desk is huge and dark walnut in color, equipped with two leather chairs in front of it. The top of the desk is immaculate: papers skillfully placed, laptop centered, and pictures of his siblings placed in perfect form.

One thing *is* lacking though… the pictures that he used to keep of me. I sigh, turning toward Chris.

He gives me a hint of a smile. "Okay, well, he should be here shortly. Sit tight." With that, he disappears through the door, closing it behind him.

I stride toward the leather sofa and plop down. The heaviness of guilt presses hard against my chest as I glance down at the divorce papers. I close my eyes, sighing in regret. "This is *really* happening." I place the papers beside me, stand, then walk over to the window, watching the busyness of the crowded downtown street. "He's actually serious about leaving me."

Like everyone else.

Tears escape my eyes as an unwanted memory flashed before me.

I anxiously waited for my mom to answer the phone. She promised her and dad would come to the school to have a meeting with the principal about the stupid girls bullying me. I mean, I know how to defend myself, my brothers taught me well, but I'm tired of all the name calling.

Since when is it a crime to be smart and get good grades? I shouldn't have to dumb myself down to fit in. I think I'm fine just the way—"

"Hello?"

"Hey mom, you didn't forget, did you?" I asked, hoping

against all hope that they won't renege.

"Um, forget what?"

"Meeting? With the principal? Bullying? Remember?"

Silence.

"We can't Kyra, I'm sorry. Your dad and I have meetings throughout the day. Can't they reschedule?"

I huffed my disbelief. "Ma, I told you and dad about this three weeks ago! This is the second time it has to be rescheduled. You promised you could make it this time!" I whined, on the verge of tears. Apparently, their daughter being bullied isn't as important as their meetings.

Apparently.

"Jakyra." Clipped and stern. That's the tone I got from her. "Stop whining. I'm sure you can handle a couple of girls on your own. You're thirteen. I'm sure it's not even that serious."

"But—"

"No buts. Handle it. End of discussion. Make sure to order you and your brothers takeout. You know where the credit card is. We won't be home until late, now I have to go. See you later honey, love you." She quickly dismissed, leaving me feeling some type of way.

"But Johnee and Jermaine won't be here. They have football practice. I'll be here alone— again." I scrambled to say, but she

already ended the call. I sighed in defeat, tears falling from my eyes. "They never put me first."

A blaring siren from the busy street drags me back to the present. I place a clammy hand on my belly, rubbing gently. "Whether you're Mike's or not, we're gonna be a happy family. I'm not giving up on our marriage." I hear the click of the door, and I turn, expecting Mike, but I'm sadly mistaken. She walks through the door with a bag in one hand and, I'm guessing, a coffee in the other. Her head is still down as she closes the door, so she doesn't notice me.

"Okay Mr. GQ, you've been ignoring me and I wanna know why? Mike, I thought we—"

"I'm sorry, Mike's not here at the moment. Who are you?" Irritation dripping with every word.

"Oh, um, I'm sorry. I thought Mike was—"

"Well apparently, he's not. Again, Who. Are. You?" I snap, raising a sharp brow.

"Um, I'm Erin Brooks. Mike— Mr. Harmon and I are business associates. I work for—"

"I'm not interested in who the fuck you work for. I'm more concerned with how the hell you get to come into my husband's office, unannounced." My brows furrow, waiting for her to explain herself. She fidgets in place, her eyes wide, chest rising and falling rapidly.

What the hell? Is this bitch havin' an anxiety attack or something'?!

"Ex-excuse me? Your… husband?" She stutters, as her hands shake, taken aback by the revelation.

*Well, we're separated, on our way to divorce, but it's not a lie. We **are** married.*

I cross the office, standing a few feet away from her.

Erin

Little Miss Energetic firecracker. I can tell by her *bubbly,* cheery voice, she's extra…. *I don't like her.*

"He n-never mentioned he was—"

"Married? Why would he mention he's married, with a child on the way, to someone who's gonna be a random fuck? What sense does that make, huh?" I goad, seeing her eyes become glassy. I know she's on the verge of shedding tears.

Who the fuck is she to Mike anyway? It's more than a damn work relationship by the way she's reacting.

Erin drops the bag and drink on the nearby coffee table, then hurries toward the door. "I-I'm so sorry. I didn't know!" The words come stammering out of her mouth; her breathing almost a pant. Her hands are visibly trembling, with a pained expression on her face that I'm all too familiar with.

She quickly swipes a stray tear away, looking anywhere but at me. She's freaking out before my eyes. I almost feel sorry for *her*. *Almost.*

"Yeah, they never do. Just leave, before Mike gets here and you make a fool out of yourself more than you already have." I mock, driving the final nail in the coffin.

Yeah, I don't think she'll be comin' back. Serves her ass right for trying to come in between me and my man. Well, he's not actually mine right now, but still.

Erin averts her eyes, gives a quick nod, and reaches for the door handle.

The click of the door opens to the sight of a speechless, gaping Mike, glancing back and forth between myself and Erin.

Shit. I just needed five more damn minutes to get her ass outta here. Five. Fuckin'. Minutes.

I release a breath I didn't realize I was holding, as I begin to hear my heartbeat in my ears, the pounding is so loud.

When Mike set his slits for eyes on me, his brows crease in anger and he grips the door handle so tight, I thought for sure he'd rip the damn thing off.

It hurts that he gives me the coldest glare I've ever seen in my life, not even knowing what happened. But what hurt more, is the fact that this bastard takes one look at *Erin* and nearly loses his fuckin' balance. The longing gaze that he gives her, the concern in his eyes. It's how he used to look at *me.*

As I stare at Mike, my feet freeze in place. His anger is palpable, like raging waves on a stormy day. I know right then that shit is about to get real.

"What the hell did you say to her, Jakyra?!"

CHAPTER 10

Mike

On the outside, my body is tense, and voice deep, almost a growl, but on the inside, I'm freakin' the hell out. What the fuck is Erin doin' here! My knees literally buckle when I see her. It's the *only* reason I'm holding' onto this damn door handle for dear life.

I take a good look at her. Erin's been…crying? What the hell happened here?

"*Jakyra*." The harshness in my tone should be a sign that I'm not for her shit right now.

Kyra rolls her eyes. "What? It wasn't anything that she didn't *need* to hear." The implication of her words make my stomach churn.

I peer over at Erin. She won't look at me. She's standing there— shoulders slumped, mascara running, and as much as she tries to hide it, shaking... *like that night at the bar.*

Shit. What the fuck did Jakyra tell her? My mind is racing with all types of scenarios… none turn out in my favor.

I finally release my grip from the door handle to move toward Erin, and she takes a step back. Stopping in my tracks, I stare in confusion. She averts her eyes once again. The knot in my stomach that formed earlier, just got a little tighter.

Kyra's exasperated sigh brings my focus back to her. "Alright, enough Mike. Let her go so we can talk. She *wants* to leave. Isn't that right…*Erin.* " Erin's head jerks up toward Jakyra, agreeing with a stiff nod.

Where's the quirky, lively woman I met at the bar on Thanksgiving night, or the feisty, seductive woman I met a couple weeks ago? It's weird seeing her like this, so lost, unnerved.

Sweeping the strands of hair from her face, Erin keeps her gaze on Kyra, not once giving me notice. "Yeah, I think that's best." She moves toward the door, and the look of betrayal that flashes across her face makes my blood freeze in my veins. "It was *never* my intention to come between you and your *husband.*"

I don't underst— Wait, what?! My eyes widen in realization, and I reach out for her, but she's already out the door.

Goddamn it!

"Erin! Wait! Please… wait!" I give Kyra a frigid glare, then bolt after her as my… *wife* stands with her arms folded, shooting me with a look death couldn't even rival.

I'll deal with her in a minute.

Erin bounces in place at the elevators, continually jabbing the button, willing it to open.

I grip her arm and she jerks away. "Please, give me five minutes." My eyes pleading and posture stiff, tensing more and more each second that passes without an answer.

"No need, Mr. Harmon. There's nothing more that can be said." Mr. Harmon… wow, that kind of hurt— *more than it should have*— but this is not about me right now.

Her professional façade has surfaced. But why am I pressing the issue? This is what I wanted, right? Just a work relationship, nothing else. *It's for the best.*

Fuck that. I thought I could stay away from her. I thought I could do this work relationship shit but seeing her today— in tears— did something to me. I *feel* an ache in my chest and the first thing I wanted to do was pull her into a warm embrace and never let her go.

I *want* this beautifully intelligent, sexy, vibrant woman, who centers me and quiets my raging storm. It scares the shit out of me, that only after two and a half weeks, I have these types of feelings for someone I don't even know that well. But I can't lie to myself anymore. There is an undeniable attraction and connection that we share that I can't explain.

Yes, I'm scared as hell that I might relapse, that I might turn into the man I used to be, but I'm more afraid of losing Erin for good. "There's a hell of a lot more that can be said, Erin. Please, let me explain." I rest my hand on her hip, not caring who's watching… and I'm sure they're watching. "We're gettin' a divorce— Jakyra and I. We're not together anymore, not even sleeping under the same roof. I didn't tell you because—"

"You just wanted a random fuck? You wanted somebody to fill the void until *your wife* was up for the task after the baby?" Her façade cracks, revealing her vulnerability.

The coldness in her tone renders me mute for a second, then I find my voice. "What? Is that what she told you?! No! That is *not* what I think of you, and the baby isn't even— look, can we *not* talk about that right now. Let's talk about *us*, and the fact that I can't stop thinkin' about you. I wanna explain all this shit to you; make you understand." The elevator pings, opening before us.

Erin slips out of my grasp, walking inside. "What is there to understand? You're still *married*, Mike. No matter how you spin it, you're *still* married, so there *is* no us." Her voice breaks at those last words. "Please, don't contact me again." She manages to say between shallow breaths.

I get a glimpse of the tears that flow from her eyes as the elevator door began to close. I clench my jaw to keep from yelling, but it's already a rumble deep in my chest and comes out before I can stop it. "Fuccck!" I slam my fist into the wall, knowing that I probably fractured it. If I didn't, it would be a miracle.

"Mike, calm down!" Chris hurries over, placing a firm hand on my shoulder.

I place both hands on the wall, eyes shut tight; my heart beating at an unimaginable pace. I inhale long, deep breaths, exhaling the same.

Chris distances himself, allowing me a bit of space. "You okay now?"

"No… Yeah… I don't know." It's all I can manage at that moment while my thoughts are scattered all over the place. My headache is in full swing, pounding from temple to temple.

Pushing off the wall, I swivel around to face him. Genuine concern for me seems to be an etched expression in Chris's facial features as of recent.

I glance around at the others, all frozen in place, *watching* me, scrutinizing, judging no doubt. "Get back to work. I'm not paying you to stand around." I return my focus to Chris, who waits patiently. I lean in closer to him. "Not. a fuckin'. word."

He gives his signature, annoying ass smirk, throwing his hands up in surrender. He gives a quick nod. "You *are* okay though, right?"

"Yeah, I'm good. I appreciate you."

"What's not to appreciate." He jokes, lightening the mood. "But seriously Mike, it's no problem. It's what I'm here for— the good, the bad, and the crazy."

I crack a slight smile, walking backward toward my office to deal with my… *wife*. "Hey Chris, no interruptions for the next hour unless the damn building is on fire, got it?"

"Got it!" Chris heads back to his desk.

I spin around to catch Jakyra standing in the doorway of my office, shifting on her feet. Her eyes are wide, and her arms cocooned around herself. She's terrified. Good. She *should* be.

CHAPTER 11

Erin

As soon as the elevator door closes, I completely break down. I can't believe I allowed myself to get sucked into the game that Mike and I were playing. He lied to me.... used me. He only wanted my body. He had no intention of pursuing me. He's... married.

I swipe at my tears as if they're burning a hole in my face, as the elevator pings and slowly opens to the lobby area. I take in deep breaths, exhaling the same, trying to stop the tremors that are currently taking over my body. My hands shake violently as I pick up my purse from the elevator floor, and step out of the lift, not bothering to look where I'm going.

My only destination is to get as far away from Mike as possible and that's why I don't see the solid frame that I collide with. I stumble back nearly falling over, but a strong grip catches me by the waist, preventing me from an embarrassing fall. After he steadies me, I lift my eyes to apologize and thank him but freeze in place when I realize who it is.

Ashton.

My ex.

The one I tried so hard to stay away from. The one who broke me into a million tiny pieces; stomped all over my heart and handed it back to me in ruins. The bastard who's standing right in front of me at the moment, gawking like he wants to devour me.

Of all the fuckin' places to run into him, it had to be here. Why is he even here?! How did he find me? Does he—

"Ren? You're the *last* person I expected to see here, but I'm glad I did." His words are smooth, dripping with lust. My body jerks away from him the moment I realize he's still holding onto my waist. He backs up a bit, a lazy smile spread across his stupid, handsome face.

Ashton is what you would call the "popular jock in high school" kinda guy. He never had a problem attracting the opposite sex, and he damn sure didn't lack in the looks department. His six-foot one lean muscular frame and low-cut wavy fade is one thing but his eyes—yes, I have a thing for beautiful eyes—his eyes are the lightest brown I've ever seen before, almost hypnotic.

They complement his light honey skin that's damn near flawless. His nose, perfectly set, and his lips, mmm, his lips. So soft, so inviting, so fuckin' kissable. He's absolutely boyfriend material, hell, husband material, but his behavior—the way he treated me, yeah that shit sucked. Aaand I'm back to reality, just like a slap to the face…with a brick.

"Why are *you* here? Did you follow me? Are you stalking me?" I ask in hushed tones, trying my best not to cause a scene in the middle of the crowded lobby. Ashton folds his arms across his stupid broad chest and chuckles.

He fuckin' chuckles.

I do a quick scan of the lobby. People are scattered throughout, busying themselves in a normal routine. Some are talking with receptionists, others are hurrying on and off the elevators, and yet others are sitting in chairs in deep discussion. No one is paying attention… good.

Returning my focus to Ashton, I glower at him. I'm so heated; it feels as if steam is coming from the top of my head. But somewhere deep inside, there's uncertainty materializing because I remember how it felt when we were together before everything went to hell. I remember how his body felt, hard and hot, as I lay underneath him. How my body responded when he touched me. I remember and I don't want to damn it. He broke me. He made me feel like I was nothing. He made me believe *I* was the problem.

"No Ren, I work here." He steps forward, closing the distance between us, lowering his voice, a deep raspy tone that sends an involuntary shiver down my spine. "But I can *work* somethin' else if you'd like." He ghosts his fingers across my jawline and despite my inward protest, fuckin' goosebumps break out all over my arms.

Shit.

This is *not* how this is supposed to be going. I don't want him anymore, but my traitorous body remembers; like it's trained to respond to his touch.

Damn it! No. This will *not* happen. I won't allow it.

I swat his hand away from my face. "Stop calling me that! You don't have that right anymore." I cross my arms over my chest and immediately his eyes zero in on my cleavage.

Pervert.

I roll my eyes so hard; it seems as if they'd roll right out of my sockets, but then it finally registers in my brain what he said. "Y-you… work here? How? When?" I don't mean for my question to come out sounding like a damn squeaky mouse, but that's exactly what the hell I sound like.

He eventually lifts his gaze back to my eyes, slowly licking his lips. "Well, you already know I'm good with numbers and Mike— Mr. Harmon was looking for a replacement in the Finance Dept. as supervisor. I applied, interviewed, and well, here I am. That was a year ago, and since then, I'm not only supervisor in the Finance Dept. but in the Accounting Dept. as well." He folds his arms across his chest once again.

I try to focus on what he's saying but my eyes travel to where his chest muscles contract, then lower, lower, lo—

"Eyes up here, Ren." I start at the sound of his amused tone, my eyes shooting up to meet his. I can't believe he just caught me ogling him. *Why* am I ogling him!

Shit. Stop it, Erin. He was your abuser—*but he was so skilled with his mouth…. and his tongue—* No, he's no good for you. He never was… that's not true. Ashton wasn't always abusive. He was sweet, attentive, understanding, funny as hell, faithful. He really *did* love me, but one night, all of that suddenly changed.

Ash had been acting strange all night. He seemed, nervous. What's going on with him? "Hey, babe, are you alright?"

He jerked his head up to meet my gaze. "Uh, yeah. Why wouldn't I be?" He bounced his leg slightly under the table as he quickly searched the dimly lit restaurant for the third time already. He said tonight was something we would never forget, so maybe that's why he's so tense. Maybe he'll propose! Oh, that would be— "You know I love you Erin, don't you?" I nodded my head, grinning like I just won the Miss America Pageant. Ashton gently took my hand in his, caressing the back of it with his thumb. He peered to the right of my head behind me for a second, stiffening briefly, then stared back into my eyes, taking in a shaky breath. "I really do love you. Never forget that." He whispered in such a tender voice; I almost didn't catch what he said. Oh. My. God. He's gonna propose! "But I can't keep doin' this shit!" He released my hand with a thud, a scowl on his face.

Wait, what?

My smile faded as quickly as it came. "Ash, what the hell are you talking about? We were just—"

"This shit!" He flailed his arms around the restaurant as he stood from his seat, pushing the chair back forcefully, causing others in the establishment to begin staring. "This fuckin' routine we have. It's as useless as you are! I thought you would get a damn clue, but your stupidity won that battle." People around the restaurant were now visibly staring, eyes as wide as my own as I listened to the man who just said he loved me, insult me to my face.

I was honestly at a loss for words. Ashton had never, and I mean never, talked to me like this before. Standing abruptly, I clenched my fists together to keep from slapping the soul out of him. "I don't know what the hell has gotten into you tonight, but you need to calm down. People are staring." I whisper-yelled.

He shot me the most intimidating glare I'd ever seen in my life, pointing stiffly at the chair that I'd just risen from. "Sit. The fuck. Back. Down." He spat each word out of his mouth as if it were venom he was spewing, wounding me more and more as the words left his mouth. "Don't make me repeat myself."

I blinked several times, forcing back tears. I can't believe he's saying this shit to me. My breathing increased and my hands started to quiver as I slowly sat back down, my eyes never leaving his.

"I'm just not satisfied with anything you do anymore, Erin. Is

that easy enough for you to understand?" He leaned on the table with his hands. "Not your cooking, your conversation, your body, or the fuckin' mediocre sex. I'm not satisfied, and you need to do something about this shit!" He pounded his fists on the table, causing me to jump a bit.

"Me??You think it's my fault?" My voice was as small as I felt. "What the hell did I do to deserve this?"

Did I... do something, say something that would cause him to treat me like this?

The tears that I'd been holding back finally fell, along with my self-esteem. I suddenly felt suffocated, as if someone were tightening their grip around my throat. I searched for my clutch, grabbed it, and with one final glance at Ashton— who looked, oddly, as pained as I felt— I rushed out of the restaurant, never looking back.

"Ren, what's goin' on? You zoned out on me." His soft caress along my cheek zaps me back into reality. Ashton wore a genuine look of care on his face, as he reaches out for me.

Taking a step back, I shake my head, trying to clear my thoughts. "I-I have to go."

"Ren, wait. We really need to talk." He holds my arm firmly.

I exhale an unsteady breath. "There's nothing for us to talk about. We've been over for a long time. It's... unfortunate we ran into one another today." I try to pull away, but his grip remains firm. Damn it. *Why won't he just let me go.*

"There's things you don't know. Things that happened back then that I couldn't tell you at the time. Please, give me a—"

"A what? A chance to hurt me again? Break me? Oh, I know!" I lift a finger as if I've come to a realization. "How about destroying my self- esteem?"

"I'm sorry, Ren. I never—"

"Save it, Ashton. I don't need your damn explanations." I finally pull free from his grip, and head toward the exit, when his next words stop me dead in my tracks.

"This has everything to do with Mel, Erin. She's the reason for everything that happened between us."

What?!

What the hell did Melanie have to do with our relationship back then? She was one of my closest friends. We shared everything, but after I left Ashton, we kinda… drifted apart. *I never got that.* Then, the car accident a year later threw me for a loop. Melanie's death really shook me. I still can't believe she's gone, but I just don't see what Ashton is getting at.

Slowly, I pivot on my feet; my ex approaching me with measured steps. "What are you talking about Ashton? What did my friend—"

"She wasn't your goddamn *friend*, Erin." The bitter bite in his tone is unmistakable. He stops a few inches from me as he releases a drawn-out breath. "Please, can we go somewhere private and talk?"

"No. I don't think—"

"She was blackmailing me, Ren." My eyes widen in disbelief. As I peer into Ashton's light brown irises, what I discover scares the shit out of me, because genuineness is staring back at me. I see concern, vulnerability. I see… *him*. The Ashton I fell in love with; the man that loved me. My God, he's telling the truth.

I take a staggering step away from him, shaking my head. "I-I can't do this right now, Ashton."

"Then, when?"

"After I get off work." I say, with bated breath.

"Where do you work? I can meet you—"

"No. I don't feel comfortable with you knowing where I work."

He sighs but nods in agreement. "Fine. Where can we meet?"

"At the park across the street from our old townhome at six o'clock."

"I'll be there, sitting inside the shed we used to picnic under." Moving closer, he takes my hand, squeezing it with the gentleness of a trusted lover. "I never stopped loving you, Ren. Never." Then just like that, he's gone, leaving me alone and… disconcerted.

CHAPTER 12

Mike

When I close the door to my office, I'm prepared to cuss Jakyra the fuck out. I'm ready to make her sign these damn divorce papers so that I can be done with her ass, but when I swivel around to face her, she's standing in the center of my office rubbing her baby bump with tears sprinkling her face. Then she speaks, and her words pierce through me like a sharp blade to the heart.

She's still the same proud five foot eight, graceful woman I have always known. Her butterscotch, smooth skin and slanted brown eyes— that always captivated me— glows from her pregnancy. Jakyra has always been her own woman, but the way she's gazing at me now— with uncertainty— is so foreign.

Inhaling a shuddering breath, she wipes away her tears. "You never ran after *me* like that." Her voice filters through the office like an echo. "You've never looked at me the way you look at *her*.

Never. You barely even *know* Erin, and you're fuckin' running behind her, trying to explain shit that's none of her business in the first damn place!" More tears escapes her eyes as I see the slight creases between her brows as she frowns." Why don't you fight this hard for *us,* Mike? I know this mess is my fault, but why was it so easy for you to give up on us? On *me*?" Jakyra's voice breaks as she swipes hard at her tears.

Swallowing hard, I feel my Adam's apple bob as I stand here— my hands on my hips— unable to utter a single word . I open my mouth to speak, but nothing comes out. Even if I *wanted* to disagree, I couldn't. She's right. Bowing my head, I feel the muscles in my jaw work. I can't even meet her accusing gaze anymore.

Unexpectedly, the guilt that I'd buried, resurfaces with an intensity so strong, I have to suck in a breath. The heaviness that's weighing on my chest nearly suffocates me as the atmosphere in the office churns with palpable tension. Closing my eyes, I exhale deeply, trying to control the sudden onset of emotions that begin shooting through me like a damn explosion.

"Say something, Michael." I hear her footsteps coming toward me. I keep my eyes shut, unable to look at her right now. She can read me like a goddamn book, and I'm afraid what she sees when I open my eyes is gonna give her hope for us, when there *is* none. "Mike, look at me." Jakyra's voice is so tender, I almost don't recognize it.

She grazes my cheek lightly with her knuckles and my breath hitches, as a lump lodges in my throat. My jaw clenches: hand immediately covering hers on my cheek. It's like her touch causes an automatic reaction from my body, and she knows it. I always respond to her touch because I'm accustomed to her body and she's attuned with mine, because… we love each other.

Shit.

No matter how much I try to deny it. No matter how much I *don't* want to, the fact is I *do* still love Jakyra, and I don't know how to stop. Our history goes way beyond marriage. Childhood friends, a family bond with her and her brothers that I thought could never be broken—that was a painful lie to discover. Yes, Jakyra and I have history, but we can't do this shit anymore.

I squeeze my eyes tighter. "We're toxic together Jakyra, and I don't wanna hurt you anymore than I already have." The words are like sand in my mouth. "Please, sign the divorce papers." Saying this shit to her is more difficult than I thought it would be.

I try to remove my hand from hers, but she catches it, and holds on. I feel stinging in my eyes from the tears I'd been holding back, so I continue to keep them closed.

She strokes my knuckles with her thumb. "Open your eyes, Mike. Look at me and tell me that."

Goddamn it Jakyra. Why are you makin' this so hard.

"Kyra—"

"Open your eyes." I feel the warmth of her body as she moves closer. Sighing, I finally give in. Our eyes lock and my heart squeezes to the point of explosion, seeing the crestfallen look on her face, but it doesn't keep her from placing her hand back on my cheek. "I *knew* it." She mutters, as if talking to herself. "You *do*. Why are you fighting us then? You *love* me, Mike."

"It doesn't matter, Jakyra. We can't—"

"It *does* matter… to *me*." She takes a breath, dropping her hand from my face, goes to grab the divorce papers and places them on my desk. "Tell you what. If this is what you really want, I'll give you an easy out." She lifts the divorce papers in her hand. "Look me in my eyes and tell me you don't love me and I'll sign these fuckin' papers… no argument."

My heart is hammering in my chest as I allow her words to sink in. Whether it's a lie or not, all I have to do is say four simple words. I already said it in my head, all I have to do is voice it.

I don't love you.

Easy.

I open my mouth, but my throat is suddenly as dry as the Sahara Desert. I swallow hard. Say this shit right now, Harmon. End both of your suffering. "I don't—" I clear my throat. "I— don't…" I tear away from her penetrating gaze, lowering my head. "I— Fuck." I walk away from her, frustrated with myself. Plopping down on the leather sofa, I put my head in my hands, Jakyra not far behind.

"So, what happens now?" She sits next to me, leaning on my arm.

"This doesn't change anything, Kyra. I love you, but it doesn't *change* anything. We can't be together anymore. We're toxic to each other, and I can't forget that this baby you're carrying isn't mine. How am I supposed to get past that shit!" I don't mean for my words to come across as harsh, but my emotions are running sky high. I have *never* been this goddamn emotional in all my thirty years on this earth, since I was a kid. I'm hurt, guilt constantly plagues me, I'm sad, then there's this big fuckin' spot in my heart with all this love I feel for Jakyra. I'm annoyed as hell.

"Mike, we can work—"

"We can't."

"Just give us a—" She tries again.

"No, Jakyra."

"Michael, I love you— please." Her cry is like a knife digging into an already bleeding wound. I turn to her, my wife's pained expression mirroring my own.

Then she does the last thing I expect her to do— leaning in, she brushes her soft lips against mine, and my body naturally responds. Instantly, I grip her face with both hands, swiping my tongue against her lips— she parts them, willingly. As our kiss deepens, Jakyra urges me back against the couch, straddling me. I strip out of my suit jacket, my hands finding the curve of her hips.

Kyra loosens my tie and the first few buttons of my shirt. She moans as I find my way to her breasts, massaging them with practiced care— they're fuller since the pregnancy. *The pregnancy. She's pregnant…with Jason's baby.*

Reality slaps me in the face… with a sandbag, stopping my movements altogether. "Jakyra—stop, I can't—"

"Mike please, I need this… *we* need this. Let's finish what we started." She moans, nipping at my ear, while grinding against me with a groan so erotic, it has me biting back a moan of my own.

In that moment, my logical reasoning takes a back seat, and I yank Jakyra's sweater dress over her head, leaving her in just a bra, panties, and boots. It's the first time I've seen her very pregnant belly. I force the feelings that bubble up, right back down. I know it will put a damper on what I want to do right now.

I'll deal with the consequences later.

Jakyra moves to unbuckle my belt, unzip my pants, reaches inside my boxer briefs, and grabs me. I tilt my head back, closing my eyes— unable to stop the guttural sound that escapes my lips— bucking into her warm hand. She knows exactly what she's—

"Oh… *shit!*" She strokes me hard. "Panties. Off." I command, hanging on to my control by a thread. Kyra climbs off of me for a moment, removing her underwear.

Of course, she has to put on a show, not that I'm complaining.

Slowly turning from me, she shimmies out of the scraps she

calls panties. She bends over a little to remove them completely, allowing me a perfect view of the wetness that glistens on the inside of her thighs. I lick my lips hungrily, watching her every move.

Yeah, keep bending over like that, and I'm gone fuc—

My desk phone buzzes for the third time, but I ignore it… again. The lack of blood flow to my brain has been replaced by sex-haze.

*This is **not** how you're supposed to run a damn business, Harmon.*

"Get over here, Jakyra." My voice thick with need as she submits, a seductive grin spreading across her face.

Something I haven't seen in a while. It's nice to see her smile again.

She ambles the short distance over, eyes hooded, lips swollen, entire body flush. As she straddles me again, taking me in her hand, she licks the shell of my ear, whispering, "Don't be gentle. You know how I like it."

"*Gentle* is the furthest thing from my mind."

You might not remember your own damn name when I finish with your ass. I'm gonna—

Knock!

Knock!

Knock!

Goddamn it! I *told* Chris not to disturb me unless the fuckin' building was on fire. This damn building better be going up in fuckin' flames, I swear to—

"Mike, Sorry to bother you. It's Ashton. Chris isn't at his desk, so I took a chance coming to your office. I need to talk to you for a few of minutes if that's okay."

Fuckin' Chris. I give him one simple task, *one* goddamn task and he— why is he even my PA if he never does what I ask him to do… that's a lie. He's covered for me more times than I can count. Chris is damn good at what he does, I'm just— Fuck! I have *never* been this sexually frustrated in my life!

Jakyra leans her head against my shoulder in disappointment, then lifts off me, putting her clothes back on with urgency.

Maybe we got interrupted for a reason.

I sigh, the lust-induced haze finally releasing me from its grip. "Hold on Ashton, give me a minute." I call out, already on my feet, zipping my pants and buckling my belt. I have never been more uncomfortable in a pair of slacks in my life than I am at this moment. Adjusting myself for the third time, I glance over at Kyra as she rises from the couch. "We almost—"

"Yeah." She smiles, blushing… *actually* blushing. "We can always pick up where we left—"

"We can't. I don't even know what the hell I was thinking.

This… *won't* happen again, I'm sorry."

She walks over to grab her purse, swiping the divorce papers from my desk, then turns back to me, her brows creased, shaking her head. "No matter how much you try, you'll never be able to erase me from your life." She saunters toward me, stopping just inches from my body. I peer down into her determined eyes. "You will *always* be mine. Your heart will *forever* belong to me. You can try to pursue Erin all you want, but in the end, *I'll* be the one you choose." Jakyra grips my tie, pulling me down, taking my breath away with a fiery kiss… and I allow her to. She pulls back, readjusts my tie, and saunters to the door, opening it to a surprised Ashton. "Hi Ashton. Mike's waiting for you." She moves aside so that Ashton could enter, then meanders out of the door confidently, never looking back.

Well, shit.

"Do I even wanna know?" Ashton closes the door behind him, then makes his way over to me, a questioning look clear across his face.

I shake my head as I round the corner of my desk to take a seat, Ashton not far behind. "Not really. It's… complicated." That's as much of an explanation I'm willing to give. Don't get me wrong, Ash is a good guy and friend, but I don't wanna get into all that shit.

Ash takes a seat in the chair in front of my desk, leaning back comfortably.

I adjust my chair. "So, what do you need to talk to me about, Mr. Ward?"

"Do you remember me talkin' to you about my ex, Ren?"

"Yeah, why?"

"I ran into her today, in the lobby. I don't know what the hell she was doin' here, but she was." He runs his hand down his beard as he continues. "Man, she's fuckin' gorgeous. I didn't realize how much I missed her until I saw her today."

"How did she react when she saw you?" I lean my elbows on the desk, giving him my full attention; happy I have something else to think about other than Jakyra or Erin.

"Needless to say, she wasn't exactly *enthusiastic* about seeing me. I knew she wouldn't be, but our chemistry is still there, whether she wants to admit it or not."

"Maybe you should try to pursue her, apologize. You still love her, don't you?" *Maybe I can help somebody else's love life since mine is shit right now.*

"Of course, I do. She's the love of my life. I got her to agree to meet me at a neutral spot, near our old townhome. That's why I wanted to talk to you. I need to leave a couple hours early if that's okay."

I shake my head, glancing down at my vibrating phone, feeling my blood pressure skyrocket in an instant. I huff out a breath, then focus my attention back to the conversation. "No, it's not a problem. I mean, who am I to get in the way of real love, right?" I smile. *Genuinely smile.* I want to see him happy. He's talked about this "Ren" since I've known him and he's finally getting a chance to redeem himself. I say, go for it. *You only live once.*

"Thanks Mike, I owe you one." He stands, then reaches over to shake my hand, relief spilling from the grin on his face. "I'm gonna get goin' so I can finish up this last report. I'll let you know how it goes."

"I don't doubt your skills, Ash. You got it."

He chuckles. "Let's hope so. See ya later." He walks over to the door, and let himself out, shutting it behind him.

I glare down at my phone, rolling my eyes. "I guess this is 'fuck with Mike' day." I clench my fist into tight balls, itching to punch something… or *someone.* I flinch a bit, still feeling the tenderness in my knuckles from stupidly punching the wall earlier, but I push past the pain. Images of me beating Jason until he's unconscious swim around in my head like a school of fish.

What the fuck does he even need to say to me at this point.

I glower at my cell for a few more seconds, listening to the sound of the vibration on my desk*, like it's taunting me.* Finally picking it up, I forcefully swipe the answer button. "What. The fuck. Do you want, Jason?" There's no damn way I'll be polite to his ass. I'm not pretending to be pleasant, or fake like I fuckin' care.

Jason not only cheated on my sister; he had sex with my goddamn wif—Jakyra. That shit calls for a fuckin' ass whoopin'. I'm not gone be satisfied until I put him in the goddamn hospital.

"Mike, I can't tell you how sorry I am. I never meant—"

"To fuck my wife and get her pregnant? To cheat on my sister and get caught? To betray my trust?" I growl out every word. Saying it aloud is like stab wounds to my gut. I grip my phone so tight; I hear the screen shatter.

Goddamn it! Rein in the anger, Harmon. Breathe. Just get his ass off the phone before you have a damn aneurysm.

I take a quick glance at my cracked screen, then put the phone back to my ear. "I don't need your apology! This shit can't be undone so—"

"MyIesha's missing." He blurts out, interrupting my one-sided rant, grabbing my attention.

"What the hell do you mean, she's missing?" I feign concern.

"The night of Thanksgiving, she wanted to stay at a hotel. I dropped her off that night and gave her a day or two to breathe, but when I went back to the hotel, she was gone. The hotel receptionist said she left the morning after Thanksgiving. I haven't seen or heard from Iesha since. I've looked everywhere for her! I don't know what else to do. I tried Marlon, but he said he didn't know anything." He's silent for a second. "You're my last resort, Mike. I know I don't deserve your help, but she's your sister, and I'm worried about her. I've been goin' out of my goddamn mind." Jason pours out every single word with urgency. It's good to know he's concerned about my sister, but I give zero fucks about how he's feeling.

"Okay?" I say, with little interest.

"*Okay*?! Didn't you hear what the fuck I said?! Iesha. is missing, and you—"

"I heard what the hell you said, and Iesha *is not* missing. *I know* where she is."

"What!? Then why the hell—"

"She doesn't wanna be found!" I snap, standing up from my chair, ambling over to the window. "Iesha called me the morning after Thanksgiving saying she needed to get away for a while to clear her head, so I made it happen. Simple as that." I let that bit of information slip…on purpose.

Now, take that, fucker.

"Where *is* she? I need to talk to her. I wanna be there for her. She's carrying my child!"

"Yeah? So is Jakyra. What's your point?" At my last snide comment, there's complete silence for several lingering seconds.

Did this asshole hang up on me? I know he—

"Jakyra was a stupid ass mistake, a lapse in judgment. I didn't want to be with her then, and I don't want to be with her now. It was a huge fuckin' mistake on both our parts, and we regret it Mike. I swear." Jason pleads with so much desperation in his voice, I would have bought it, had he not been the one to fuck me over. "I need me and Iesha to be okay. I want to show her how much I love her and wanna be with *her*. Please Mike, tell me—"

"No, leave her the hell alone. If she wants to talk whenever she returns, fine, but until then, back the fuck off!" I roar, walking away from the window to sit on the nearby couch. "If I had it my way, I wouldn't allow you near my sister again, but it's not up to me. So, until she contacts you, leave her the fuck alone! This is my first and last warning, Jason. Don't test me." Ending the call, I throw my phone on the couch, shaking my head. I exhale a ragged breath, gripping the leather armrest so hard I puncture it.

Shit. This day just keeps gettin' fuckin' better and better.

CHAPTER 13

Erin

The run-in I had with both Mike and Ashton today has my mind reeling. I'd been distracted for the rest of my workday and ended up leaving early with the lame excuse that I wasn't feeling well. It gave me a chance to go home, change clothes and mentally prepare for this dreaded meeting with Ashton. I don't know what the hell I was thinking, agreeing to meet up with him.

I sit in my car clutching the steering wheel like it's my salvation, as I glance back across the parking lot of the picnic area where Ashton has been waiting for the past fifteen minutes. I know I said six o'clock, and he, as usual, is on time. I, on the other hand, stall, debating whether I should even talk to him.

Do I really want to hear what he has to say? Do I need to know what happened back then; why he treated me like shit?

Yes. Yes, I do. Then, I can move on and finally heal.

I draw in a trembling breath, steeling myself, before releasing my vice grip from the steering wheel and open the car door. The gush of brisk winter wind causes an involuntary shiver to flow through me.

Ugh, I hate winter.

I slowly trudge over to where Ashton sits on top of the picnic table. His head's down, and he hasn't noticed me yet, so I stop several feet away, taking the time to really observe him. He hasn't changed at all. A bit more muscular and the addition of a scruffy beard, but he looks the same… beautiful, in a manly kinda way. I sigh, recalling the first time we were here at "our" spot.

What the hell is Ash doing? He knows we have a long day tomorrow. I just want to finish unpacking these last few boxes, eat and relax. I'm so damn tired from this move. I literally can sleep for a week but his ass has me blindfolded, strolling around outside like I'm walking the damn plank. I want to unwind in our new townhome and—

"Okay Ren, take the blindfold off." His voice was even and calm, as I feel the warmth of his body behind me, resting his hands on my hips.

I untied the loose knot from the blindfold, slipped it over my unruly hair and stilled at what I saw before me. "A-Ashton." His name was all I could manage to get out of my mouth. I'm blown away by his thoughtfulness.

The picnic table was laid out with all my favorite finger foods, fresh sliced fruit, several types of cheese and crackers to pair with the two bottles of wine that are set in the center of the table, with two large wine glasses. He even decorated the table in my favorite color— emerald, green— with hints of gold throughout.

My eyes mist over as he pulls me closer to him, kissing the side of my head. "You needed a break, and I wanted to do something to help you to relax. You work too hard, baby."

I turned in his arms, tears finally escaping. "Thank you. This is the most romantic, thoughtful, sincerely heartfelt thing anyone's ever done for me. This is the last thing I was expecting." I swiped the lingering tear away, as I graze his cheek with my knuckles, boring into his loving eyes. He smiled brightly at me, and my heart melted a little.

If Ash keeps this up, I'm gonna be a puddle on the concrete under this damn shed.

"Then I guess I've successfully surprised you then." He kissed my forehead, then reached down to grab a bouquet of red and white roses from the bench they lay on.

Oh wow, I hadn't even noticed those.

He placed the roses in my hands. I inhale the fragrant scent of the roses as he leads me to the table to sit. "These are beautiful, Ash. Thank you."

"You deserve this, and so much more. I would do anything for you. You know that don't you?" I nod, smiling sweetly at him, as I *placed the bouquet beside me. Ashton takes a seat on the opposite side of me, closing the gap between us.*

I took a grape, bringing it to my mouth with alluring intent. "Can we do this again?" I asked, hopeful, placing the grape between my lips, careful not to put the entire thing into my mouth.

Ash wet his lips, focusing solely on the grape. "We can do this every week... make this our spot, our thing." He leaned in to kiss me, taking half the grape that was visible into his mouth. "If you keep trying to seduce me like this, you're not gonna get a chance to eat."

"Well, maybe I'm not hungry for food anymore. I'm hungry... for something else."

He lifted a brow. "Really?" He kissed the edge of my mouth, causing my breath to catch in anticipation of what he's going to do next. "Well... too bad. We're eating food first, then we'll get to desert." He chuckled, pulling away from me, as I smack him in the chest.

"Asshole." I rolled my eyes at my tease of a boyfriend. I turn to pick up a turkey club sandwich from the container, Ash following suit.

He gives me a quick peck on the cheek. "I've been called worse."

I wipe away the tear that unknowingly escaped my eye, as I shake my head, trying to clear thoughts of my past with Ashton.

But isn't that what we're here to discuss?

My heart is pounding like a drum as I begin the trek toward him again. He notices me and stands, the both of us meeting at the edge of the grass where the concrete begins.

"Hey." I say in a small voice, rubbing my hands together to get a bit more warmth.

"Hey." He shoves his hands into his jeans—that fit him perfectly, might I add—giving away is nervousness. I'm no better, as I wring my hands like I'm squeezing the water out of a dish towel. "You're tense."

"So are you. The hands in the pockets gave it away." I giggle as Ashton yanks his hands from his pockets, running one hand over his beard. "Another tell-tale sign." I add.

"Okay, maybe I'm a *little* nervous." He admits. "Damn, stop readin' me, woman."

"S-Sorry." I stammer, averting my eyes from his.

"I'm joking, Ren, breathe." He places a hand on my shoulder. Ashton's touch is the same every time—gentle, soothing, calming. I release a trembling breath, swallowing hard; my mouth dry, and my palms beginning to sweat— it's always like this when he touches me.

I back away, allowing his hand to drop from my shoulder, then we stand in awkward silence for a few seconds before I clear my throat. "So, what is all this talk about Melanie blackmailing you?

Why was she even blackmailing you in the first place?" Sauntering over to the picnic table, I take a seat on the cold surface, Ashton not far behind.

As he takes a seat beside me, I instantly feel warmth emanating from him, engulfing me like a blanket. Ashton leans over, placing his elbows on his knees. He's quiet for several seconds, and the atmosphere around us becomes heavy.

What the hell happened?

Just as I'm about to voice my thoughts, he meets my gaze. Ashton's eyes reveals the same haunted, pained look he had that night at the restaurant.

Oh no. This can't be good.

He exhales, apprehension rolling off of him in waves. "I regret hurting you every single day. If I could take it back, I would but she made it near impossible to walk away without you getting hurt in the process." He turns his body to face me. "Melanie was always manipulative. She was jealous of you, but you couldn't see it for some reason."

I scrunch my face up in confusion, still unable to grasp how he came to this conclusion. Melanie *never* acted differently around me. "I'm not understanding. Melanie was always—"

"Mel blackmailed me with something she had on *you*." My eyes bug out of their sockets. "She was jealous of our relationship. She wanted *me*. She approached me one day after work and—"

"Wait a minute? How did she know where—"

"She admitted that she'd been stalking me for weeks."

I'm astonished that all of this was happening without my knowledge. How the hell had I *not* noticed her behavior?

"Anyway, Mel approached me after work and confessed to wanting a shot with me. She said you would never be enough for me. How you weren't my type and that I should leave you."

I'm speechless. My shoulders instantly sag, and my stomach roils. All that time I believed Mel was my friend. I thought we'd bonded, but the whole time she was trying to steal Ashton away from me?!

I shake my head, anger igniting in my belly. "I-I can't believe this!" I stutter, shooting up from my seat.

Ashton rises as well, standing in front of me; his sad eyes revealing so much guilt and regret I had to look away. "It gets worse." He releases a breath, long and deep. "When she demanded that I leave you, I laughed in that crazy bitch's face. I had every intention of walking away from her, until Mel said she had something on you. Something that would ruin your reputation… your career." He walks further into the shed, pulling something from his coat pocket.

Is that a… phone?

He's still faced partially away from me, but I see the phone as he stares down at it. "I warned her to stay away from us, then walked away when my phone received a video message. I heard her saying behind me that I'd change my tune after this; then the bitch laughed." Ashton turns back to face me, moving to where I stand— glued to my spot. "This is what she sent." He holds a phone out to me; my hand trembling as I take the phone from him and press play. "She threatened to not only send this to your boss and co-workers, but Mel swore she would post it across every social media platform that she could. She promised to make it her mission to destroy your career if I didn't get you to leave me."

As I watch the video, my eyes fill with tears. How the fuck did she get this?! I was a fuckin' junior in college when this happened!

"Before I could even say anything, Mel had already made it known that she had a copy and if I told you or went to the police… to anybody for help, she'd send that video out. Not only did she force me to make you leave, she *insisted* I humiliate you until you did." I can hear the agony in Ashton's voice as he speaks, but I can't tear my eyes away from the blackmail video. "Mel was everywhere *we* were. Home was the only place that seemed safe, and even then, I was on edge because she knew things that went on inside our home at times."

I blink the tears away as I continue to watch myself have sex with two guys I knew in college. It was *one* goddamn night at a party. I got pissy drunk and had sex with dudes whose names I don't even remember! The anger that ignites in me turns into a raging fire, but shame and humiliation creeps in, as my hands begin to shiver violently.

Ashton removes the phone from my hands, enveloping me in a warm embrace. I heave copious amounts of air into my lungs as he kisses my temple, rubbing soothing circles along my back.

My thoughts travel right back to every demeaning thing Ashton said to me when we were together. "You didn't think I was inadequate, or repulsive or—"

"God, no, Ren. I'm so sorry I put you through that. I *thought* I was protecting you at the time. I thought that by doing what she said—"

I push away from him, but he holds me tighter. "You hurt me, Ash! I had a breakdown! I had to go to therapy for almost two fuckin' years! I had to rebuild myself! Because of you, I didn't know who I was anymore! Y-You destroyed me!" I scream into his chest, gripping his coat so tight, I'm sure I tore it.

"I'm so sorry. So sorry." He continues to murmur into my hair. "I'm gonna spend the rest of my life makin' it up to you, showing you how much I love you. How much I never *stopped* loving you." He kisses my temple.

I sob deeply into his chest for what seems like hours but is only minutes. After my mini breakdown, the fog in my head begins to clear, and I'm finally able to regain focus. I draw back from him, knowing I look like a hot mess, and meet his gaze. To my surprise, it seemed as if he shed a few tears himself. "Why do you still have this video, Ashton?"

My question is direct and his answer is just the same, as he wipes my tears away. "I kept it for the sole purpose of letting you *see* what Mel was blackmailing me with in case you didn't believe me. I knew you wouldn't." He brushes the few stray strands of hair out of my face. "I searched for you soon after I heard of Melanie's death, and I never stopped. It was pure luck that I saw you today. I thought you had moved out of state." He clings to my waist like it's his lifeline. "I never looked at that video again after the first time, and now that you've seen it, I'll delete it and destroy the phone. In fact…" Ashton reluctantly releases me, then hands me the phone. "Please, do the honors." Without hesitation, I press delete, and instantly a weight lifts from me.

Ashton takes the phone from my hands, drops it onto the cold cement, and stomps on it with his foot, shattering it completely. "There *are* no more copies, so you don't have to worry. I wouldn't do that to you."

"But, how do you know Mel's copy is—"

"For some reason, she always kept it with her, so I'm fairly sure it was destroyed in the car fire when she died. Besides, I *made sure* she had no more copies myself. I give you my word, so please, don't worry." I feel relief, because if Ashton isn't anything else, he *is* a man of his word. I dare not ask *how* he knew Mel's copy was with her when she died…. I don't wanna know.

"Ren, I need you to understand, now that I found you, I'm never letting you go. I *will* pursue you until you're *mine* again." I avert my eyes from his heartfelt gaze, but he captures my chin turning me again to face him, and my breath seizes. "I love you. I always *will.*" He leans down, brushing his lips against mine, so light that it causes my knees to weaken a bit. "I don't care how long it takes; I'll wait for you." His declaration floors me.

I just find out things weren't as they seemed back then, and now he drops *this* bomb on me? It's all too much at one time. "Ash…." I whisper, my mind a muddled mess.

He shakes his head, his thumb rubbing my bottom lip softly. "We don't have to talk about this now. I just want to let you know where I stand." He kisses my forehead, then backs away, entwining my fingers with his… and I allow him. "Let me walk you back to your car." He offers, but not before disposing of the crumpled phone into one of the waste baskets nearby.

As we make our way to my car, I twist to face him, still baffled about everything he confessed to me. "Ashton, I don't even know if I'll be able—"

"As long as it takes, Ren. I'll wait." He repeats like a mantra. It's all he says before kissing my lips as light as a feather, then turns, heading toward his own car, leaving me with a whole new set of jumbled emotions to work out.

Shit. This just got a lot more complicated.

CHAPTER 14

Mike

New Year's Eve

I *did not* wanna bring in the New Year like this. Shit with Jakyra is nowhere *near* being resolved. Jason has a damn death wish to keep texting me about my sister, and Erin has been avoiding me like the plague for the past three agonizingly long weeks.

Fuckin' ironic. I did the same thing to her just over a month ago.

I know I should respect her wishes and just move on, but I can't. I tried, and I can't. I've made up my mind that I want her to be mine. I'm going to chase after her until she *is* mine. I'll find a way to deal with Jakyra, to get her to sign those damn divorce papers.

But is that really what you want though?

I close my eyes, blocking out that very unsettling thought. Of course, I want a divorce. I *want* Erin!

*You **want** both of them.*

I shake my head in defiance when the sudden blaring of my ringtone sounds off. I start at the unexpected noise, then glance around, noticing I'm still sitting in my SUV in the driveway of my house.

Come on Harmon, pull yourself together.

Reaching into the center console, I grab my phone; jaw set tight. A soul-destroying scowl seems to be my trademark expression these days.

Jason.

Take a breath. Relax. You're not gonna do this coming into the New Year.

I decline the call, block his number, then hop out of the SUV, and make my way to the front porch. The wind is blowing harshly, and the temperature is frigid, but there is still no snow, for which I'm thankful. I quickly unlock the door and step inside. "*Shit*. It's freezin'." I lock the door, rubbing my hands together to get them warmed a bit.

"Took you long enough." I jump at the booming sound of his voice.

"What the fuck, Marlon! Didn't you move out?!" I yell, throwing my keys— full force— at my irksome brother. "Why are you here, and where the hell is your car?" I question, meandering toward him, picking my keys up from the floor.

"I came to check on you, since you don't bother to call anybody…and that was rude." He rises from the seat he was just reclined in. "And my car is in the garage that you *never* use." He finishes, sarcasm dripping from his words.

I meet him where he stands, removing my coat in the process. I toss it on the sofa, then pull him into an embrace. "Sorry, I've been busy. We're about to start the Leeman International project in January, so it's been all early mornings and late nights for me." I make my way to the kitchen to prepare us hot chocolate, Marlon following along.

We sit at the center island, waiting for the pot with milk I put on the stove to heat up.

Marlon leans an elbow on the counter. "Other than that, you've been… okay though?" I know exactly what he's getting at, and I don't blame him. My track record isn't that great.

"I'm fine, really. I haven't taken a drink in almost four months. I'm good… well, not *good*, but… one day at a time, right?"

"Right." He sighs in relief, but the uncertainty in his voice is as clear as day... again, I can't blame him. "I'm sorry, Mike. I just— I know you've been dealin' with a lot of shit, and I don't want you to… relapse."

"I won't." I answer, more confident than I feel. Pushing away from the island, I walk over to the stove to turn it off, then pour the steaming milk into the two coffee mugs on the counter next to me, with cocoa mix inside. Grabbing two stirring sticks, I head back over to Marlon, placing his mug in front of him before taking a seat, as he watches me with justified caution. "I get why you might think that, given my past behavior but I promise you, that's not me anymore, bro." My heart feels as if it's been crushed with cement, knowing Marlon doesn't trust my words. I stir my cocoa aimlessly, the desire to have the sweetened beverage, gone. I'm not even able to meet Marlon's skeptical gaze anymore.

"Hey. Mike, look at me." Taking a drawn-out breath, I force my eyes to meet his. "I'm sorry I'm pushin' you so hard. I don't—" He exhales. "I don't wanna lose you to this… to the alcohol. I can't see you take the same road as our sperm donor."

I hear the strain in his tone the moment he utters the words. The pain etched in his face, in his voice. The devastation of losing not one, but two parents on the same day. My heart twists in agony, bile rising quickly in my throat, as the horrid memory of that day comes back unmercifully.

"It's the weekend, it's your birthday…. What are we doin'?!" *Marlon asked me, brushing against my shoulder, as we made our way toward the house. Today was my eighteenth birthday. I should be happy. I should wanna celebrate makin' it through another year of my dad's shit, yet I've had this sinking feeling in my gut all day*

while we were at the mall.

I've been jumpy, almost anxious. Even now, my heart was pounding outta my chest as I unlocked the door and stepped inside. "I'm thinkin', since I saved up some money for the past few months, me, you, Iesha, and Ma can get a hotel room downtown. Go out to eat, go to the festival and hang out there all weekend. We just need a break from—" We hear a familiar, disturbing scream coming from upstairs, and terror gripped me like a vice.

Not again.

Marlon and I raced up the stairs, taking two steps at a time. We rushed into our parents' bedroom to find dad leaning over mom, his bloody hand wrapped around her throat. The blood drained from my face as I watch mom literally fighting for her life, but before I had a chance to react, my sixteen-year-old brother bolts toward them.

He shoves my dad so hard that he nearly topples. Nearly. "No!! Get your damn hands off momma!" Marlon shoves him, full force, again.

Dad loosens his grip around my mom's neck, swinging wildly at him, connecting his fist with my brother's chest, knocking the wind out of him. Marlon tumbled back, falling over the broken lamp that was on the floor.

I looked at mom, then over to my brother and my mind drew a complete blank. With a few quick strides, I was towering over my dad, hands balled into tight fists, jaw set tight with fury seeping out of my pores. I snatched dad by his shirt, dragging him back and away from mom, then punched him so hard, blood from his mouth splattered across my white t-shirt. "What the fuck did they ever do to you! What the fuck did *I* ever do to you!" I tried to hit him again, but he caught my arm, yanking me down with him, and we tumbled to the floor.

He quickly recovered, kneeling over me, takes me by the throat and tightens his grip. I clawed at his hands, trying to loosen his hold, but he wouldn't budge. I heard mom yelling in the background to stop, then seconds later, her grabbing him from behind and pulling with all her might.

My dad's empty eyes were set on me as he pushed her away from him. "You know what you did to me you little bastard! Huh?! You were born! You and your stupid ass brother! You were born!" He screamed at me, all the while squeezing harder. "If your sister were here, she'd get the same treatment. You can't hide her forever." He spewed; his eyes eerily void of any compassion.

"Fuck you! You won't **ever** touch her, Ma, or Marlon anymore! I'll kill you before you do!" I managed to choke out, beginning to get dizzy as black spots invaded my vision, but I refused to lose consciousness. I gave him two quick jabs in the side to get him to loosen his grip, but he only tightened more.

That's when I see, through blurred vision, my mom cracking him in the head with something. I'm not sure what, but it was hard enough to make him get off me. I instinctively gulped in enormous amounts of air, as I felt Marlon's hands tugging me up. That's when I heard a loud bang. I peered over to see mom's head bouncing from the corner of the nightstand, her body crashing to the floor with a thud, then.... Silence.

I froze, as I see my mom laying on the floor, still. "Ma? Ma!" My quivering voice called out to her, unshed tears distorting my vision . I glowered, with murderous intent, at my dad, who stood just off to the side of her, motionless.

The terrorized look on his face said it all... dread. Dread of what he had just done. It's the first time I have ever seen him afraid, but I don't give u fuck about him. I'm gonna kill him. I already made up my mind about it... but—

I have to think about Marlon and MyIesha now. What's going to happen to them if I kill him? Who's going to take care of them? No. I can't kill him, but he's damn sure gonna rot in prison for the rest of his worthless life, you can bet that shit.

My heart was tattered as I stalk toward mom's battered body. "What did you do!" I roared, barely able to contain the devastation that poured out of me. I saw Marlon, as he dropped to his knees on the side of mom's lifeless body. He was bawling in agonizing grief, shaking her, hoping she would wake up, but I knew she wouldn't. She's dead. My mom is dead. He killed her. He took her from us. "No!!" I sobbed, tears finally escaping my eyes.

I jump at the light touch of a hand on my shoulder. Marlon gives me a knowing look. "Don't go there. It's not your fault...

and *you're not* him. I'm just worried about you, that's all." I blink a few times, trying to bring myself back to the present. "I trust you Mike, but you gotta talk to me." I can *feel* the positive energy flowing from him as he removes his hand from me.

His identical chestnut-colored eyes always reminded me of Ma when she stared at me like she could see right through me, and tonight is no different. I look away, unwilling to throw a pity party for myself—and the fact that he looks like a male version of our mom doesn't help.

From the contour of his cheek bones, the shape of his lips, eyes, and nose, to his African mahogany skin, to his compassionate nature and protectiveness. I could never keep anything from her, and I can't keep anything from him either. I push my cup of, now cooled, cocoa away, peeking over at him again. "I'm just dealin' with a few personal issues."

"What kinda issues? You gotta be more specific, Mike. I can't help you if you don't tell me everything."

I exhale, knowing he's gonna give me shit about this. "I kinda have a situation with Jakyra…"

"Okay, well we can deal with—"

"—And Erin." I finish.

Marlon tilts his head, burrowing his brows for a second, then his eyes widen as clarity dawns on him.

"What the fuck did you get yourself into, Mike?" He

accuses— with good reason— so I tell him everything that happened— from the time we left the bar Thanksgiving night to the present.

We make it back to the living room where I recline on the couch and Marlon sits on the chaise. He leans on his elbows. "You know Kyra's not gonna let this go. You opened the door to this shit and there's no way she'll let it close now."

"Didn't you hear what I said happened between me and Erin? I don't *want* Jakyra!

"You almost had *sex* with Jakyra." He points out matter-of-factly.

I roll my eyes in irritation. "That was a lapse in judgment."

"If Ashton hadn't knock on that door, you *would* have."

"*I don't* want Jakyra!" I snap, knowing he's getting a little too close for comfort.

"You don't know *what* the fuck you want. You're stuck, and you don't wanna admit it."

I throw a pillow at him, refusing to admit he's right. "Fuck you and your logical reasoning."

He chuckles, then flings the pillow back at me. "And if Erin told you to leave her alone, why don't you—I don't know— Leave. Her. Alone."

"I tried; it didn't work. I'm gonna pursue her until she gives in or gets a restraining order against me for being a fuckin' stalker, because you can guaran- damn- tee, I'm not givin' up." I'm serious as hell. I may still have feelings for Jakyra, but I'm *not* lettin' Erin go.

Marlon lets out a boisterous laugh, shaking his head. "You have serious issues, bro."

"Well, you already knew that, so…" I shrug, lifting up from the couch and move toward the hallway walking backward. "Gotta take a leak. Be right back."

"Too much information." He hollers, leaning back on the chaise. I give him the middle finger, then continue to my destination.

CHAPTER 15

Marlon

Sometimes I feel like *I'm* the oldest, because both Mike and Iesha can be a bit irrational… and impulsive… and immature. Okay who am I kiddin', they can be fuckin' outta control sometimes, but I guess that's why I'm here to balance us all out. If not, it would be a zoo of goddamn chaos. But hey, you can't choose who your family is, right? Not that I *would*.

I love them to death, and I wouldn't change a thing about'em…. and Mike? Mike gave up a lot for us, before *and* after mom died… I mean, after she was murdered, because that piece of worthless shit killed— I can't allow myself to go there. I have to be strong for my brother. I didn't suffer *nearly* as much as he did when Don, our sperm donor, was on the rampage. Iesha didn't experience the beatings, but she couldn't escape being yelled at, the unnecessary punishments, and seeing our mom get abused.

She has no idea, to this day, the extent of what me and Mike went through and if we have anything to do with it, she never will. We couldn't shield her from the devastation of the day our mom was killed though. It was one of the hardest things we've ever had to do.

The ride back to Aunt Lea's house was hauntingly quiet. The air was thick with anxiety and pent-up grief. Mike was as stiff as a statue, as he held MyIesha's hand firmly.

I glanced over at my clueless sister as she fidgeted in her seat, as restless as always when we're in any type of vehicle. She doesn't know what happened to mom yet and if I'm in the room with Mike when he tells her, I might break down in front of her before he even has a chance to get the words out.

The car came to a stop as Iesha darted her eyes around in confusion. "Why are we at Aunt Lea's? I thought we were going home. I wanna tell momma I made the team!" She pulled her hand away from our brother. "And I thought we were doing something for your birthday, bro?"

Mike's jaw tightened as I took a quick peek at him, and my heart plummeted in anguish. I think of holding Ma's hand for the last time. Tears escaped my eyes before I had a chance to stop it, and MyIesha noticed almost immediately.

"Mookie, what's wrong? Why are you crying? What happened?" MyIesha has called me that stupid nickname since she's been able to talk. Over the years I've come to love it. She's

the only one who gets to call me Mookie... well, and Mike when he's teasing me.

I swiped the tears away and got out of the car, my other two siblings right behind me. "Something happened, Iesha, and I don't—"

Mike shakes his head. "No Marlon, not yet just... wait for me. I need to talk to Aunt Lea for a second." He took our sister into the ranch style home, leading her to the couch in Aunt Lea's pristine living room.

I watched my brother as he instructed Iesha to sit, then went into the kitchen to talk to our aunt. As I looked around, I saw that Auntie's place hadn't changed a bit. The eggshell-colored walls with dozens of family photos, a fireplace that sits on the far wall in front of us, where we used to roast marshmallows and the small dining room off to the side. It's a cozy home and we have always felt comfortable here, but now being here just felt... incomplete.

As I took a seat next to Iesha on the navy-blue couch, she turned to me right away. I tossed the blue and white throw pillows aside as her questioning gaze caused me to nearly spill my guts. "Mookie?"

"Just wait until Mike gets back, then—"

"Why can't you tell me? Why are we here? What's going on? Why won't anybody tell me anything?"

The questions kept coming in rapid succession, causing my

heart to ache and my eyes to water. I'm trying damn hard to wait for Mike, but the look she gave me—anxious, scared, unsure— was wearing me down. I can't keep quiet anymore. She needs to know. I inhaled a ragged breath, taking her hand in mine. "Iesha, we can't go back home. Something terrible happened."

She gripped my hand a little tighter. "Wha-What happened?" Her voice was trembling with fear. "Momma and Don had a fight and..." I faltered for a second, the words feeling like gravel in my mouth. "Don... he—"

"Shit Marlon, I thought I told you to wait for me?!"

"She needs to know, Mike. We can't protect her from this!"

"I know we can't, I just wanted to—"

Iesha jumped to her feet, silencing us with a yell so full of emotion, I wanted to cocoon her from the pain we were about to inflict on her. "Stop arguing and tell me what's wrong! I'm fourteen, not a little girl anymore. You don't need you to protect me!" She roared, tears threatening to spill from her eyes. Her hands trembled and breaths teetering the fence of hyperventilation. "I just wanna go home. I wanna go home and see momma. Why can't I just go home?" She begged, her voice cracking.

I peeked over at Mike. The apprehension, the pain that radiated from him was intense. His jaw was clenched tight, and I noticed his hands shaking vaguely before he shoved them in his pockets. "You can't Iesha— we can't." Mike answered, his voice straining with every word.

"Why not?"

"Because... Don, he.... hurt Ma and—" He attempted to explain, stumbling over his words.

"Oh my god! Is she gonna be alright? Is she in the hospital? We need to go see her! Take me to—"

"Iesha." I uttered, causing her to turn her attention to me. I knew Mike was about to lose it. His eyes gleamed with unshed tears, as we stepped closer to our distraught sister. "Momma's... dead. Don killed her." As the words finally spilled out of my mouth, tears followed.

I watched as Iesha took a sharp intake of breath, her eyes widened, then tears fell, but she didn't say a word. After a few seconds, I noticed she hadn't exhaled.

"MyIesha, breathe!" I yelled, gripping her shoulders with contained force.

Mike cradled her face with both hands so that her devastated gaze met his own sullen one. "Breathe for me, baby girl." I have never heard Mike sound so loving, as he encouraged our sister. I knew inside he was all over the place, but he'd never let her see that side of him.

As Iesha finally released her breath, she let out a deafening cry that shook me to my core. She crumpled to the white carpeted floor, sobbing painfully, as Mike and I joined her; all of us on our knees, embracing and comforting one another. We let go of all the unreleased grief that we'd been holding back. I knew that after this, nothing would ever be the same.

My phone buzzes on the glass end table next to me, jolting me out of my thoughts. The pain of the memory weighing heavily on my mind. I run a hand over my face, trying to refocus, when I notice wetness on my cheeks.

Damn.

I release a lengthy breath, fully back in the present. My phone stops buzzing but starts right back up seconds later. I pick it up, glancing at the screen.

Koko.

I swipe the answer button. "Hey baby, what's up?"

"You've been gone all day. Me and Eva are missing you, that's all." She feigns honesty.

My wonderfully sweet girlfriend, who is always there when you need her. With her knock-out smile, beautiful personality, and come-hither light brown eyes, Koko is one in a million, but right now, I'm calling her out on her bullshit.

"Yeah right. It's just time for daddy duties and I'm late. Don't pull that, *I miss you*, shit with me. I know you too well, Koko." I laugh, knowing that she *knew* she was caught. "Hello? You still there Ms. Hobson?" I chuckle again, as I hear her huff out a forceful breath on the other end.

"Damn it. Fine, you caught me. I was really trying to see what time you were coming home, cause this lil' girl is driving me crazy. Only three months old and she's taking advantage of the situation." I laugh so hard; my side begins to hurt. "You know she's a daddy's girl. She knows where the winning side is."

"Whatever, smartass." She huffs. "Anyway, G called to check on me and Eva today."

"Uh, doesn't he realize there's a third party in this situation? He's always been a rude bastard."

"No he hasn't. Your brother is the rude one." She laughs. Can't argue, she's right. "He's in Missouri right now."

"What the hell is he doin' in Missouri?"

"Searching for our brother."

"What?! Mick's… alive?" I'm stunned speechless. Miguel— we called him Mick— and George are twins. Even though they aren't identical, you couldn't tell them apart when they were younger. George witnessed his twin get kidnapped when they were eleven years old and after unsuccessful attempts to find him, the cops closed the case. Told their family that Mick was most likely dead. Just like that. G hasn't been the same since. "How is that even possible?"

She sighs on the other end of the line. "I don't know, but he hired a P.I. back in November before he left the day after Thanksgiving." Koko is silent for a second then, "He says Shylah, his investigator, thinks it's a strong possibility that Mickie could have been the victim of human trafficking."

I sit up a bit straighter after hearing that. "Wow. They think he could be in Missouri, and what about his job?" My brain is firing on all cylinders. This shit is crazy. Mick could actually be alive!

"He took a leave of absence. He said if he needs to be gone longer he'll either work from where he is at the moment or quit. He has more than enough money saved so he should be okay."

"I guess it pays to be the one in charge, only second to the big boss. I can't blame him though. If there's even the slightest chance that y'all brother could be alive…." I trail off. This is some major shit. "Did he say—" There were several rapid knocks at the door, interrupting our conversation. "Baby, I'll be home soon. Give me about an hour, okay?"

"Alright. I love you."

"I love you more." I end the call and trek over to the door.

The moment I touch the handle, a bad feeling washes over me like ice water. I hesitate a second before finally pressing down on the handle.

Shit. This is *not* gonna end well.

"You really shouldn't be here, Jason. You need to leave. *Now*." I place an arm across the doorway so he can't pass.

Jason looks horrible. I do a quick once over; he's a total mess.

His eyes have shadows underneath them; it seems as if he hasn't shaved in weeks, his usual low-cut hair is now in short twists, and his mix-matched clothes are wrinkled. I've *never* seen Jason look so out of place. I understand he's worried about Iesha, but he brought all this on himself, and if Mike sees him, I'm afraid—

"I just wanna know where she is. I tried callin' Mike earlier, but he wouldn't answer, so I came over. I knew he was home. I need him to tell me where—"

"Let it go! Mike's not gonna tell you. In fact, if he sees you at his house, he might break your damn jaw. Leave Jason. It's fucked up what happened, and as much as I wanna kick your ass, I'm not. I can't say the same for my brother though." I try to make the threat sound as intimidating as possible but it's like talkin' to a damn brick wall. His ass can be so stubborn sometimes.

"In all honesty, I came here expecting a fight. I know Mike hates me, but I will *not* give up looking for her, Marlon. What if it was Koko? Would *you* give up?"

What kinda dumb ass question is that?! Of course, I wouldn't give up! I would go through anything *or anybody* until I found her! I would— I see his point. I remove my arm from the doorway, knowing that I'm making a huge mistake. "No, I wouldn't, but I didn't have sex with Mike's wife and get her pregnant. I don't know what he's gonna do if he sees—"

"I know what I'm walking into. I'll take my chances." He slips past me and into the living room.

I shake my head at my own stupidity, then close the door, following after him. "For the record, I tried to warn you."

"Duly noted. Iesha is my—"

"Son of a… *bitch*!" Mike roars as he storms toward Jason. "What. the fuck. are you doin' in my house?" Every word Mike spews from his mouth is like a snake striking its prey. Then, he turns his death glare my way, his eyes murderous.

Oh shit.

"What is he doin' in my house, Marlon?" Suddenly, his voice is eerily calm. I don't like eerily calm Mike. Eerily calm Mike is a dangerous, uncontrollable Mike.

Fuck.

"I— Mike, breathe. You don't need to go there. Remember your progress. Remember—"

"It's not his fault. I forced my way inside. I just wanna find MyIesha. I need to know she's okay." Jason pleads; his stance unguarded…. not wise.

Mike snaps his frigid gaze back to Jason, his jaw so tense, that the vein in his neck is twitching. I shoot a quick side glance at Jason, wondering why he decided to lie at this very crucial moment, knowing that the wall of Mike's control is crumbling before our eyes.

"Mike." I drawl, noticing his fists clench into tight balls; the exact moment his control snaps. I reach out, to restrain him a second too late.

Mike's fist connects with Jason's jaw, causing him to stumble back, tumbling over the cherry oak coffee table, and fall to the floor with a thud. Mike doesn't give him time to recover. He kneels over Jason so quickly; I never get a chance to grab him.

Mike delivers every blow to Jason with so much force that I'm sure something has to be fractured. There is nowhere on Jason's face or upper body that Mike's fierce blows didn't make contact,

but what's even more disturbing is Jason isn't trying to fight back or even defend himself, not once. He's blocking as many blows as he can but never throws a punch.

I tear myself out of the initial shock of Mike's fury and force my feet to move toward my rabid brother. "Mike! That's enough! He's still Iesha's boyfriend!" I peel him from a groaning Jason. "Bro, get a fuckin' grip!" I push Mike back farther.

Jason gradually pushes to his feet, holding his left side. I'm pretty certain something's wrong, with how he's gasping for air and the grimace on his face, which honestly has me a bit concerned.

Mike jabs at him a few times, as I keep my forearm to my brother's chest. "I warned your ass, Jason, but you keep pushing me. You keep fuckin' pushing me!" Mike suddenly shoots past me, catching Jason with a blow so brutal, it sends him barreling into one of the end tables; the back of his head colliding with the edge of it.

Jason crashes onto the floor, then nothing. It's like déjà vu. I swallow hard. My heart is in my throat as I rush toward his still body. My hands tremble as I check for a pulse.

I can't feel one.

Shit.

No, this isn't happening again.

My heart races, fearing the worst. I shoot my eyes over at Mike, frozen where he stands, his blind rage evaporating like water on a scorching surface. The haunted look in his eyes, revealing the terror his stiff stance displays. Mike's breathing so hard, it looks as if he's having a panic attack.

"Mike, I can't find a pulse! H-He's dead!" I choke out, barely holding my distress.

The tone of my voice must have jolted my brother back to the present because the next thing I know, he's on his knees beside me, taking Jason's arm in his hand, checking his pulse. After a moment, I can see him visibly relax. "He has a pulse. We need to get him to a hospital." Mike speaks with controlled precision, although there's a strain in his voice. I know my brother well enough to see he's worried about Jason and regrets his actions. Whether he hates him at the moment or not, Jason's still one of us. He's still one of our best friends, regardless of the fucked-up situation between them right now.

I glance at Jason, noticing a pool of blood slowly beginning to pool around the wound and I have to force the bile back down that rises in my throat. "Mike, we need to—" I start, then realize Mike already has his phone in hand, giving directions to the person on the other end of the line. I exhale a sigh of relief, standing upright. When I go to help my brother up, I see him holding onto Jason's hand, unwilling to let go.

"Bro, he's gonna be fi—" I begin, but he shakes his head, brows deeply furrowed. I know then, if I say anything more, he'd lose it.

I nod, giving him a tight squeeze on the shoulder, then amble over to the chaise to have a seat. As I sit, I hear the faintest sound of sniffling, then two words echoing through the house like a whisper.

"I'm sorry."

CHAPTER 16

Mike

Guilt.

Guilt consumes me as we wait for the doctors to come with news on Jason's condition. I'm sure he's gonna press charges. I don't blame him. I didn't mean to hurt him this bad, but my rage swallowed me whole, leaving no room for logical reasoning, and this? This is the result of unchecked anger. I thought I had it under control. I assumed my anger problem was behind me.

I sit in one of the chairs of the waiting room, staring at my hands, still tinged with Jason's blood. I suck in a deep breath as my hands quiver in my lap. If only he would have— no, this is *not* Jason's fault. It's mine.

Fuck! I'm no better than Don! I could have—

"Don't. This is *not* the same situation." Marlon says, as he plops down next to me. Sometimes I honestly believe he *can* read my mind.

"How is it *not* the same? Jason could have died if I hadn't been so reckless. He still could—

"Stop, Mike. You're not our father, okay. Yes, you could've handled this shit a different way, but it was a mistake. This was a different—"

"How?! How the fuck is this any different from what Don did to momma?! He pushed her, she hit her head, and she died. I punched Jason, he hit his head, he could have died… there still may *be* damage."

I shoot up from the chair and amble toward the door. I need fresh air, it's too stuffy, too closed in. My chest is tight, so much… guilt. It's eating me alive. I have to get out of here. I have to…. I need a drink. I need something to calm my nerves, ease my guilt, to make me… forget.

"Mike." My brother calls out, as he makes his way to me. "Breathe. Deep breaths, come on." He coaxes. I didn't realize my breathing had become so shallow. My heart stutters in my chest. I stare into Marlon's eyes, conforming to his instructions until my breathing stabilized. "Better?"

"Yeah. Thank you." I choke out, as my wall finally crumbles. Marlon pulls me into a tight embrace as I release years of grief, anger, and guilt. He hugs me until I'm able to pull myself together. Only then, does he let go. I wipe the tears from my face and exhale.

He squeezes my shoulders. "You needed that."

"Yeah." I breathe.

Marlon wraps an arm around my shoulder, leading me back to sit down. I scan the room, content it's still only Marlon and I occupying the space. "So, you good now?"

"I don't know about *good*, but I'm better." There's still a tiny voice tempting me to get that drink… and the voice is winning.

"I'll take that. It's a start." The worry lines in Marlon's forehead visibly disappear. "Oh, I talked to MyIesha." He adds, as he peeks over at me. "She knows… everything. Ironically, Iesha called me a few hours ago when I was… vulnerable. She heard the panic in my voice and asked what happened." He sighs. "I spilled my guts faster than an inmate pushin' for immunity. I had to tell her, sorry."

Shit.

"Was she mad?" It's a dumb ass question. I know MyIesha's mad, and she's gonna let me know *how* pissed when I talk to her.

Marlon looks at me like I'm a damn fool. "This is our sister we're talkin' about. She had some…. choice words for you. Said she'll talk to you when she sees you." I crease my brows. "Iesha's on her way back home. She should be here…. at the hospital, in a couple hours." I lower my head.

MyIesha? Here? Fuck.

"She said somethin' about her foot, your ass, and you seein' stars." He shrugs, I groan.

The sound of footsteps catches my attention and I look up to see the doctor enter the waiting room. "Mr. Harmon?" Marlon and I stand simultaneously.

"Yes." We both respond in unison.

"So, I have good news." The tension instantly leaves my body at his words. "Mr. Morrison is going to make a full recovery. There is no internal bleeding, but he does have a moderate concussion, bruised ribs, and pretty bad facial and body bruising." He glances at his notes briefly. "All of his tests came back normal. He does, however, have a nasty headache, and he may be a bit dizzy, but other than that, he should make a full recovery."

Relief floods my body. I extend my hand to the doctor. "Thank you so much for taking care of him."

"You're welcome. It's what I'm here for." He shakes our hands and heads toward the door. "If you want to see him, he's awake." Marlon nods, peering over at me.

I shudder at the thought. "Thanks, we will." The doctor exits the room, and I take a seat. "You go ahead, Marlon. I'm not ready yet."

"Mike—"

"I'll come and see him; I promise. Just not yet." Marlon reluctantly agrees, then departs, leaving me alone with my thoughts.

CHAPTER 17

Erin

I am out of my damn mind to be doing this! I said I was done with Mike, yet here I am on my way to the hospital on New Year's Eve to see about him instead of going to the small gathering I planned to go to with Ashton— as friends of course. I was doing so well ignoring his calls—although I listened to every single voicemail he left me—I was getting over him, but one phone call from his brother and my defense collapses like a house of cards.

Marlon called from Mike's phone so as usual, I waited until a message was left. When I listened, it was Marlon speaking in hushed, panicked tones that set the hairs on the back of my neck on edge. When I called back, he told me everything; from Jakyra cheating and getting pregnant by one of their best friends, to Mike putting said friend in the hospital.

But what made my stomach bottom out is when he told me

Mike wasn't doing great. It brought to mind the night I saw him on Thanksgiving—the despair in his eyes, the lost, defeated gaze he had when he thought I wasn't watching. The internal battle he was having with himself whether to take a drink or not. *That*'s what I fear most right now. If I can help him from giving into that urge, I will…. whatever it takes.

I slide the key out of the ignition and release a long breath. Opening the car door, I step out. A strong gust of brisk winter wind meets my body causing me to shiver. I press the alarm for my car and quickly scurry across the snow dusted parking lot, into the hospital where I'm met with a receptionist.

I saunter further into the lobby area. The place smells of disinfectant and air freshener. It's well lit, but the hallways are nearly empty. A nurse here, a janitor there, but empty with an unsettling quiet that gives me goosebumps. I take in a breath.

Concentrate. Mike is here somewhere, and I need to find him.

An older, chubby-faced woman scans me with curiosity. I know it's way past visiting hours, but Mike's in trouble. "I'm sorry Miss, visiting hours ended two hours ago. You can always—"

"I understand that, but I was called here for an emergency."

She shakes her head and releases a breath. "Hospital policy states that—"

"Fuck your hospital policy! I need to know where Mike is, right now!" I shout. The receptionist's eyes widen in disbelief; her lips pressed into a thin line. I don't mean to be rude, but the more time I waste here, the worse—

"Erin? What… are you doing here?" I twist around to see Mike's six-foot frame meandering toward me. His clothes are a disheveled mess—tie undid, shirt untucked, pants wrinkled, and is that…. blood?

What the hell did you do Mike?

Completely disregarding the receptionist's disapproving scowl, I rush over to him. "Mike!" I fall into his arms, wrapping him in a tight embrace. "Why didn't you call me? I would have been here sooner."

He returns my embrace, relaxing as he releases a shaky breath. "I've been *trying for* three damn weeks now, but you wouldn't answer— haven't so much as come to any of the meetings I attended. You've been MIA." He pulls back, resting his hands on my hips. I shiver at the innocent gesture.

Calm down, Brooks. Mike needs you. No time to be thinking inappropriate thoughts right now. Behave.

"Right. Sorry about that. I had to put as much distance between you and I as possible or I would have—" I catch myself before I can finish. We don't need to do this right now.

"You would have what?" He presses, eyes boring into my own.

I avoid his intense gaze, feeling heat rise to my cheeks and…

other areas of my traitorous body. "It doesn't matter. Right now, I'm here for *you*. Where were you going? Is your friend going to be alright—*if* he's still your friend, that is." His grip tightens on my hips and an emotion I can't quite place, flashes across his face… regret?

"He's still… a friend, but it's… complicated." Mike frowns as he releases my hips and stalks toward the exit.

The receptionist clears her throat as she watches the entire interaction. "Mr. Harmon, we have visiting hour policies in place and—"

"Thank you for pointing that out, but I know your fuckin' policies." He snaps. "If you have issues with either myself, Ms. Brooks, or my siblings coming to visit my friend, take it up with his attending physician. He's the one who gave us permission to see Jason after hours." Mike's voice echoes through the empty lobby. He's intentionally being rude, I *knew* that, but it's…. turning me on.

Damn it. Just. Stop.

The short, plump woman's face reddened, then gives a tight-lipped nod, going elsewhere.

He continues toward the exit, but I call out to him. "Where are you going, Mike?"

"Why does it matter?

"Answer the damn question and stop being so stubborn."

Mike tilts his face upward; his hands behind his head and breathes out roughly. "I need—"

"A drink?" I finish his sentence.

Mike's arms drop to his sides and his tired eyes shoot from the ceiling to glowering directly at me. I can't say that the way he's staring me down isn't a bit… frightening, but I refuse to let him intimidate me.

I stalk toward him as he clenches his jaw so tight, I see the muscles working. "No, you *don't* need a drink. You need to work through all these damn emotions that you're trying to drown in alcohol."

"Leave me the fuck alone, Erin."

I grab either side of his face, forcing him to make eye contact. "No. Talk to me."

"Like you talked to me these past three weeks?" Yeah, I ran right into that one. "I just wanted a chance to explain myself to you, but you completely shut me out."

"You're deflecting, Mike. Right now, we're talking about what's happening with *you*. We'll talk about everything else later." I stroke his jaw with my knuckles. "Talk to me." Mike glances around the hospital lobby. It's damn near a ghost town here. I gently guide his face, returning his focus on me.

He sighs, swallowing hard. "I was supposed to be doing better; thought I had a handle on my anger, but the fact that I just tried to kill Jason….” His words stammer over one another as he speaks. He gulps hard; his breathing begins to quicken. “I’m… scared I’m gonna hurt somebody worse than this. I’m terrified of hurting… you.”

I tilt my head and scrunch up my face. “Me? I know you wouldn’t—”

“I used to be abusive, Erin. I physically abused Jakyra; it’s why she left me the first time.”

I’m speechless. My hands shake violently as I take his hands in mine. I can hear the deep pounding of my heart in my ears. He can tell that I’m shocked, by my saucer sized eyes and sharp intake of breath, but I don’t falter. I refuse to shrink away. I won’t bail on him. His past is just that… the past, but I see the shame in his beautiful brown eyes as he continues.

“I eventually changed for her, because she didn’t deserve to be treated like shit because of my fucked-up childhood. By the time I got it together, she ended up getting pregnant with Jason’s baby and it crushed me.” Mike pulls away from me and trudges toward the vacated receptionist station. I follow quickly behind him. “Jakyra dealt with my shit for three years before she separated from me, and at the first sign of trouble, I left her.”

“You have a right to be upset with both Jason *and* Jakyra. She slept with your sister’s boyfriend— one of your best friends. You have a fuckin’ right to react that way, Mike.”

He jerks his head in my direction. “How do you know about—"

"Marlon… filled me in on some of the details of what happened when he called me earlier. He's worried about you, by the way."

"I know." He agrees. "And that just adds on to everything else I'm dealing with. His worry. I'm the eldest of us; he shouldn't be worrying about me. I'm supposed to be taking care of *them*, protecting them, and I can't even—"

"Yes, you *are* the eldest, but you're not invincible, Mike. You're human. You make mistakes like everyone else."

"Yeah, but my mistakes might cost someone their life one day…. just like Don took my mom's." Enclosing my arms around Mike's waist, I hold him tight.

Marlon told me unsettling incidents about their childhood too, and one thing he is *not*, is his father.

"I'm ashamed of what I've done to Jakyra, Jason… you." His arms tighten around me as I hear the break in his voice as he speaks. "I know we haven't known each other long, but my feelings for you are strong and I'm scared as hell of losing you. I need you, Erin. You're my calm, my peace." He whispers.

Tears sting the corner of my eyes, as I listen to his heartfelt confession. His feelings mirror my own, and *that* is terrifying. We've known one another for a little over a month, but it seems like I've known him all my life. I don't know how to explain it; he's the quiet to my storm. The calm to my anxiety. The heat to my desire, and I can't shake the feeling that we've met before.

I pull back from him, staring deeply into his beautiful mocha irises, and in that moment, I understand him— his pain, his struggle, his grief, his shame. My words are automatic. "You're not gonna lose me."

CHAPTER 18

Mike

Erin's words are like someone releasing their grip from my lungs; I can breathe again. Hope flickers in my heart once more as I hold her close. "You can't take that back, it's too late. I'm not letting you go."

She tightens her grip around me gazing up at me with a smile that reaches her eyes. "It wasn't my plan to take it back. You aren't gonna lose me, and I won't run anymore." She pulls away to take my hand. I have to suppress the shiver that creeps up my back from her touch.

Calm down, Mike. You just got her back.

Dimples begins leading me to the elevators. I get a glimpse of her outfit through her open black pea coat as we make our trek over. She's wearing a sleeveless silver and black sequin fitted jumpsuit, with an embellished bowknot at the collar. She has on black spiked heels, and her hair is pinned up to perfection. I lick my lips, as she leads us into the elevator. "Were you going out tonight?"

"Uh, yeah, I was, but it's not a big deal." She answers. "What floor?"

"Four." I feel horrible that I interrupted her plans. "You didn't have to come here for me, you missed your—"

"It's fine, Mike. It was my decision to make, and I made the right one. Now, end of discussion." She says with finality. Erin pushes the floor number, then leans against the back wall. "You need to deal with Jason."

Shit. Jason. Right.

"I know. I owe him an apology. I could have killed—"

"But you didn't." She brushes up the length of my arm with the same nails that I've fantasized about marking my back as I— "Look, I know you guys have a lot to work through, but baby steps, right?"

I drag a hand down the length of my face. I need to refocus my attention before an extremely noticeable bulge in my slacks make an unexpected appearance. "Baby steps, right." I repeat, as the elevator pings, opening the door to the fourth floor.

My heart pounds, and palms start to sweat as I lead us to Jason's room on the far end of the agonizingly quiet floor. I come to an abrupt stop just shy of his room, Erin nearly crashing into me.

"You can do this, Mike. I'm right here with you." Erin rubs my back in long, smooth strokes. My stammering heart calms at the command of her touch. *She's definitely an angel.* With one last shaky exhale, we entered the room.

At the sound of the opening door, Jason lifts his eyes to meet mine, and my steps falter. I scan his face… he looks bad. A busted lip, black eye, bruised jaw— not to mention, the injured ribs the doctor told us about— and the bruises, that I'm ninety-nine percent sure, he has on his torso from the vicious body shots I gave him.

I catch sight of the bandages at the back of his head, bringing me back to the harsh reminder that his fate could have been the same as my mom's if—"

"I didn't think you would show up." He sluggishly hoists himself up on the bed, interrupting my spiraling thoughts.

Glancing over to the lounge chair, I see Marlon passed out from fatigue. I turn back to Jason; my quivering hands resting securely in my pants pockets, as Erin encouragingly strokes my back, keeping me grounded. I lick my dry lips, swallowing around the lump in my throat. "Jason." I shake my head. "I didn't mean to…. I wasn't trying…" My emotions are jumbling together, as I let out a frustrated breath. "I'm sorry. It wasn't my intention… fuck!" The damn words just won't come out.

Erin leans into my side, offering the comfort of her touch, and my body instantly relaxes.

Jason adjusts his pillow, flinching as he gets into a comfortable position. "I don't blame you, Mike."

"You should." I make my way to his bedside at a snail's pace, with Erin glued to my side. "I let my anger control my actions and it almost cost you your life. No matter how pissed I am at you, I shouldn't have—"

"I get it, Mike. If the shoe were on the other foot, I would have done the same… maybe worse."

"Don't make excuses for my damn problems, Jason. I have anger issues and I need help. I thought I had it handled but… I don't." It's hard to admit your failure to someone else. And for me, there are too many to count. "I don't blame you if you wanna press charges. I deserve it."

"I'm not pressing charges, I'm not mad, and I don't blame you. *I* came to *your* house, knowing I was pushin' your buttons. I saw you were furious. I *knew* you were on the warpath. I realized what I was getting myself into when I showed up on your fuckin' doorstep, but that didn't stop me from comin'." Jason grimaces as he changed positions. "You have every right to wanna beat my ass. I… slept with your *wife*; got her pregnant, Mike. I deserve this shit." He leans back against the now upright bed, grabbing hold of his left side, as he blows out a ragged breath. I feel like shit for doing this to him. "I'll never give up looking for Iesha, just so you know."

"I don't expect you to." I say, experiencing his bullheadedness firsthand.

Jason peeks over at Erin, who I grip tightly around the waist. "I don't think we've met. I'm Jason. The asshole friend who did some stupid shit that landed him in the hospital and now has some suckin' up to do to both his friend *and* girlfriend." I don't wanna react because I'm still pissed at his ass, but I can't help the smile that creeps on my face as I shake my head at him.

Erin smiles brightly, exerting a calmness into the room that wasn't there before. She steps a few inches in front of me, waving cheerfully. I swear, she can take the most awkward situation and make it natural, radiant, and lighthearted, like herself. "I'm Erin, Mike's…. friend?" She glances back at me as if to say, what *are* we?

A grin breaks out across Jason's discolored face. "You don't sound too sure. From the chemistry you two are giving off, I thought you were—"

"It's… complicated right now. That's all you need to know." I quickly intervene before he can say anything else.

Jason settles back deeper into the bed, releasing a quick yawn. "Fine, I won't dig. Friends it is." He agrees with a stupid ass smirk on his face that makes me wanna throw something at him. "Seriously though, don't blame yourself, this shit is on me, and I—"

Marlon's phone blares in the quiet space causing him to jolt up out of his sleep. "— No Koko, it's too late to be lickin' the cherry off of—" He blinks, fully aware now and his gaze lands directly on me.

I raise a brow in curiosity. "You were sayin'? What kinda fishy business are y'all *into*?"

Marlon gives me the middle finger before answering his phone. "Hey baby. No, I fell asleep in Jason's room." He yawns, pushing himself up from the chair. "He's doin' better, so I'm on my way home. Okay, love you." As Marlon ends the call, he stands, stretching in the process. "Don't ask." That's directed at me. He scowls, I laugh, but don't say a word. "Jason, I'll check on you tomorrow." Jason nods, his drooping eyes giving away his exhaustion. "Erin, always a pleasure." Marlon pats Dimples on her shoulder as he passes us. "I'll call you tomorrow, bro." And just like that, he's gone.

I turn toward Jason, who's dozing off. His head rests against the pillow; his eyes half closed. "Hey, we're gonna get going too. Get some rest." Jason nods his approval, and we quietly leave his room.

We end up back at Erin's place; a two-bedroom modern style luxurious apartment that's so clean, I'm afraid to step foot inside. The first things I notice are the vaulted ceilings and the floor to ceiling windows. There's also an open concept living area with crisp white furniture that's arranged a couple of feet away from that spectacular view. Splashes of yellow, blue and green make the entire area lively, vibrant and bold… like her. As I turn to check out the rest of the apartment, I spot an eat-in kitchen and an unusually large dining area. Impressive…. But I didn't expect anything less. Not even a speck of dust on the white tiled floors.

Dimples slips her heels off and sits them by the door and I follow suit— Don't wanna mistakenly scuff her spotless floors.

Definitely a neat freak… but I can work with that.

"Make yourself at home. I'll get us something to drink." She calls out, heading toward the kitchen. Before I open my mouth to respond, Erin peeks over her shoulder. "Don't worry, no alcohol." She winks, smiling that soul-warming smile of hers.

Seriously, where the hell has she been hiding all my life.

As I enter into the living room, I find myself nearing the windows. An amazing view of Lake St. Claire greets me. Glimmers of light shine over the frozen lake, but it's still a beauty to see. With an appreciative sigh, I make my way to the oversized sofa and lean back into the plush leather cushions. "Your apartment is amazing." She sashays over, planting herself beside me; so close that I can smell the gentle coconut scent of her shampoo. I inhale again, the familiar scent invading my senses. She smells so good, like cucumber melon and honeydew.

"Thank you." She blushes. "Here you go." Erin passes me a long stem wine glass. "Sparkling white grape." She says, not missing a beat. "We still have a couple minutes before the New Year." Erin continues, smiling.

"Damn, I thought we'd missed it." I take a generous gulp of the sparkling grape juice, relieved that I get to bring in the New Year with this gorgeous woman. I place my wine glass on the white marble coffee table, then take her glass and sit it next to mine.

As I return my attention to her, intending to continue our conversation, all words dry up in my mouth, as she drinks me in. I have *never* seen Erin as immersed in me as she is in this moment; her eyes hold so *much:* passion, unmistakable need and…. love?

No, not love. It's too soon. I don't think I'm ready for that yet, am I? She can't—

"You ready to watch the ball drop?"

"Yeah." I clear my throat; the first to break eye contact. "Yeah." I repeat, trying to regain my composure. By the time I get enough control of myself—to keep from spreading her out like a Thanksgiving feast— and peek over at her again, the flat screen is on and she's watching with anticipation as the ball begins its descent.

I take in her beauty: glowing copper-like skin, thick lustrous hair that I long to break free from that damn updo. Her plump lips, and deep-set dimple; her heart-stopping body that would have any man on his knees, begging for the honor of being her husband.

It's not only her looks, it's her…. everything. Her positive attitude, the way she lights up the atmosphere, the peace she brings into a room. The way she makes me believe I *can* be different, better. I *want* to, for myself… for *her*. Erin is everything I didn't know I needed!

How the hell did this happen so quickly?

"5....4.....3...." She counts down.

I think I'm—

"2....1...." She finishes.

In love with Erin....

"Happy New Year, Mike!" She shouts, as I gaze into her gleeful eyes, stunned speechless at this self-realization.

Fuck.

"Mike?" She calls out.

Shit.

"GQ, what's wrong?" Her concern is clear, as she touches my cheek, a slight frown on her perfect face.

I force myself out of the daze I'm in. "I'm sorry. I realized something a second ago, and it caught me by surprise. I'm fine." A smile that reaches my eyes, spread wide across my face.

I grab both sides of her face and pour everything I feel into the kiss that I plant on her; my passion, my desire for her, my love, and from how eager she returns the kiss, she feels the same.

Erin twists her body so that she's flush against me, sending me into a heated frenzy. I lift her from the sofa onto my lap, so that we're chest to chest. My hands find their way to the back zipper of her tightly clad jumpsuit, as I nibble and kiss up and down her neck. Erin makes moaning sounds of approval, but I stop.

As much as my willing dick protests, I don't want to do anything she isn't ready for.

"Erin, if this is going too fast—" I start but halt on an unexpected moan that rumbles from deep within my throat, as she slowly begins to grind on me.

"Don't… stop." She groans, her voice raspy.

I pull her in for another wet kiss, sliding my tongue into her willing mouth; jumpsuit already to her waist. When I go to tug on the thick strap of her bra, I freeze. Staring me in the face is a distinct birthmark in the shape of a butterfly on Erin's shoulder. I blink a couple of times, making sure I'm not seeing things.

Nope, still there.

No. Fuckin.' Way.

"What? What's wrong now?" Erin whines, but I can't speak past the boulder of a lump in my throat. As I gape at the birthmark; my heart thumps like a rhythmic drumbeat. "Hey?" She guides my head to face her. "What is it?"

"Brook-lyn?" I manage to choke out.

Erin leans back, in shock, her body tensing. "Where did you hear that name from? There's only one person who called me that. How did y-you—" I put my finger to her lips to quiet her, then unbutton and remove my shirt, my shallow breaths in competition with my racing heart.

Erin's eyes instantly fall on the cigarette burn marks on the upper left side of my chest. As she inspects me, she notices the silver bracelet with the engraved initials, B & H on my wrist. She gapes at me, then back at the burns on my chest; her quaking fingers gently tracing the outline of the burns that formed the letter D. Erin's breath hitches as her glistening gaze meets mine. "Harmone?"

CHAPTER 19

Erin

I can't believe Harmone is… Mike? The same boy that I met at the park every day since age eleven? The same battered boy that confided in me every time his dad hurt him? My first crush…. first love? The swoon-worthy teen that promised me when we were old enough, he was going to marry me? Mike is…. him?

My mind is swirling with jumbled emotions that I want to express but can't articulate. The anger issues, the drinking, the abuse— not that I approve of any of that— all the signs were there. He has been struggling with anger since I've known him. His asshole father. Everything that Harmone's going through right now is *his* fault. I hope his dad is somewhere in prison getting butt—

"I came to the park, waiting for you every day, for two months hoping you'd show up. Two damn months, Brooklyn! I was goin' out of my fuckin' mind looking for you. I thought something awful happened! You never called me back; even a simple text would have eased my worry, but you just… disappeared. You left me. Why did you stop coming? I needed you." His voice is rough and strained as his devastated eyes search mine for an answer.

"I'm so sorry." I cry, choking back a sob. His hands grip my hips tighter as I caress his scruffy bearded face. Mike's beautiful mocha brown eyes display a swirl of emotions; the dominant one— hurt. Eyes I should have recognized. "We left overnight. Some once in a lifetime job offer, my dad said. It required us to relocate." I explain, wiping a lingering tear from my eye. "He had already made plans to move us but didn't let us know until the night we left… on my birthday." I watch as Mike's chest rises and falls in short bursts. My heart aches for him as I place a trembling hand over the burn marks on his chest. He needed me and I couldn't be there for him. "We didn't even take any furniture; only our most valuable things. The worst part?" I blink back tears that well up in my burning eyes. "I never got a chance to say goodbye." I whimper, my voice a whisper.

"But you could have called…. Something to let me know you were alright. You don't know the thoughts that—"

"Everything was such a mess at home, that I lost my phone in the process. I kept calling you from my sister's phone from the airport, but you didn't pick up." I swipe away stray tears. "After we got to our new home, I tried again, but your phone was disconnected." My heart is in my throat as I watch Mike's face scrunch up in anguish. "I tried, Mike. I swear I tried!" I cover my mouth, choking back a throaty sob. "Mike? Please, say something."

His grip loosens on my hips, as he leans back against the sofa. He's silent for several long seconds, then pins me with a stare so consuming, I can't look away, even if I wanted to. "Months after my mom's funeral, I started searching for you again. I never forgot you; always thought about you." He admits; his fingers tenderly caressing the swell of my hips.

"I thought about you, too. Believe it or not, you're the reason I came back." I confess. "I guess making up nicknames was dumb, wasn't it? I mean, when it came down to it, we lost years because we decided not to tell each other our real names." I shake my head at our naivety.

I move to lift from his lap, but he keeps me glued in place, tilting my chin down to meet his gorgeous eyes. "Fifteen years… four months… two weeks… and a day." I gape at him, speechless. He really didn't forget me. "If you hadn't left, I would be married to *you* right now." His mouth is inches from mine; my breath hitching from the feather light touch of his fingers ghosting trails along my thighs.

I lick my dry lips while being sucked into his hypnotizing gaze. "Harmone…."

"I didn't forget my promise. I *am* gonna to marry you. I

wanted to fifteen years ago, and it hasn't changed Brooklyn—Erin." He corrects himself.

What exactly is he saying? He *still* wants to marry me? After all these years! Does that mean…. Does he *love* me? But he's still married to Jakyra. Does he still love her *too*?

"Mike…." I whisper, but before I can say another word, his lips brush against mine and my brain turns to mush. I clasp my arms around his neck, deepening our kiss. I hear a guttural moan rumble deep in his throat, causing a moan of my own.

Mike stands with me wrapped around him like a tightly laced ribbon. "Bedroom." He manages to say between kisses.

We come up for air, long enough for me to direct him. "Down the hall, to the— Mmm, Harmone, yes, just above the collarbone— bedroom is to the right." I moan in ecstasy.

He takes slow deliberate steps, until he reaches my bedroom, one arm looped securely around my waist, the other at my nape as he devours me with his skillful mouth. This kiss isn't like before at my office: rushed, lustful, frenzied. No, this is…. different; gentle, sensual; warming my heart with his unspoken words.

Before I realize it, he's setting me back on my feet at the foot of the bed. Mike slowly turns me, so that my back is to his chest. He dips his head to my shoulder, softly kissing my birthmark, sending a current of electricity straight to my core. My body's on fire from his delicate touch. I need to touch his body, hold him. It's time someone took care of *him*.

"Harmone, let me take it from here. I need to touch you. Please." I whimper, on the verge of begging, but he continues his slow torture, teasing me through my lace bra while using his other hand to unzip the rest of my jumpsuit.

"Don't move." Mike growls, need thick in his voice, as he makes quick work of my jumpsuit and underwear in one fluent motion. I sense his closeness as he scales his way back up my body. I feel a gentle bite on one butt cheek, a kiss on the other, then a pleasurable moan. I inhale a sharp breath, biting the inside of my lip to keep from whimpering like a needy bitch.

"Mike, please."

"Shhhh." That's the only response I get before I feel the quick tug of my bra being ripped from my body. Now I stand naked in front of him, needing him more than I've ever needed anyone in my life.

He places soft kisses between the crease of my neck, driving me insane with desire for him.

With one last kiss, he says, "Turn around." I turn as if in a trance, exposing myself to him. My breathing is a steady pant now, in anticipation of what he's going to do next. "You're beautiful, do you know that?" He skims over my body once before stepping closer.

Mike caresses my cheek, as he gives a gentle tug to the clip that holds my updo in place, allowing my hair to cascade freely down around my shoulders. "Perfect."

I swallow hard, as he unbuttons and removes his pants, boxer briefs and socks unhurriedly, never taking his smoldering eyes off mine. The longing in his heated stare has me reaching out for him. "I need you, Mike." He backs me onto the bed, lays me back and hovers above me.

Leaning up, I kiss him deeply, willingly spreading my legs for him, like an offering. I'm not just giving my body to him, but my heart as well; a heart that was already his fifteen years ago.

CHAPTER 20

Mike

I can't believe Erin is the same sixteen-year-old girl I have been infatuated with for the past fifteen years. My first love…. and I fell for her all over again.

I close my eyes, savoring the soft caress of her tongue tangling with my own, as I lower my body, supporting my weight with my elbow. Breaking our kiss, I press my forehead to hers, entering her at a snail's pace. I let out a low groan, trying to maintain my control.

As I open my eyes, hers flutter closed, encasing her arms under my own and up to my shoulders. Erin releases a moan so erotic, it reaches my soul. As she begins to grind into me, I still. It's gonna be over before it begins if she keeps that up. "Brooklyn, baby, hold on. Stop movin' for a minute." I groan. "I just found out *you're* my Brooklyn; I thought I would never find you." I remove the strands of hair from her face. "It's been fifteen damn years of wantin' you. Give me a minute to get myself under control."

"Yours?"

"Yes, mine. You've always been mine. I loved you then, and I—" I stop, pressing my forehead back to hers.

Erin unravels one of her arms from me, stroking my jaw. "And you what?" She asks, her voice a whisper.

I lift my head, staring into her misty eyes, and exhale a breath that I didn't realize I was holding. "I still love you now, Erin." The glittering eyes that gaze at me, now leak with tears, as she smiles.

"Say it again." She says, her bottom lip quivering.

"I love you." I repeat, gradually moving again, brushing my lips against hers.

"Again." She moans, moving with me.

I groan, thrusting deep, falling into a rhythm. "I love you, Erin." She holds me closer, gripping my back like the most valuable thing she's ever owned, because she does. She owns me.

My thrusts are brutal, as her legs lock around my waist. I grind into her, causing friction where she needed it most. "Erin…" I moan.

She pants heavily, as she stares deep into my eyes. "I loved you… when I knew you as Harmone." She begins. "And I love you… now…" She finishes on a moan, as her orgasm hits hard. Words escaping her, as she releases a silent scream. Erin's body shutters against mine, as I continue to pump into her faster. "Mike…" She breathes out, entwining her hand with mine.

"Say it again, baby." I pant, close to my own release. "Say you love me." I thread my fingers through her hair, as my other hand holds onto hers.

"I love all of you, Mike. You're mine! Ah, Mike!" She screams. I feel her body shutter against mine as another orgasm rips through her. My own release quickly follows, and I moan her name as I come so hard, my body is vibrating.

We both lay there for a moment, bodies glistening with sweat, breathing heavily, then I roll over to my side, cocooning her in my arms. "And you're mine." I murmur into her hair.

"All yours."

I kiss her temple. "Happy New Year, Brooklyn." I tighten my hold around her, more at peace now, than I've been in a long while.

"Happy New Year, Harmone." She presses closer into my side, as if she's trying to meld herself with me. I don't mind one bit because against all odds, I found my Brooklyn… and I'm *never* lettin' her go.

CHAPTER 21

Last night was one of the best nights of my life. We made love until we passed out from exhaustion. I admire Erin with wonder as she sleeps, like the damn creep I am. I realize some subtle things about her that I should have recognized all along. The scar just above her eyebrow, her infectious laugh, her lively, positive personality. She is the same as when we were kids. How could I *not* have known it was her?

I run my hand up and down the curve of her hip, tempted to go further.

Erin exhales an airy sigh, turning in my arms to face me. Her hair lay wild on the pillow, and she has sleep lines on her cheek, but to me, she's the picture of perfection. "Good morning." She smiles, her tone sultry and inviting. I know it isn't her intention, but she sounds damn sexy right now, and I'm ready for round five.

"Good morning." My lips find hers, as I hungrily takes what

she gives me. My body sparks to life like a car battery getting a boost, as she skims my arm with her nails. "You know, I'm turned on by the sound of your morning voice. We should do somethin' about that." Cupping the curve of her ass, I give a firm squeeze.

Erin pushes the comforter down and sits up, her perfect size DD's bouncing with her movements. "I think you're right. I know just what you need." Her hand begins travelling southward. I hiss, as she strokes me, her head slowly descending.

I unhurriedly lick my lips in anticipation, my breathing heavy and wanting. Erin's eyes meet mine as her tongue makes its glorious appearance, inches away from where I need her to be. "Erin…." I pant, my voice raw and raspy. She shoots me with a mischievous grin that promises a dirty time, flicking me with her tongue and—

My phone booms with a familiarly annoying ringtone that I'm growing to hate. Christopher fuckin' Daniels. I swear, I'm gonna fire him today.

Erin and I glance at one another. She places her head on my thigh, and I fall back onto the pillows; both of us groaning in unison.

"I'm sorry, it's Chris. If he's calling, it's important. Gotta take this. To be continued." I promise, giving her a peck on the lips before, reluctantly, lifting myself off the bed.

"To be continued indeed." Erin teases, slapping me on my naked ass, as I stand up. My phone stops ringing, then starts right back up again. I promise, I'm gonna strangle his ass.

I swipe the answer button, quickly. "Chris, what could possibly—"

"Do you know what fucking time it is?!" He whisper-yells. "Did you forget what today is? Where the hell are you?!" Taking a glance at the giant crystal encrusted clock on Erin's wall, my eyes almost pop out of their sockets.

Shit. *Shit*!

"Let Nate know I'll be there in an hour, and that I'm so sorry for this. Fuck! I can't believe I forgot! Chris—"

"I already told him you had a family emergency this morning and you would be a bit late. Nate understood, but you're a fucking hour and a half late, Mike! I can't keep stalling him. I asked him to give you another hour so make it count, asshole." Chris gripes in frustration, and rightly so.

"I'll be there in forty-five. Thanks for covering my ass."

"Yeah, yeah. You owe me in full details, beers, and a two-week vacation around my birthday."

"How do you know there's even anything to tell?"

There's silence on the other end for a second, then he says, "Really, Mike? Okay, are there any details?"

"That's not what's important right now." I deflect.

"Whatever. I said what I said. Now, get your secretive ass to the office."

"I'm on my way. I'll see you soon, jerk." I end the call, rushing to gather my clothes. "Erin, we're late!" I call out.

She's already showered and half-dressed when I find her in the bathroom. Erin's hand trembles, as I watch her place the deep red lipstick back into her make-up case. "You can borrow one of my brother's suits in the second bedroom. You're both about the same size." She rushes to say, while trying to apply eyeliner. Erin's gonna be a mess if she doesn't calm down. "Nate called me five times this morning! Five times! I've never been late. Never! He's gonna—"

"Breathe, baby." I massage her shoulders in soothing circles. Erin closes her eyes, inhaling deep, then releasing. "Did he sound upset when you talked to him?"

She opens her worried eyes and looks at me through the mirror. "No, he sounded…. concerned, but—"

"Relax. You'll be fine." I give her a quick peck on the cheek. She blows out a puff of air; the trembling already subsiding. With a nod, she continues to finish her make-up. I rush out of the bedroom and down the hall— in all my naked glory— to find something to wear for the biggest project of my career.

CHAPTER 22

Erin

Hurrying off of the elevator, I rush toward the conference room where everyone is waiting patiently. The clicking of my heels on the dark tiled floors matches the pounding of my heart as I pass Mike's office. He's not here yet. I left my apartment minutes before him, so he shouldn't be too much longer.

The door of the conference room is already open. I hear my jovial boss, talking up a storm. He doesn't sound angry or irritated, just the opposite. Maybe I *have* been overreacting. I brush the stray strands of hair back into place. I didn't have time to wrap it into my usual bun this morning, so I opted for straight and flowy. Damn it, I'm so out of my comfort zone right now, but the night I had with Mike was so fuckin' worth it. He was so dirty in the most delicious ways, and I can't wait—

"Good morning Ms. Brooks." Chris greets, in an exaggerated

whisper. I spin around, eyes wild; heart jumping out of my chest. He stands there, with a knowing grin on his face, which has me fidgeting in place. He *couldn't* know, could he? "Funny you're just getting here. Mike called me not long ago; said he's on his way up. Should be here in about…" He glances at his watch, then gives an annoying smirk.

"Chris, is Nate upset?" I hear the worry in his voice, as he stops beside me. Chris flashes a quick look at me, then Mike, lifting an eyebrow. Shit, he knows. "What?" Mike asks, finally glancing over to me, lingering a little too long on my cleavage before quickly turning away. He clears his throat. "Good morning, Erin— Ms. Brooks." He corrects, shoving his hands in his pockets.

Chris takes a step closer to us, nodding his head as if he were agreeing with himself. "Yeah, I'm gonna take a chance and assume you two were… together." He says in muted tones, amused with our awkwardness. "No need to be shy, we're all adults here. Just… try not to be so… obvious next time." He folds his arms across his chest, chuckling to himself.

Mike shoves past him, heading toward the conference room. He turns, sporting a scowl and middle finger, directed at Chris. "Mind your damn business, jerk. I'm this close to firin' your overly observant ass. Now, come start the meeting." Chris throws up his hands, laughing as we walk toward the conference room.

He stops in front of his boss, slapping him on the shoulder. "Better go in first. Wouldn't want anyone getting the wrong idea, would you?" Mike rolls his eyes, walking into the room, Chris trailing behind him, still snickering.

I exhale a nervous breath, smoothing imaginary wrinkles out of my black and white pinstripe pant suit. "Shit. This is gonna be a long meeting." Bracing myself, I finally walk through the doors. As soon as I enter, I see Mr. Leeman shaking hands with Mike, then his fatherly eyes meet mine. He smiles, then continues his conversation. I breathe out in relief, meandering over to the conference table where Chris watches me with perceptive eyes.

I place my things on the table, avoiding his stare, but acknowledging his presence. "Mr. Daniels."

"Ms. Brooks." His eyes twinkle with amusement.

I do an obvious once over at Mike, admiring him in the black-on-black suit with a burgundy and black tie that he picked from my brother's wardrobe. I nibble my bottom lip, to suppress a moan, when my balance decides to take a break and I stumble a bit, taking hold of the edge of the table. I shake my head in humiliation. Chris laughs. Yes, a long meeting indeed.

The meeting lasts about two hours; something about expanding, reinventing, projected costs, figures, graphs, and some other shit that I failed to pay attention to. I'm glad I recorded the meeting because I damn sure wasn't listening.

For that matter, Mike wasn't either. We were too busy

undressing each other with our eyes to focus on anything else. Thank God for Chris. He ran the meeting like the professional he is. Us, on the other hand? Yeah, we were acting like two damn horny teenagers who couldn't keep their hands off one another.

Shit. I hate not being focused. I usually bring my A-game, but Mike comes steamrolling back, disrupting my controlled, planned out life. Now it's all tingly body, lustful thoughts, and dirty dreams that occupy my time…. like now. Mike is talking to Nate, all calm. The picture of professionalism. Meanwhile, I'm leaning against the doorpost, imagining all the ways he can fuc—"

"Ms. Brooks. It's lovely to see that you didn't listen to a word I said earlier." Chris comments, sarcasm oozing through each word. He sidles up next to me, leaning against the wall. "Way too obvious."

"Huh?" Tearing my indecent gaze away from Mike, I give my attention to the nosey man beside me. "What do you mean?" I feign innocence.

He shakes his head, giving me a lopsided grin. "So, we're playing *this* game, okay." Chris leans in a bit closer. "Look, we've already established the fact that you and Mike… had sex, made love, had coitus, fucked; however, you wanna put it. No one needed to tell me, it's pretty damn clear to see." My eyes widen at his bluntness.

I scan the room immediately, to make sure no one heard him, then return my attention to Chris. "We did *not* have—" I start, but he shoots me with a look that says, *don't insult my intelligence*, causing me to stop mid-sentence.

"If you don't want the entire office to know what I so plainly see, I would advise you two to stop eye-fucking each other while you're working." He gives a pause, as if he's contemplating. "Unless you don't care about people finding out; then by all means, let the eye-fucking commence." He finishes, taking pleasure in my awkwardness.

I push off of the doorpost, looking everywhere but at Chris. The non-existent lint on my suit jacket seems quite interesting at the moment, as I fidget in place. "I… see your point, and I'll be sure to take your advice." I speak in a hushed tone. Finally working up the courage, I look at him "You're a good friend to Mike."

He smirks but he doesn't say another word, just a head nod. "Mike likes his privacy, but sometimes he can be… careless. I'm just looking out for him, like I know he would for me."

I smile at his genuine words. "I understand. Thank you."

He shakes his head. "No, thank *you*, Erin. You're good for him." He compliments me. "Mike's a little rough, hell, he's more than a little rough around the edges, but he's a good guy." He seems as if he's going to say something else but stops himself. Instead, he gives me a light pat on the shoulder and walks out of the door.

As I turn to make my exit, my phone buzzes with a text from Mike, telling me to wait for him in his office. I peek over to see his seducing eyes promising me a fun time in the filthiest possible way. I shiver at the thought, quickly walking out of the door and down to his office where I notice Ashton standing.

Damn it. Not now.

"Ash, what... are you doing here?" I ask, meeting him at Mike's office.

He leans in and kisses my cheek, smiling. "I work here, Ren."

"You know what I mean. Why are you waiting here... at Mike's office?"

He raises an eyebrow, folding his arms across his broad chest. "Oh, you *know* Mike. Good, you can convince him to let me take an extra hour for lunch so we can go grab a quick bite and talk. Maybe tell me why you bailed on me last night?"

"You had plans with *Ashton* last night?" Mike interrupts, swallowing the atmosphere with his presence.

Ashton grins, turning toward GQ. "Yeah, me and Ren were going to a New Year's Eve—"

"Wait, *she's* the Ren you've been telling me about?! Erin is the one I told you to pursue?!" Mike yells, in horrid disbelief.

I notice on-lookers stopping to see the shit show that's about to take place— live in living color. Touching Mike's arm, I guide him toward his office. "Why don't we discuss this inside. People are starting to stare." He looks down at me, jaw clenched, frowning, and eyes as dark as a starless sky.

Shit.

Without another word, Mike unlocks his door, and we all enter in, Ashton closing the door behind him. I open my mouth to explain, but Mike starts in again.

"When the fuck did this happen with him, Erin?"

"Uh, *he* is right here, Mike, and don't talk to Ren like that. What the hell is your problem?" Ashton defends, as he stops a few feet from the door.

"My problem is— Wait, wait. Ashton, you told me Ren was your ex. That means…" He trails off. I don't know what conclusion Mike comes to, but it can't be good from the way his body stiffens and the terrifying scowl on his face.

Not good at all.

Mike faces me, his anger rolling off of him in torrential waves. "Ashton is the ex?! He's the one who verbally abused you?! The reason you had a—"

My entire body tenses as my heart plummets into my stomach. "How the hell do you know that? Who-who told you that, Mike?" I stammer out, my hand trembling as I sweep the hair from my face.

Ashton glances between us, clarity beginning to take shape. He looks at me, hurt flashing across his face. "You were with *Mike* last night?"

I can see the vein pulse in GQ's forehead as he moves closer to me. "Correction, she still *is* with me. Now get the fuck out of my office before I beat the shit outta you." Mike growls.

Ashton whips his head in my direction. "What the hell is that supposed to mean?"

I move toward Ash, but Mike grabs my arm, pulling me back. Looking down at my arm, then up at Mike, I glower my disapproval. "Let. Me. Go." My glacial tone is all he needed to snap him out of his caveman act, as he realizes what he's doing.

He releases my arm, as if he's been scorched by hot coals. Mike steps away to move behind his desk; his hands flat against the smooth cherry wood, breathing roughly.

I return my focus to Ash, who stands motionless; a knowing look on his face, expressing to me with his eyes, that he knows what I'm gonna say. My heart hurts for him, but I can't let him think we're anything more than friends.

CHAPTER 23

Mike

My hands shake with barely restrained rage, as I remain planted behind the desk; my eyes burning a proverbial hole in the dark cherry wood surface. Why the hell would she still be friends with his ass after what he did to her! He abused her! He made her feel like nothing! He—

The rest of the unspoken words taste like gravel in my mouth. I have no right to judge him. I was just *like* him… worse, but I changed. What makes me think that Ashton can't? I'm a goddamn hypocrite.

Before I found out he was Erin's ex, he was a good friend and an all-around nice guy. If I'm being honest, he still is, but my anger— no, I'll call it what it is—my jealousy, is overriding my logic right now.

I peek at them, studying the expression on Ashton's face:

determination, hope, loyalty… love. He's not gonna give up. *I* wouldn't. He told me Erin is the love of his life, his soulmate, but Erin is *mine*. I will *not* lose her again!

I notice Dimples fidget with her fingers as she stares up at him. "I'm sorry I wasn't honest with you sooner Ash, but Mike and I are—"

"Together. With each other. In a relationship. Whatever the fuck you wanna call it. She's mine, Ashton. Are we clear?" I interject, standing to my full height, folding my arms across my chest.

Erin glares at me, sending a chill down my spine, but that green eyed monster is keeping me pretty heated. "I don't need your aide, Mike. Let me handle this."

"Why are you sugarcoating this shit? Ashton's a grown ass man. He can manage rejection."

"What? Like you?" She shoots back, her icy glare cutting through me like a sharp blade.

"Brooklyn—"

"No! I don't wanna hear another word from you, Mike!" She bellows, rendering me speechless, as I clamp my mouth shut.

She turns her attention back to Ashton, who had this defeated look, as he ran his hand down the length of his face, shaking his head in denial. I feel bad for him, but this is Erin we're talkin' about. If it were anybody else….

Ashton shakes his head again. "I never had a chance, did I?"

"I'm sorry, Ash. I didn't mean to hurt you. We can still be friends, but anything more is not an option." She places a hand on his forearm.

I flex my jaw tight and swallow the words that are trying to force their way through, as Ashton lifts his eyes to meet mine. In that instance, I know he's never gonna give up.

His eyes flash with purpose; a blazing fire that has me ready to jump across my desk and throttle him. "Yeah, I'd love to remain friends, Ren." He smiles at her, then his eyes lift to meet mine again; a coldness replacing the warmth that was there mere seconds ago. "But I don't plan to give up on you. No. I won't stop until you're mine again. I don't care *who* you're with."

"Get the hell out of my office, Ashton!" I nearly leap across my desk to get to him, but Erin stands between us, gripping my biceps like a rubber bands grip around a newspaper. "Don't come back!"

"I expected that. I don't need you or your damn job… but I *do* need Ren, and I won't stop until I have her. So, consider yourself warned… *Mike*." He turns to strut toward the door.

I twist from Erin's grasp, rushing toward the bastard before he can leave.

She secures her arms around my waist, pulling with all her might, allowing Ashton to walk out unharmed, which pisses me off even more. "Mike! Let him go! Calm down! What the hell is wrong with you!" She shrieks, releasing her iron-clad grip. "I had it *handled*!"

I turn so fast; I could have gotten whiplash. "Did you not just hear this conversation the last ten minutes?! No, you *didn't* have it handled! He threatened my relationship with you, and I take that shit seriously! You're *mine*!"

"Are you even listening to yourself?!" She throws back, smoothing the front of her pants down.

Willing my thudding heart to settle down, I suck in a huge breath, taking a closer look at Erin. Her eyes are wild with panic, shallow breaths have her on the verge of hyperventilation, and her hands are shaking violently.

Shit.

"Calm down, okay? Just… breathe. I'm sorry. I was outta line." I say, as calmly as my voice will allow. I don't wanna escalate the situation more than I already have. "Maybe you should sit for—"

"I don't want to sit down! I don't wanna be here with you right now!" She rails, in a piercing cry that registers deep in my chest. "Do you know how humiliating it was for you to claim me like I'm a cheap trophy?! Nobody owns me, Mike!"

"That's not what you were sayin' last night." I regret the words before they even leave my mouth.

Her eyes gleam with unshed tears, as she grabs her briefcase from the floor.

Shit.

"Erin, sweetheart. I'm sorry. I shouldn't have— I didn't mean it like that." I rush to say, as I make slow steps toward her quaking body.

Unexpectedly, her body jerks fully toward me, holding up her shaking hands; her glare so severe, it can be felt. "Don't! *You are the most inconsiderate bastard I've ever known!*"

I stop dead in my tracks, the ground suddenly feeling like quicksand beneath me. Her words rip through me like a bullet to the gut.

Her words. The same words Jakyra hurled at me the first time I'd hit her.

You are the most inconsiderate bastard I've ever known.

I take an instinctive step back, my heart echoing so loud in my ears, I can barely hear. I tug at my tie; it feels like it's too tight around my neck. I sense beads of sweat beginning to form on my brow, as my breaths come in short pants.

You are the most inconsiderate bastard I've ever known.

The words keep replaying in my mind like a bad dream that you can't wake up from. "Erin—" I strain to say; the rest of my words becoming stuck between the bile rising and the lump in my throat.

"No! I don't wanna talk to you anymore!" She bolts toward the door, as Chris hurries in, assessing the situation quickly before his eyes land on me.

"Mike." He drags out. I scramble to the door that my Brooklyn just ran through.

Chris catches me by the arm, holding firmly. "Let her go. You need time apart."

"How the fuck would you know!" I shout my disagreement, jerking out of his grip.

Chris glances outside of my office, to see employees gawking at the full-on circus that I've put on for them. He softly closes the door, then eyes me with a pissed off glower that I haven't had the displeasure of seeing in a long time. "Because you're not thinking straight right now, and she needs the fucking space. So, you either settle the fuck down or *I'll* settle you down. Your choice." Each word that leaves his mouth is controlled, but stern; a warning bubbling underneath the surface.

We stand in silence for a moment, the sound of my labored breathing, the only thing cutting through the suffocating tension. Finally, I give in, slumping my shoulders then flop down in the chair in front of my desk.

Chris ambles over to me, placing a firm hand on my shoulder, sighing. "Wanna talk about it?"

CHAPTER 24

Chris, once again, steps in, taking control of the mess I made. He rescheduled all of my meetings this afternoon, dealt with my nosey employees; all while sending me off to Marlon and Koko's to get my mind right. So, that's where I am currently, waiting for Chris to join Marlon and me.

I hold my soon-to-be four-month-old niece like she's a glass doll. I swear, I don't know the first thing about babies. "Don't you wanna come and get your daughter now?"

My douche of a brother is threatening a damn stroke trying to hold in his laughter at my awkwardness. "Nah, you're doin' a superb job, bro." He bursts out in a hearty laugh.

I shift in my seat on the recliner, trying—and failing—to position Evie on my shoulder to burp her. "Marlon, come and get her please."

"Alright, alright." He finally gives in, swiping the tears from his eyes as he carefully pulls her from my unrelaxed grip. I breathe a sigh of ease. "So, to recap what you told me: not only is Erin *thee* Brooklyn you were in love with for fifteen years, she's also the love of *Ashton's* life, who emotionally and verbally abused her, who she's still friends with." He looks at me, his brow raised. "You fired Ashton because of your jealousy. Treated *said* girl you're in love with like she was property, then publicly bragged about the vocal declarations she confessed to you while being intimate. Is that about, right?"

In a nutshell, but I refrain from saying that.

"I didn't *brag*, it just came out, and I did *not* fire Ashton because I was jealous." I did. "He was threatening to take what's mine."

"Like I said, jealous, and do you hear yourself? *Take what's yours?* You can't say shit like that, Mike. You sound like a chauvinistic ass." He's right, but she *is* mine. I don't know how else to put it.

I have been in love with her for so long, the thought of losing her again after all this time has my mind scrambled. I don't wanna lose her, but if I keep this shit up, that's exactly what'll happen.

I push up from the recliner, pacing the length of the family room, which looks more like a baby factory with Evie's things scattered around. Before my niece came along, the family room was an absolute guy's dream; equip with a seventy-inch flat screen, a huge leather sectional and every video game you can think of. Now, it's Evie's world and we're just livin' in it. "You're right, Marlon, but what's done is done. I need to beg her forgiveness, simple as that."

My brother nods, as he puts Evie in her bassinet. He makes his way over to me, as I think of ways to say I'm sorry for my idiocy. "Apologize. Tell her how you feel. Be honest with her." He pats me on the back.

There's a quick knock, then the sound of an open and closed door. Seconds later, we hear footsteps, then we see the tall, tanned, and brooding bastard in the flesh. There are very few people who can come into our home without being invited. Chris is one of them.

"How did you know we were in here?" Marlon asks, as Chris steps over a pile of stuffed animals entering into the door.

"Just followed the stench of assholism. Led me right to you." Chris shrugs as if his response is the greatest thing in the world. Marlon burst out in laughter.

I raise my hand in acknowledgment anyway. "Guilty." I say in earnest. "Thanks again for earlier, Chris. I owe you one."

Chris raises a brow. "You owe me *several*; a vacation, a drink and dinner, but who's counting." He jokes. At least I think he's joking, but he's right. There are no words to describe how much I appreciate his level headedness. He makes his way over to us, giving Marlon a quick bro hug, and me, a side hug, then goes to sit on the sectional, as my brother heads to the kitchen. When he returns, it's with a beer and two cold pops.

Chris focuses his attention on me. "So, Erin is her…*Brooklyn.* Wow, I didn't see that shit coming." He drapes an arm over the back of the sofa, as he accepts a beer from Marlon, popping the lid to take a quick swig. My brother hands me a pop, then plops down on the recliner.

Settling in the recliner opposite Marlon, I balance the can on my thigh, holding it in place. "Yeah, my mind is still reeling from it. I can't believe I didn't recognize her." Shaking my head, I recall over the past few months. The way Erin's infectious laughter always had my heart trapezing in my chest. How she tugs at her blouse when she's nervous, or the— barely there— crease between her brows when she's angry. How could I *not* know it was her? "After I finally processed it all, we fell right back in sync, like all those years ago." Even now, this conversation brings back every recollection, every feeling, every conversation with her. But memories of the shouting matches and beatings from my dad were never far behind and I don't wanna go down that rabbit hole right now.

I shift to Marlon, who gulps down his pop in record time. *Damn.* "If you wanted a beer, you could've had one. You don't need to tiptoe around me because *I* have a problem. I can manage people drinking in front of me."

"It's not that. I don't wanna drink when I have Eva. So, sorry to burst your conceited bubble, but it's not about you." He grins, placing his empty pop can on the coffee table.

"Fair enough…. Ass." I hurl one of the throw pillows at him.

Chris puts his beer on the table and rubs his hands together. "You need a plan. Do you know what you'll say to her?"

I shake my head, clueless as to what I'm actually gonna do. "I don't know. I figure I'd go to her apartment and lay it all out. Be spontaneous. All or nothing type thing."

"Terrible plan." My brother and best friend say simultaneously, as if they're Siamese twins.

I blow out a puff of air. "What then, because I don't know what the hell I'm doin' here."

"Apologize. Lead with that." The command of Chris's tone would have been intimidating if I didn't know deep inside, he's as soft as a cotton ball.

Marlon wastes no time giving his two cents. "Be honest about your feelings and trust her. Follow up with that."

"And don't say anything stupid." They both warn.

Watching Marlon lift Evie out of her bassinet, I stand, putting the unopened can of pop on the coffee table before leaving the family room. I head for the front door, Chris and my brother rallying behind me. "Guess I'll try my luck now. No time like the present, right?" I grab my coat, and zip it up. Hopefully, she doesn't throw my ass out. "Thanks for listening, Marlon, Chris."

The level of respect I have for them is unexplainable.

Marlon pats me on the back, as he cradles Evie in one arm. "I'm always here bro, you know that."

Chris leans against the wall, his hand in the pocket of his slacks. "I've got your back, always. Even when you do stupid shit." He's not wrong. The amount of stupid shit I've done over the past year *alone* would have the *Pope* ready to beat my ass. It would be well deserved.

Marlon and Chris are right though. I need to get my shit together. I love them both for always tellin' me the truth… even when I don't wanna hear it. "I'll let y'all know how it goes. If I call with despair in my voice, you'll know it didn't go well." I joke—not really— opening the door, only to run right into my, "V for Vendetta," sister, staring me down like she's ready to blow my mouth out. "Hey Iesha! I didn't know you were comin' over. I missed you." I coax, hoping for a peaceful reunion.

MyIesha slaps me in the chest. "Don't give me that. You put Jason in the goddamn hospital! If I wanted him hurt *that* fuckin' bad, I would have put him there myself!"

Guess not.

I glance back at Marlon, and he shrugs. Asshole. He could have given me a heads up.

I go back into the house as MyIesha continues her rant. I knew I would have to deal with her at some point, but I don't have time for this. I need to—

She jabs her prickly nail into me so hard, I can feel it through my coat. "Are you even listening to me, you ass!"

Shit.

CHAPTER 25

Erin

I am so fucking pissed at Mike. How dare he treat me like a trophy. I am *not* anyone's play toy! Then he shares what was supposed to be an intimate moment between us with the whole damn office?! I'm fairly sure everybody heard us.

I get that Ashton was out of line, but I had it under control. I wouldn't leave Mike for Ash. Doesn't he know that?

Of course not, because he doesn't trust me. That's what hurts the most.

"Erin? You still there?" My older sister, Anyah asks.

I need to vent and she's a great listener…. A better listener than our younger brother Zeke. He's a "knock you out, ask questions later" kinda guy, and that's why I'm not telling him what happened.

"Yes, sorry. I'm here. I just…" I breathe in deeply, shrouding myself in a chic black and white print throw. Leaning my head against the cool window, I settle on the chaise. "I know Mike is hot-headed, he always *has* been, but he took it *way* too far. He doesn't trust me, Ann." I force the words out, my voice wobbly, and eyes glistening.

"Oh Erin. I'm sure he trusts you. He's just having a tough time. He was abused for years, and from what you told me, his wife cheated on him and is pregnant with someone else's baby. His walls are high and thick, just like yours." I balk at her words. If *I* have high and thick walls, his must be like The Great Wall of goddamn China. "I'm not saying he's right, I'm just saying, try to be understanding. You know how Ryan was before I broke through his walls. It's not the same situation, but the fear, the anger, the pain is the same. Be patient with him."

Tears trickle down my face as I remember how many times I had to clean Mike's cuts and put bandages on his arm. How he would call me on nights he couldn't sleep, sometimes crying because he was in so much pain. The fear he carried for his mom, brother, and sister. The weight of the world on his shoulders; burdens that no teenager should have to carry. Anyah's right. She helped her late husband with the demons he faced, and he was better for it. I smile at the memory of me and Ryan battling against Anyah and Zeke in Monopoly. "I miss Ry. He was a good man and an awesome brother-in-law."

"Yeah, I do too, but what can you do. I can't change what happened and missing him isn't gonna bring him back. Now, back to you, girly." She deflects. Anyah still won't talk about the fire that happened six years ago and I won't push her.

I glance at the large round mirror clock that's mounted on the wall nearest me. "He hasn't even called me. It's been almost seven hours."

"He's probably trying to get his shit together."

"You have an answer for everything, don't you?" I joke, sitting upright.

 She giggles. "I wouldn't be me if I didn't."

My mood brightens a bit, but I still wish he would— A knock at the door has me jumping to my feet to look at the monitor.

It's *him*. He's here!

Okay, breathe.

"Ann, I have to go. Mike is at the door." I hurry to say.

She chuckles in an "I told you so" kind of way. "See, he got his shit together. Now, listen to him and get out of your head because you tend to do that when you're afraid."

"I'm *not* afraid. I have to go, Ann. I'll call you tomorrow. Love you." I end the call before she can say anything else because I know she's right. *I am* terrified of letting all of my walls down. Wiping the remaining tears from my face, I open the door. "Mike."

"Erin." His Adam's apple bobs up and down as he swallows hard. His fingers twitch ever so slightly. He's nervous, that much is for sure— if the deep intake of breath and shifting of his feet is anything to go by. "Can I come in?"

Without a word, I move aside, allowing him to enter. As I close the door, I catch sight of him removing his shoes before he moves further into the apartment. My heart melts a bit.

He always did notice the little things.

Following him into the living room, I stop just short of the coffee table, where he stands. His eyes are full of regret, and something I know all too well… fear. I know why *I'm* scared, but what is *he* afraid of? Suddenly, the rhythmic thumping in my chest intensifies and I begin to feel tingly all over.

He takes a step toward me, then stops. "I'm sorry. I'm a jealous idiot, Erin. I didn't mean to bring up, what was supposed to be, a private moment between us. I didn't—"

"Why are you here, Mike?"

"To apologize, and…"

"And *what*?" My heart is in my throat. I don't understand why I'm so anxious all of a sudden. I cross my arms over my chest to keep him from commenting about my trembling hands. Trying to regain moisture in my – dry as a desert– throat, I swallow hard.

Mike opens his mouth, as if to speak, then closes it again. He licks his lips, then, "…And to be honest with you." He allows the words to linger in the air for a second, as he steadily approaches me, entering my personal space. "I *need* to be honest with you." The flash of vulnerability in his eyes catches me off guard. I'm prepared for a fight, not… his willingness to open up.

I sway on my feet, feeling off balance, but he grasps me at my elbows, steadying me. "You, okay?"

"Y-Yes, I'm fine. What do you need to be honest with me about?" I stammer the words out, my pulse thumping against my neck.

Mike frees me of his grip, inhaling deep before releasing it. "What happened today was more about me than anything else." He begins, meandering over to the window, staring out into the chilly winter night. He loosens his tie and removes his suit jacket, placing it on the chaise, then turns to me. "Yes, I was jealous. I didn't want him touching you. I don't want you to still be friends with him, and I didn't want him fuckin' talking to you." He says through clenched teeth. Mike closes his eyes for a second, before opening again. "Ashton told me he was in love with you on many occasions. It never occurred to me that it was *you* we were talking about. He always used the name Ren." He sits down on the chaise.

I want to say something, but words won't form on my lips, so I stand there, tugging at the hem of my blouse.

Mike's eyes swirl with worry. "I gave him advice about you; told him to pursue you! I pushed him right into your arms!" What the hell is he afraid of?

I move to the chaise instantly; my eyes on him the entire time. Grasping his head, I angle it up toward me. "You didn't know, Mike. How could you?" I graze his cheek with my knuckles. "I don't want Ashton."

"But he wants *you*, and I can't—"

"Don't you trust me?" I stifle out, my hands leaving him all together.

"It's not that I don't trust you, Erin. It's just that—"

"It's just what? Can't you believe that I would never do that to you? I would—"

"People that I love hurt me one way or another. My dad, my fuckin' best friends, my mom…. Jakyra. They either betray me, hurt me… or leave me." As his eyes find mine, they shine with tears. "I'm sick of being hurt all the damn time! I'm tired of being the strong one! I'm exhausted being the one who has to have it all together, because I don't! I don't have it all together goddamn it!" He cries out, his voice breaking as he lowers his head. "I'm afraid I'm gonna lose you; that Ashton will take you from me. I can't lose you again, Brooklyn." He chokes out, his voice low and gruff.

I immediately drop to my knees, tears falling like raindrops across my cheeks. I embrace him so firmly that I thought I would squeeze all the air out of his lungs. "Harmone." I bawl, as he circles his arms around me, squeezing gently. "I'm not going anywhere. I won't leave you. I promise." I press my forehead against his, wiping the few stray tears that escaped his eyes. "I love you, and

I'm sorry if I made you think otherwise." The tension seems to drain from Mike's body as I make my declaration to him.

Pulling myself up from the floor— dragging him with me— I stalk to my bedroom, as Mike trails behind. With him still in a melancholic state, I lead him to the bed to sit, then search through the emerald, green and silver jewelry box—that my grandma got me for my sixteenth birthday—on the dresser until I find what I'm looking for. "Look." I hold out my hand as I sit next to him.

He glances down, then back at me in sheer wonder. "You still have it?" He takes the emerald birthstone ring from my palm and replaces it with the caressing grip of his hand. My heart swells with so much love for this man, I think it might burst wide open.

"Yes. You made me a promise, and I never forgot it." I force the words out past the thick lump in my throat.

He draws my hand to his lips, kissing it, then slips the ring on my left ring finger. "And I'm gonna keep it." Mike peers down at our entwined fingers. "I didn't think it would still fit."

"I had it resized a few years ago. I wear it on special occasions."

"Well, now you'll wear it as a reminder. I *will* marry you, Erin."

My body tingles with anticipation at the certainty of his words. I smile. "Promise?"

"I *promise*." His voice drips with assurance, and I believe him.

He pulls me onto his lap, brushing his lips against mine. "I love you, Dimples."

"I love you too, GQ." I whisper into his gentle kiss.

He's the one I let slip through my fingers, but he came back to me. Now that I have him, I'm going to do everything in my power to hold on to him…. because he's worth it.

CHAPTER 26

The next day, we both call off work. This is something new for me. I have never taken a personal day for myself before. It feels kinda weird, but at the same time, much needed. Mr. Leeman was *more* than enthusiastic about me not coming in to work though. I don't know whether to be touched or offended.

I peek over at Mike, who's sprawled over my bed, bare chested in boxer briefs—which leaves nothing to the imagination—on my laptop searching for a new home. He admitted to me this morning that it's time for him to start fresh. That means moving out of the house that holds memories of Jakyra— both good and bad— that he wants to put behind him.

Jakyra. Whom we *still* haven't dealt with. Who, even now, won't sign the divorce papers.

He still loves her, I'm no fool. I can't say that I don't feel a tad bit of competition…. Who the hell am I kidding? I feel a mountainous amount of competition when it comes to Jakyra. He could go back to her at any—

"Hey, come look at these. I narrowed it down to two." I start in my recliner, jerking my head in the direction of his voice. "You okay?"

"Couldn't be better." I lie, unwanted insecurities crowding my thoughts. I push them way to the back of my mind and leave them there so that I can be with him in the present. "Let's see what you've got." I rise up off the recliner and meander over to the bed, stretching out on my stomach next to him. Mike scoots the laptop over to me and I scroll down to look at his first choice. "This is *gorgeous*." I click through the pictures of the house. "And it's not far from your company… perfect."

"Yeah, it's ideal for *me*, but take a look at the second one, then say that again." He engulfs his arm around my waist.

"I'm not gonna change my mind, GQ. This first one is perfect for you. It's literally ten minutes from Adira. Five bedrooms, four and a half baths, finished basement, den, large living and dining room, huge kitchen, attached three-car garage, huge backyard, *beautiful* landscaping, and not to mention, fully furnished. What could be better than that?" I argue, listing off all the things he said he's searching for. Of course, he ignores me, clicking on the next house. I roll my eyes, glancing at the screen and my mouth flies open. "This is where *I* live!"

"Good catch. Nothing gets past *you*, Dimples."

"No one likes a smartass, GQ." I keep scrolling through the pictures. "Why have I never seen this type of apartment here before? "

"It's their penthouse floor plan. I would be on the top floor… the *entire* floor."

I peer over at him; my eyes as big as headlights. "No goddamn way. Are you *serious*?"

"Very."

"This is so far from your company… almost an hour away."

"But closer to *you*." I still at his words. He would give up a perfectly located house that suits his needs, to be closer to *me*?

My heart surges with love and an overwhelming need for him to ravage me. I close the laptop and place it on the floor, then climb back on the king-sized bed, straddling him in the process. He doesn't object. "GQ…. I don't know what to say. You would do this just to…"

"Yes. All you have to do is say the word. Can you manage me being so close to you?" He caresses the swell of my hips.

I lower myself until I'm inches from his lips. "Is that even a question? Yes, I would *love* for you to move into that penthouse." I purr, stroking his nipple with my thumb lightly, causing it to harden under my touch.

Mike's breathing becomes rough, and his grip on my hips tighten. "Just a warning… I'm insatiable." He darts out his masterful tongue, skimming my bottom lip.

"Who says I'm not?"

"My kinda woman." He grins, bucking his hips upward. I return the gesture, grinding into him. I hear a lustful moan echo throughout the room. I don't know if it's Mike or myself but a wild hunger swirls around us and it's not my intention to waste a moment of it.

I feel him harden even more as I continue to grind my slick core against him. "GQ?"

"Hmm?"

"I didn't wanna be the one to have to say it, but you have… stalker tendencies." I say, smiling into his feather light kisses.

He chuckles, then in an instant, I'm under him, my wrists restrained by his large hands. "Maybe so. Is that a problem?" His soft, hot tongue marks a path from my neck to the peaks of my breasts.

"I never said I *didn't* like it. It's… kinda hot." I moan, breathless from his seductive attack. Mike releases one of my wrists, leaving a trail of goosebumps as his fingers move, lazily, from my arm to my waist, down to the waistband of my panties to—

His phone vibrates on the nightstand, breaking the haze of

sexual tension that encircled us. He kisses my chest, reluctantly detaching his hand from inside my underwear.

Damn it.

"Sorry, it might be Chris." He lifts off the bed and moves toward the nightstand, swiping answer without looking at who's calling. "Chris, I swear you have terrible timing. Is there something—" I see his shoulders tense. "Why are you calling me?"

Yeah, definitely not Chris.

"Good, Johnee turned himself in. What does he want, a fuckin' medal? It should have never taken him this damn long in the first place." His voice is callous as he stands straighter. I crawl across the bed, stroking his back in a circular motion. "Okay, if that's all— are you signing the divorce papers?" He plops down on the bed. "Then no, I don't wanna see you." Mike's shoulders are so tense, you can break a two-by-four over them. I begin to massage his shoulders and instantly he gives a low groan of approval. "It's none of your business who I'm with. I'm not having this conversation with you." He ends the call, flinging his phone across the bed.

"You have to deal with Jakyra, Mike. There *is* no getting around it. You know she's not gonna stop."

"I know." He sighs, lying back on the bed.

"You still love her?" I don't know why I asked him. I already know the answer, and when he doesn't respond, it confirms my rising worries. "You don't have to say anything, I know you do. It's only natural. You have history."

"Not like the way I love *you*, but… yes, I do. Kyra didn't used to be this way. She was one of my best friends. We've been through a lot of shit." He closes his eyes, shaking his head. "I don't wanna love her, but I don't know how to stop."

Settling next to him, I encase my arm around his waist. My heart is lodged in my throat, but I manage to speak. "I know this has to be hard, but you can't keep this up. It's going to destroy you, Mike. You *have* to face her." I drape my leg across his.

He turns his head toward me, eyes glossy with unshed tears. "I don't want to hurt her anymore, Erin. I've done enough."

I touch his face, with a quivering hand. "I know, baby. I know." I cuddle deep into his side, as my insecurities come raging back with a vengeance. He has to deal with Jakyra, I understand that, but I can't help wondering if he will give in and go back to her. My head is spinning. I don't want to think about the answer because I know I can very well lose him.

CHAPTER 27

Jakyra

Why Mike decided to pick this crowded ass café beats me, but if it gets me a chance to talk to him in person, then I'm all for it. Zelle's isn't known for its *privacy*, but it's either this, or back to Mike ignoring me. Surprisingly, the café isn't super busy. I mean, it's *never* empty, but it's not-counter to door- crowded, so that's a plus. I must have just beaten the afternoon rush. After glancing down at my phone for the third time, I lean back against the wall.

My heart is hammering as I peer at the door, willing him to walk through it. I sigh, ambling over to an empty table by the window and sit down. If anyone would have told me a year ago that I would be six months pregnant with someone else's child, on the verge of divorce, and fighting to save my marriage, I would have laughed in their face. I would have told them to get a fuckin' life, but as it stands... here I am.

"Good afternoon, welcome to Zelle's. My name is Aaron. I'll be serving you today. What can I get for you?" The dark-haired waiter smiles, awaiting my response and all I can do is cringe at his name. *Aaron.* That's the last name I need to hear right now. Definitely can't be a good sign.

Steadying my breath, I look up at the friendly waiter and force a smile. There's a sinking feeling in my chest and it's getting worse as each second passes. "I apologize." I clear my throat. "There's someone else who'll be joining me shortly, but I'd like to go ahead and order for the both of us and you can bring his order out when he arrives." Aaron nods his head and takes out a notepad. "I'll have a mocha latte and my companion will have a caramel macchiato." It's Mike's favorite. I'm sure he'll appreciate the gesture.

"I'll get your order right out to you, ma'am, and congrats by the way." He gestures to my protruding belly. I swallow past the thick lump in my throat. If he only knew.

I subconsciously rub my tummy. "T-Thank you." Aaron smiles, then heads to the counter. Blowing out a breath, I shake my hands a little, trying to stamp down my nerves. I need to convince Mike to give us a— The rest of the words evaporate from my thoughts along with the dying hope of us reconciling as I watch Mike and Erin— from the window view I have— ambling toward the café door. His arm snugly over her shoulder; her arm securely around his waist.

What. Fresh hell. Is. This?!

My heart plummets. I *know* he's not with her after what *we* almost did. He cann*ot* be serious! "Why the hell did he bring… *that?*" I frown as Mike holds the door open for *Ms. Energetic.*

"I'm sorry, didn't you order the mocha latte?"

"Oh, yes, I did. I apologize. I wasn't.. referring to you. Thank you, it smells amazing." The waiter places the hot beverage in front of me. "You can bring the caramel macchiato out now. My companion is walking in." Aaron nods, then heads to the counter once more. My gaze, however, is on my husband and the man-stealing bitch beside him.

"Jakyra" Mike's tone is cold, impersonal; like he doesn't even know me.

My brows crease as I grip my phone tighter, anger igniting like wildfire. "Don't greet me like I'm some stranger, Mike."

Did you forget we almost had sex in your office not that long ago?

The words are on the tip of my tongue; trying to pry my lips open like a vice grip. "Despite everything, we *were* best friends. Or did you forget about that?" His jaw tenses, then he sighs, pulling out a chair for Erin then sitting himself.

Oh, *now* you want to be the perfect gentleman?! Un-Fuckin'-Believable.

"No, I haven't forgotten. That's what makes this so— I'm sorry, Kyra. I didn't mean to be rude." He peers across the table at

me, the frigidness gone from his eyes, but now it's replaced with…
sadness? Shit. This can't be good.

"What is *she* doing here?" I can't even pretend to be cordial.
Her very presence pisses me the hell off. Sitting there, uninvited,
in her white Michael Kors coat with *matching* purse and boots.
Come on, give me a fuckin' break. I swear, the level of
disrespect—

"*She* has a name, and I asked her to come."

I tilt my head. "Oh, I'm sorry? Am I supposed to greet the
home wrecker that destroyed our marriage?" I turn my focus on
the enemy. "Please forgive me. How are you, Erin? How does it
feel to know you broke up a marriage?" I glare at Erin as sucks in
a breath.

The vein in Mike's neck is literally bulging. "Kyra, what the
fuck—"

"Caramel macchiato for you, sir?" The waiter interrupts, what
I'm sure would have been, Mike going from zero to a hundred in
three seconds flat.

Mike scrunches his brows in confusion. "I didn't order—"

"*I* ordered for you. I know it's your *favorite*." Ha! The look
on Erin's face…. Priceless. "Thank you, Aaron. Just put the drink
there." I gesture to the spot in front of Mike as he silently glowers
at me. "That'll be all, thanks." He nods with hesitation, glancing
between the three of us, then leaves. "What? It *is* your favorite.

Isn't it?" I blow my steaming mocha latte, then take a cautious sip. "Aren't you going to thank me, Mike?"

He leans back in his seat. "You said you wanted to talk. Let's talk."

"Yes, but I didn't think we'd have an *audience.*" I cut a sharp eye at the intruder, then back at Mike. "But fine. If this is how you wanna do it."

Erin glances over at my husband, leaning into him, the shoulder of her puffy white coat brushing against his. "This is a bad idea, GQ. I can wait in the car." She begins to stand, but he grips her hand, tugging her back down.

"No, Erin. We already talked about this."

"But GQ—"

"I need you here with me." Erin rests her hand on his and nods.

GQ?! Oh, *hell* no. Now they have *nicknames?!* I don't think so. This shit ends today. My stomach churns at their interaction. Tilting forward on the table, I laugh the driest laugh I can possibly muster. "This is unbelievable. Why couldn't I get *this* version of you, Mike? Why did I get the abusive, drunken bastard?" Mike jerks his head in my direction, gorgeous brown eyes full of guilt. "I suffered through a lot of shit because of you!" Curious heads turn toward us in the café, so I inhale a deep breath to calm myself.

One of Mike's fists clenches and unclenches as he looks down at his drink, then back at me. "I know, Kyra and I'm sorry."

He hesitates, then, "But what we had—"

"Have. What we *have*. Or don't you remember what happened in your office, not even a month ago?" Mike draws in a sharp breath. Erin withdraws her hand from his, staring at him in shock, and *I'm* mentally slapping myself for allowing that small piece of information to slip.

Damn it. I wanted to use that as a last resort to keep him near, but I screwed *that* up. Oh well. Go big or go home, right? I know I don't have a chance in hell of getting him back now.

Erin cocks an eyebrow. "I'm sorry, *what* happened in his office?" Her voice is steely, eyes staring a molten hole into the side of Mike's head, but *his* eyes remained on me.

Just the way I like it.

Mike shakes his head with slow movements. "Jakyra, don't—
"

Sipping my cooled coffee, I lift a brow. "Oh, I guess you two *don't* tell each other everything." I glance at my husband, who pleads with his eyes for me not to continue.

Erin turns her focus to me, eyes overflowing with anger. "Apparently not. Please, continue." Oooh, I like this feisty side of her. She's still enemy number one, but I like this version of her better than the sniveling, panicky bitch I saw at Mike's office.

The vein on the side of my husband's neck strains as he grips the side of the table with bare knuckle force. "Jakyra—"

"Mike and I got into a pretty intense argument in his office…."

"Stop it, Ky—"

"Then it got hot and heavy. We would've had sex right there on his leather sofa, if Ashton didn't knock on that door when he did." Mike closes his eyes, lowering his head. "It was… passionate. A type of burning need that we've never experienced before." I smirk, allowing those words to sink in a second or two. "I don't have to tell you how… demanding he can be."

I feel the vibration of Erin's leg bouncing up and down under the table as she crumples the napkin in her hand. "When?"

"The day you and I met." The three of us sit in silence for a long suffocating second, then Erin's chair screeches back, and she's on her feet. I lean back against my chair, rubbing my belly.

Mike holds onto her arm, a desperation in his eyes that I've never seen before. "Erin, let me expl—"

"Let go. I need to leave." She tries wiggling out of his hold.

"Give me a chance—"

"Let me go!" He releases her as if she were red hot coals. Grabbing her purse, my enemy storms out of the café.

Well, my job is done here.

Mike returns his penetrating glare on me. His eyes grow dark as his jaw twitches. "We're done." His voice is eerily calm, yet his body is as stiff as a board.

I purse my lips, shaking my head. "Not if I don't sign the divorce papers, we're not. There's nothing you can—"

"You have ninety days to sign the papers, after that, I will pursue a divorce with or *without* your consent. So, sign by February… or don't. Either way, this divorce *will* happen." He stands, zipping his coat.

"You can't do that! I won't let you!" I screech as panic claws at my chest. I had *no* idea you could do that shit.

"You can't stop me. Don't contact me again unless it's through a lawyer." Mike turns away, heading for the exit.

"You asshole!" I scream at him, but he's already out the door and searching for that… that…bitch!

No, no, no! This is *not* how this is supposed to turn out. My hands tremble as I unlock my phone. Scrolling down in a frenzy, I search for the two emergency contacts Mike gave me for his office when we were together. One is Chris and the other is Ashton. I press Ashton's number. "Please, pick up." My breathing is shallow, so I take a cleansing breath, then refocus my attention to the phone call. "Shit, he's not gonna answer."

"What do you want? I don't work for that ass anymore, so why are you calling me?"

"I thought you weren't going to answer for a minute."

I wasn't. Again. What do you *want*?"

"Mike and Erin don't belong together. I think we can help

each other out." There's silence on the line for a minute.

"I agree, but how do you even know anything about me and Ren's relationship?"

"I have my ways. Never mind that. Are you willing to hear me out?" I await his answer; my nerves shot to hell. Ashton is my last hope.

"I'm listening."

CHAPTER 28

Mike

As soon as I step out of the café, a burst of frigid wind smacks me in the face. Flecks of snow swirl in the air as people hurry along to their destinations on the busy strip. Boutiques, restaurants, a local bookstore and a little mom and pop bistro line both sides of the street.

I focus my attention on the bodies shuffling around on the sidewalk, as I begin my trek, opposite the parking lot where my SUV is. My eyes scan the crowd. I see at least a dozen people with white coats.

What are the fuckin' odds?

I grab my phone out of my coat pocket, dialing Erin's number. Ringing…. No answer. "Shit. She couldn't have gone far." My heart is beating out of my chest as I walk down two more blocks, dialing her number several times, all ending in the same result…

nothing. I stop in my tracks; people give me side eye for making them go around me. "Dimples, where the hell *are* you?" My chest feels as if there's a boa constrictor squeezing my heart, my breathing shallow.

Heading inside one of the boutiques, I dial my brother's number. He answers on the second ring. "You're a little late, but I'm guessin' it didn't go well with Erin."

"Erin's not answering her phone and I can't find her, bro." I rush to say, as I quickly search around the store before heading back out. "She walked out of the café after—"

"Whoa, Mike. Start from the beginning. Where are you?"

"I'm headed back toward Zelle's. We went to meet Jakyra, so that I could end things officially, but—"

"Why in the hell would you bring the woman you're with now, to a meeting with your soon-to-be ex-wife?" A valid question. It *was* pretty stupid of me.

"I needed her there, but that's not the point. The point *is*, I can't find her and I'm freakin' the fuck out!" As I enter the bookstore, all eyes zero in on me as I unashamedly walk through the aisles searching for Dimples. "I tried calling her, but she's not answering her damn phone, Marlon. How am I supposed to find—"

"Have you checked your car yet?"

"No. My keys are with *me*, so she wouldn't—"

"Just… humor me, Mike. Go to your car and search around there." Marlon's voice is steady and his tone brings me to a place of calm. My breathing regulates and I can think more clearly.

Looking around at the patrons in the bookstore, I put a placating hand up. "I'm so sorry for disturbing you." With that, I leave out in haste, practically sprinting to the parking lot near the café. When I round the corner, there she stands, leaning against my SUV, chin tucked into her coat and hands in her pockets… waiting for me. I release a thankful breath, walking toward my SUV. "I found her…"

"You're wel—" I end the call, stuffing the phone back into my pocket. I'll thank him later… after he cusses me out for hanging up on him.

Erin's face is a tinted pink from the harsh wind. She looks up when she hears the snow crunching beneath my feet.

"I'm sorry, Dimples. I should've listened to you. I tried calling, why didn't you answer your phone?" She points inside the SUV, and there in the center console is her cell. I hold my arms open in invitation. "Can I?"

Erin glances up at me, eyes gleaming. "You don't have to ask, Mike. I wasn't upset with you." Erin wraps her arms around my waist, as I swathe my body around her, shielding her from the wind. "I can't be mad at you for something that happened when we weren't even together." I kiss the side of her head. "I knew she was manipulating the situation and I fell right into it." She unravels herself from my arms, the loss of her touch immediately felt.

I take her hands in mine, warming them up. "Still, it was a bad idea, and that's on me."

"I didn't mean to yell at you, GQ, but I needed to remove myself from the situation before I threw your coffee in her face. After I left out, I realized I didn't have the keys and I sure as hell wasn't coming back in to ask for them after *my* grand exit." I chuckle, bringing her fingers up to my lips, kissing each one. "What really upset me…" She lowers her eyes "I thought that… you might… go back to her. I've been a little insecure lately, but I didn't want to be *that* girl, so I kept my thoughts to myself." I'm speechless. This fierce breath of sunshine, energetic-is-my-middle-name, woman is having doubts about us?

I lift her chin as another gush of wind whirls snow from the ground. "Listen to me, Erin. I am all in. I'm not going anywhere. I *love* you. You're wearing my ring; I'm getting a penthouse in your complex to be closer to you. That's as real as it gets."

Her cold hand finds my scruffy beard, stroking it. "Yeah…. Real stalker-ish if you ask me." She smiles, but it doesn't reach her eyes. "I'm sorry I caused a scene."

"No apologies. It's over. Jakyra won't be contacting me without her lawyer. It's finally done. By August, I will officially be a free man. And believe me, if I can get things sped up, I will." I give her a peck on the lips. "You have nothing to worry about, Dimples."

"I love you, Mike…." She leans into me, nuzzling into my coat. "But can we get in the truck now? I need to thaw out in places I didn't know needed to be thawed." I unlock and open the door for her, and she hops in. Shutting it, I run over to the driver's side and jump in.

After cranking up the heat, I turn to her. "Still need to be thawed?"

"I know two things that can defrost my frozen parts like no other. Your mouth…. and your di—"

"I aim to please." I wink at her, as my fingers skim her warming thigh.

"You know what they say? Dirty minds…"

"So, when am I gonna meet this mystery woman, Mike? You *talk* about her, but I haven't seen any evidence of an *actual* person. You sure Erin's *real*?" I roll my eyes at my annoying ass sister, as she rubs her baby bump, awaiting an answer.

Things moved quickly since that disaster of a meeting I had with Jakyra. In just over two months, I sold my house, moved into the penthouse, got the divorce process started— let's just say, Jakyra was *not* happy— and in full swing recreating Leeman International. Yeah, I've been busy.

I sit MyIesha's orange juice on the black granite coffee table, then relax on the leather recliner, draping my leg across the armrest. "She's real Iesha; as real as that shag on top of your head you call hair." My baby sister hurls a throw pillow at me. "Erin's working late today, but she'll be here later, I promise." Iesha waves me off, then simultaneously grabs her juice and the remote to the wall mounted flat screen, switching it on.

I focus my attention on the layout of the penthouse, still trying to process the fact that I moved out of the house that I once shared with family; with friends… with my wif— soon-to-be *ex*-wife. I shake my head at how much has changed in the past year.

I scan the room again, admiring the open floor plan. It's a mirror image of the pictures I'd shown Erin two months ago: A panoramic view with floor to ceiling windows, dark hardwood floors throughout with beige and chocolate brown walls to match. It has an eat-in kitchen with built in black and chrome appliances, an in-wall oven with black and gray marble countertops and backsplash— Dimples said it was her second favorite part of the penthouse. The first being the master bedroom… no explanation needed. A large living and dining room, a guest room, office space; not to mention, an immense walk-out balcony that gives a fantastic view of lake St Claire, although it's frozen over right now. The pictures didn't do this place justice.

It still doesn't feel real though. I finally made a clean break; a chance to start over with my Brooklyn. Noticing movement from my peripheral view, I turn to see Chris wandering back and forth across the length of the hallway clicking away on his phone.

Shit, I forgot he was here.

"Whatever you're doing on that damn phone must be life-altering because you've been at it since you got here. Hell, I forgot you *were* here. Christopher Benjamin Daniels' mouth is like the energizer bunny. He never fuckin' stops."

Chris pauses; his face scrunches up. "First off, don't ever use my middle name again. Second, my mouth has gotten *your* ass out of trouble many a time, and third, shut the fuck up." He flips me the bird, then goes back to texting on his phone.

I fling a pillow at him. "Who have you been texting?"

"Uh, nobody?" He picks up the pillow and throws it back, hitting me dead in the face.

Accurate bastard.

"Well, *nobody* has occupied your time since you got here. What happened to family time? Don't you love us? He doesn't love us, Iesha." I glance at my sister as she peers over to me, then we both look at Chris with pouty faces.

Chris takes a seat on the oversized sofa and tilts his head toward us. "Don't do that shit. Don't try to make me feel guilty for texting to my…." He stops himself from finishing.

"Your *what*, Chris?" I tease, turning fully toward him. MyIesha flicks the T.V. off, then makes her way over to Chris, sitting beside him.

He leans back. "It's… complicated. Never mind."

I lift a brow. "It wasn't that complicated when you were texting whoever you were texting for the past forty-five minutes." I love getting under Chris's skin. He's just so easy to rile up.

MyIesha bounces up and down, patting Chris on the leg. "Oh, oh, I know! Chrissy has a *girlfriend!*"

My best friend's tanned skin flushes a faint pink as he put his phone away. "No… that's not… I don't…. shut up, and don't call me that." Iesha pats him on the leg again, as we both laugh at his discomfort. At that moment, my intercom buzzes, and Chris shoots up from his seat, stalking toward the door. "I got it!" We laugh even harder.

I lift from the recliner and move closer to MyIesha, sitting on the armrest of the sofa. Rubbing her belly, I grin. "How's my nephew doin' in there?"

"Active. He keeps me up at night, kickin' the hell out of me; movin' around like he's a damn acrobatic." I chuckle, continuing to stroke her firm tummy in awe of this gift inside of her. "You know…. Jason *is* gonna be a part of my son's life…. And mine. Can't you… I don't know, tolerate him? You put him in the hospital, Mike. You owe him *that* much."

"I don't owe him a goddamn thing. You *do* know he cheated on you right… with my—" I'm not finishing that sentence. Jakyra is no longer my wife. I need to let this go. I remove my hand from her stomach and stand, walking over to the beverage cooler to grab a bottle of water. "Look Iesha, whatever you and Jason do is between you two, but don't expect us to be like we used to be because that shit is *not* gonna happen. I can tolerate him for my nephew's sake, but I can't promise you anything else." Ambling over to the sofa, I sit next to her. Opening the bottled water, I take a swallow.

MyIesha peeks over at me, leaning her shoulder against mine. "Don't think that I've forgiven Jason… I haven't, yet, but I don't want my son in the middle of this shit. He doesn't deserve it. So, me and Jason *will* work this out." She rests her headon me as I wrap my arm around her shoulder, setting the bottle on the table. "He has another child on the way, too. A child that's gonna be my son's half- sibling, so that's something else I have to come to terms with." She sighs, gesturing for me to help her stand. "Just so you know, I owe that bitch a beat down after we have these babies."

"I knew it was just a matter of time before you brought that up." I take her empty glass, placing it on the kitchen island. "That's between you and her. Just don't end your ass up in jail."

"No promises."

"Hey family!" Marlon waltzes through the foyer into the living area with my niece in her car seat.

I take a few steps forward, meeting him at the edge of the living room. "What the hell took you so long coming up? I was about to call out a search party. Where's your better half?"

Marlon places the car seat on the oversized ottoman, taking Evie out. "We were having issues with the code you gave us for access to the floor, so we had to get one of the staff members to help. Turns out, you forgot the pound sign… jerk." He hands off Evie to MyIesha, who's bouncing on her toes with excitement. "As for Koko, she's comin' in with Erin. She got on the elevator, I'm guessin', from her floor, on our way up."

My ears perk up at the mention of Dimples name. "Oh, she's here?" I swivel toward the growing sound of footsteps to see Erin taking her shoes off at the door and toss her keys into the glass dish on the accent table near the entrance. My fingers instantly tingle in anticipation to touch her. My feet start moving before my mind can catch up to what I'm doing.

Erin's smiling eyes lock with mine, heat simmering just underneath. "GQ." She beams, sauntering my way.

I meet her between the foyer and the kitchen, cradling her face in my hands. "Dimples. You're early."

"My workload wasn't as strenuous as I thought. I missed you." She brushes her lips against mine.

My body ignites like a match to gasoline. "I missed you, too." I manage to say between kisses. "You ready to meet my sister?"

She smiles into my lips as she gives me one last peck. "Of course, I am."

"Erin is real after all. Good for you, Mike. Now I don't have to commit you." MyIesha jokes, making her way over to us with my niece, in a slow stride. "Nice to finally meet you. I'm

MyIesha.”

Dimples untangles herself from my grip, extending her hand. “Hi! I'm *thee* real Erin Brooks, not the cheap imitation he was married to.”

“Oooh, I’m sold! I like her already, Mike! We will get along *just* fine.” Iesha leans in, giving her a one-armed hug, grinning from ear to ear.

I feel a slight shove as Koko maneuvers around us, punching me in the arm. “Next time you overlook me, it’ll be *other* precious extremities that’s in pain, you ass.” She rolls her eyes.

I give her a side hug. “Sorry, Koko. I didn’t ignore you on purpose.” I kiss the side of her head and she pushes off me.

“Whatever. Don’t let it happen again.” Koko gently removes Evie from Iesha’s arms as she continues her conversation with Dimples.

I glance back at the closed door. “Where the hell did Chris go?” Pulling out my phone, I dial his number.

Marlon removes the cap from my niece’s bottle, testing the temperature. “Oh, he said he had to take care of something. He was headed into the elevator when we got off.”

I walk toward the hallway for a little more privacy as I hear Chris's voice on the other end of the line.

“Let me explain, Mike.”

"Why the hell would you leave without telling me? Does it have anything to do with who you were texting earlier?"

"Yeah, but I don't want to talk about it over the phone. I'll tell you soon, but not now, okay?" I hear the pleading in his otherwise rough voice.

I sigh. "Fine, but you still could have told me you were gone. That was rude as fuck."

"I know, I'm sorry. I'll be back in about an hour." There's silence for a second, then, "Tell Iesha she was my first real crush."

"What?!" I didn't mean to yell, but he came way out of left field with that one. This is the first I'm hearing about the shit.

"I'm kidding, Mike. I just want her to feel as flustered as she made me." I make my way back to where everyone is.

"So, you were *flustered*?"

"Bye, Mike." He ends the call. I laugh, then stroll into the living area where everyone is sitting.

"Iesha, my beautiful, clueless sister. Guess what I just found out...."

CHAPTER 29

"Hey, baby. I'm on my way to Kyra's lawyer office. I'm meeting Carl there. If all goes well, the divorce will be expedited from August to May." I turn the corner, approaching the office building. Carl, my lawyer called me earlier in the week with the good news that I could get my divorce finalized sooner than expected.

It's sunny out this afternoon, the snow has finally melted, and the weather is decent for mid-March. To top it all off— not without difficulty, of course— this shit is finally about to be over. Nothing can spoil my mood today.

I catch shuffling on the other end of the line, then a harsh sigh from Erin. "Well, that's good news. I'm happy for you— Liz, can you get me the Carnelli account from Mr. Leeman's office— I'm sorry, Mike. There's so much to do before the International Software Convention."

Pulling into the parking lot, I disconnect my phone from the car. I manage to hear Dimples yelling orders over the whistling of the wind. After hitting the alarm, I hightail it across the parking lot, to the glass doors of the law firm, entering. "You got a lot goin' on right now, Dimples, so I'll call you back later, then we can celebrate. Sound good?" Strolling up to the receptionist's desk, I wait for the thin faced, pale skinned woman to finish her conversation on the phone. Doing a quick scan of the quiet lobby, I notice everything here is stark white and caramel colored, including the walls, hardwood floors and furniture.

I hear loud clatter, then Dimples screaming in frustration. This is so unlike her. She's usually the picture of professionalism.

"Shit. Somebody please, pick that up and move it into the conference room." I feel her anxiety through the phone. "I'm so sorry, GQ. Yes, going to celebrate sounds like a victory well deserved."

"Dimples?" I say in an even tone.

"Yes?"

"Stop what you're doing and take a minute to breathe. You gotta calm down."

"I *am* calm. I just—"

"Close your eyes and breathe, baby." I hear Dimples inhale deeply, then exhale. She repeats it a couple more times, each breath becoming steadier.

"Thank you, Mike. I'm okay now." The tension in her voice has faded. My bad-ass— take charge— woman is back.

That's more like it.

"I really need to get back before these people destroy something they won't be able to replace. I'll talk to you soon, love you."

"I love you more." I end the call, just as the raven-haired receptionist— Debbie it says on her name tag— finishes her call.

"I do apologize for the wait, Mr.—"

"—Harmon. Mike Harmon."

"Yes, Mr. Harmon, your lawyer is waiting in room 102. Let me take you back." Debbie leads me down a hall, which reminds me of a doctor's office; ivory walls and tiled floors to match. The door is already open when we approach. Carl raises his head as I walk through the doorway. "Mrs. McCoy-Harmon will be here with Mr. Malone in ten minutes."

"Thank you." I nod in appreciation, and she smiles, leaving the room. Removing my coat and hanging it on one of the available hooks near the door, I take a seat next to my lawyer. "Hey, Carl. You ready for this circus act today?" I joke— not really— taking in the space we're in.

Everything is bland from the eggshell walls to the dull brown carpet. Even the wall art and conference table are lackluster. Not the best décor, but hey, to each his own.

I can't help it, it's the interior designer in me.

"Jakyra has *not* made it easy for us, Mike but I don't believe there will be an issue with finalizing today. Everything should go smoothly." He boasts. Yeah, Carl is one cocky bastard, but he can definitely back up his talk.

He adjusts the cufflinks on his white shirt sleeve under a dark gray suit, leaning back in the leather seat like the arrogant son of a bitch he is. "Just let me handle everything, and you'll be leaving this office today, a free man, Mike." He smiles, with confidence. His pecan-colored skin almost a glow in the sunlight beaming from the floor length windows. "Trust me."

"If I didn't trust you, you wouldn't be here beside me, so I'll let you do your job and I'll concentrate on what's important." *Keepin' my shit together*. Of course, I didn't voice that, but it's settled into the back of my mind. I *cannot* fuck this up.

Forty-five minutes into this meeting and all hell breaks loose. Jakyra has been on a rampage since the moment she waddled into the room. She is *definitely* eight months pregnant. Her face is the chubbiest I have ever seen; stomach is as big as a beach ball. Her complexion is more of a darker caramel now, rather than her normal butterscotch skin tone, but that pregnancy glow is unmistakable.

Her poor salt and pepper haired lawyer can't even talk without Jakyra interrupting him. I have to give it to him; he's managing her like a champ. There are few people who can get Kyra to shut up when she gets started, but Mr. Malone is handling his business. Controlling her *case* is a different story, though. Carl shut down everything Malone proposed, sending her into even more of a frenzy. She knows she can't win.

Kyra stands to her feet, glowering at me. If looks could kill, I'd be six feet under with cement blocks for feet, gagged and tied with my eyes gouged out.

She slams her hand on the table. "Why do you get the easy way out? I cheated, yes, but you did far worse. I *still* stayed after everything you put me through!" I flinch at her words. She's not wrong. What I did to Jakyra is unforgivable compared to her cheating. Guilt is slowly slithering up my spine, attempting to wrap itself around my throat.

I inhale a sharp breath before speaking. "I couldn't be who you needed me to be. I'm sorry it took me so long to change." I lean forward. "But I told you before that we're toxic for each other. One of us had to stop this cycle."

"Tell me the fuckin' truth. Do you want me out of the way so you can be with that *bitch?* Is that it?"

"*She* has nothing to do with it. *This here?*" I gesture between us. "Has been happening for a while." I notice Jakyra rub the side of her belly, scrunching up her face a bit.

"Bullshit. If she wasn't around—" She inhales sharply, gripping her stomach on both sides. Then, I see a tint of red spreading quickly on the inner thighs of her white dress pants.

No.

I stand, the chair tumbling over behind me. "Kyra? You're… bleeding." I barely get the words out before she glances down at herself, then at me, eyes sheening with tears.

"Mike?" At the call of my name, I'm beside her. "Not again." She cries, her scrunched up face now wet with tears. Jakyra doubles over, as far as her belly will allow her. I can almost feel her pain myself.

I toss Carl my keys, his eyes bulging from their sockets, as he hands us our coats, then rushes to get the SUV. I swiftly help Kyra into her coat, her breathing borderline panic. I throw mine on, then peer into her worrisome eyes. "Listen to me, Kyra." I try to stay calm, but inwardly, I'm freaking the hell out. "You're gonna be fine. The baby will be fine. Do you hear me?" Tears continue to fall as she nods, unable to speak.

Walking Jakyra toward the door, I peer over at Malone, who's even paler than before. "Can you grab the rest of her things?" He gives a quick nod, collecting all that she brought.

I hear his footsteps from behind. "I called EMS, Mr. Harmon. They're on the way." I *hear* him, but I don't respond. My focus is solely on Kyra and the baby. Thoughts of *our* loss invade my mind.

Us arguing.

Her storming out of the house.

The rain.

Me trying to pull her back inside.

Her slipping.

The sounds of sobbing…

Her pain.

The blood.

I blink a couple of times, swallowing hard. No, I'm not going there. This isn't the same. This isn't my fault. I force the bile back down that's in my throat.

As if she were a rare flower, I carefully guide her out to the reception area, where I notice Carl pulling my SUV up to the front of the building. I already made up my mind, I'm not going to wait for the EMT's. I need to get her to the hospital myself. She won't lose another child… not if I can help it.

Several hours later, I find myself in scrubs, being led by a nurse to the OR, where they've prepped Jakyra for an emergency C-section. Her Ob-Gyn gave me the nerve-wracking news that Jakyra suffered a Placental Abruption and the baby's movement had been decreasing. My heart damn near self-detonated hearing those words come out of the doctor's mouth. I don't think Kyra can take another loss… I don't think *I* can.

Erin is waiting in the lounge area. She rushed down as soon as

I told her what happened. Marlon and Koko, I'd dialed next. Koko is with Dimples and Marlon stayed with Evie. I haven't been able to contact MyIesha *or* Jason.

Fine fuckin' time for them to try and reconnect.

In the past four hours, I've nearly passed out… twice, had a panic attack and puked up my spleen. Right now, my hands are as sweaty as a teen going on his first date. My heart's racing so fast, you would think it's competing in the Grand Prix.

Alright Mike, breathe before you pass out again.

I take deep breaths as we stop in front of the OR doors. The nurse had to make sure I was okay more than a few times in the past couple of hours.

She turns back, smiling. "You ready, Mr. Harmon?" Her smile soon transforms into a look of concern. "Are you alright?"

Right on cue.

I gulp and nod.

"Everything is going to be fine. The baby just needs to come out sooner rather than later. You're going to see your little one in no time." I don't have a chance to correct her because she opens the doors of the OR, where my gaze immediately lands on Kyra.

Her eyes are puffy from crying and the fear twisted into her features mirror my own. I push every negative thought I have into a metal box and lock it, shoving it way back into the depths of my mind. I need to pull myself together. Jakyra needs my strength and support. If I can't do anything else, I can do this for her.

I'm led to Kyra's side, where she instantly latches onto my hand. Leaning over, I place a chaste kiss on her forehead, squeezing her hand lightly.

She looks up at me, another tear trailing down her frightened face. "I'm scared, Mike. What if—"

"No, don't go there. Everything's gonna be fine."

"But they said she's in distress. Her heart rate has dropped. I don't wanna lose—"

"Stop, Ky. You won't lose her. The doctors are gonna save her." I haven't used that nickname for her since we were kids. I caress her cheek, my eyes beginning to sting from tears I'm willing back. "She *will* be alright, Ky." I whisper into her hair; memories of us losing our daughter intruding like a thief in the night. Taking in a shuddering breath, I blink away the tears.

The doctor peeks over the makeshift curtain that separates us. "We're going to begin now. I'll do a quick test. Let me know if you feel anything?" I glance over the curtain to see her giving little pricks— with a silver pointed... something... I don't know— in different areas of her belly and upper thighs. "Anything?"

"No, I don't feel anything." Kyra answers, her voice rough from hours of crying.

"Good. Now, we're going to be moving quickly to get her out of there. You'll feel a lot of pressure, but I assure you, no pain.

Take a deep breath and try to remain calm for me, okay?”

“Okay.” Kyra breathes. “Please, don’t let her die.” My heart breaks for her. This is the woman I fell in love with; not the vindictive, manipulative woman I’ve been at war with over the past several months. The woman beside me— compassionate, loving, trust-worthy— she’s back, and I missed her.

I have never seen Kyra so broken…. except for when I made her lose our— no it wasn’t my fault. An unexpected tear escapes my eye and I wipe it away as the doctor begins the procedure.

They make quick work, cutting into her lower abdomen, then, “Alright, lots of pressure, Jakyra. Hold tight, she’s almost here.” After a couple short minutes, “You have successfully delivered a baby girl!” There’s shuffling behind the curtain, but no sound of crying and my heart does a nosedive into my stomach. Jakyra grips my hand tighter. I’m on the verge of pulling that curtain down to see what’s goin’ on when the thunderous ring of healthy lungs sound throughout the OR. “There it is!” The doctor lifts her up so that we can see her. Jakyra chokes back a sob, covering her mouth with her hand; my eyes wet with tears that I no longer care are falling.

She’s alive.

We didn’t— *she* didn’t lose her.

That sobering thought has me sucking in a sharp breath. She isn’t mine. She’s Jakyra and Jason’s. Glancing back down at my soon-to-be ex-wife, I smile. “She’s okay.” I smooth her hair back.

"You did good, Ky. I'm proud of you." And I am. I kiss her forehead.

She grabs onto my arm pulling me into a hug. "Thank you. You didn't have to be here with me after the way I've treated you."

"I wasn't gonna let you do this by yourself, Kyra. You don't have to thank me. I'm glad I was here." My heart twists in turmoil. I'll never get to hold my daughter and it brings up emotions that I kept buried behind a cemented wall for years. I force a smile, as the doctor brings the baby to Jakyra to hold. I exhale a shaky breath. My heart is in ruins, but she's alive. Kyra's daughter is alive and that's worth all the pain in the world.

CHAPTER 30

Jakyra

Rays of the bright afternoon sun pour into the living room as I fold the last of my daughter's receiving blankets. It's been a month since threat of a miscarriage. Thirty days since I gave birth to my beautiful baby girl.

I smile as she opens her bright cocoa-brown eyes. There's no mistaking it. Aside from my pouty lips, she's a reflection of Jason. From her straight raven black hair to her cashmere complexion. "I can't believe how stupid I've been." My delusions of Mike coming back to me even after what I did, had me making irrational decisions. In the end, it drove him further away and into the arms of another woman.

Jordyn, my daughter, closes her eyes once more as I rock the bassinet until she settles. Sinking back into the sofa, I push the laundry basket off to the side.

I glance over at a picture of me and Jermaine on the end table beside me. He sits on the stairs of the front porch with his eyes closed, face scrunched up. I stand above him laughing with the bucket of water I'd just poured on him. I remember that day well. It was scorching hot and sunny, and we had just called a truce from bombing each other with water balloons.

He's worked hard all his life and he still is. Jermaine has been going to therapy sessions religiously and the change in him is like night and day. I'm proud of him… I always have been.

Mike and I haven't been in contact with one another since we shared that moment together at the hospital. I mean, he's checked to make sure me and Jordyn were alright a couple of times, but other than that, nothing. I can't say that I'm surprised though. I've made his life pure hell these last few months. *I* wouldn't wanna be bothered with me either.

As I glance around the quiet town home, I notice another photo on the vanilla-colored wall closest to me. It's of all of us in our early teen years; between ages nine to thirteen years old, at least. "Wow, so much has changed since then." I sigh. We were happy. No drama. No worry of cheating or lying. No betrayal. "I wish we could just go back to how it used to be." The photo was taken in front of our childhood home. It was the fourth of July; humid, and sunny.

Mike and Johnee leaned against one another. Jermaine had MyIesha on his back while Jason pulled on her hair. Marlon and I held George while Koko hit him with a water balloon. Every one of us with a smile on our face. It was simple back then. What happened to us… what happened to *me*? I shake my head.

"I need to let this shit between Mike and I go and move on." I'm tired of holding on to someone who clearly doesn't want me anymore… not that I blame him. He's no saint. Mike's done some shitty things to me, but somewhere along the way, he changed. I see it in the way that he treats Erin, how he talks to her. I might not like it, but she may *be* better for him than I ever *could* be. That realization pours over me like hot chocolate on a sundae. I suck in a breath, then shakily exhale.

"Our marriage… our relationship *was* toxic." Mike tried to tell me, but I didn't wanna hear it. When he walked out that door Thanksgiving night, I should have let him go then. But this is what happens when you allow pride to step through the wide-open door that you provide. "It's time to put an end to this."

Ambling over to the charging port on the desk at the far end of the living room, I pick up my phone. "I need a clean break, and Ashton does too." Scrolling down my contacts, I find Ashton's number. As I'm about to dial him, there's a knock at the front door. I'm expecting Jordyn's dad today. Ninety nine percent of the time, Jason knocks at the back, so this is unusual for him. I trek over swiftly to open the door and I'm met with the last person I expect to see.

Ashton.

My heart drops into my stomach as my eyes bulge from their sockets. *What the hell is he doing here!* "Are you out of your fuckin' mind?!" With the speed of Flash, I skim over the courtyard and parking lot, making sure there's no one who would recognize him. "You have some goddamn nerve." Pulling him inside, I shut the door, then jab my finger into his chest. "I told you never to come here! What if my brother was home?!" I whisper-yell, careful not to wake my daughter.

Ashton strolls into the living room as if he didn't just show up here uninvited. He plunks down on the sofa, peering up at me with eyes full of menace. It's unsettling. "I'm doing good, thanks for asking, Jakyra." He rolls his eyes. "We need to get started with our plan. It's been two months now. The longer they're together, the closer they'll get. I'm tired of waiting, Jakyra." The way he says my name, has me on high alert. Ashton is calm as he speaks, but it's the dangerous undertones of his voice that propels me straight to fight or flight mode. I need to get him out of my damn house.

I instinctively stand between him and my baby. This is the first time I have ever felt uneasy around Ashton. I clasp my clammy hands together; my heart thumping so fast, I think I might pass out. "Yeah, about that." I gulp. "We need to rethink this plan."

"What is there to think through?" He leans forward, pinning me with a glacial stare. "I invite Ren for coffee to personally apologize for my behavior in Mike's office. *You* take pics of us when I hug her, reach for her hand, kiss her… because I *will* kiss her; anything that makes it look as if we're being intimate. You send the pics to Mike and let nature take its course.

We both know that Mike can't survive another betrayal. You did a hell of a job making sure of that." He gives a lopsided grin. "This should break him though, then you can swoop in and save the day and *I* can console my sweet Ren's heartbreak. It's a win-win." His face lights up as he goes over my plan. He is *way* too eager… then again, so was I, not too long ago.

I fold my arms across my chest, my hip cocked to the side. "I changed my mind, Ashton. I don't wanna go through with this stupid plan anymore." He furrows his brows, leaning forward, more than he already is. "It's time for me to let Mike go. Besides, I don't want to do this to him. He deserves to be happy… even if it's not with me." I can't believe the words that are coming out of my mouth right now. A couple of months ago, I was ready to fight tooth and nail to keep Mike. "Let's forget about them and move on with our lives. We deserve better than sloppy seconds, Ashton."

"Well, whoopty- fuckin'-do, you had an epiphany. You suddenly grew a goddamn conscience. Now where does that leave me?" His voice is callous, causing an icy chill course down my spine as he stands to his feet. "*You* may have reconsidered, but *I* haven't. Ren belongs with *me*, and I *will* make damn sure that happens… with or without you."

"Ashton, don't force my hand. I don't want to get the police involved. Just walk. Away."

"Go ahead. You can't say anything without implicating yourself. It was *your* plan, Jakyra. What do you think would happen if I started running my mouth to your *husband* about things only you and he should know, hmm?"

"It's your word against mine. Honestly Ashton, who do you think Mike will believe?" I'm grasping at straws. There is no way in hell Mike will believe my ass.

He moves closer to me until we're inches apart. His eyes relay a void that reaches my soul. I shiver in response to his intimidating glower. "How would you explain the calls to me? The texts? I can easily send all of this to him." Shit. That means if he goes down, I'm going down with him. A sinister smile slowly appears as he stares me down. He knows he has me. Damn it. "Checkmate." My breath hitches as he grabs my chin, gripping it with barely contained force. "I have my own plans for Ren. Stay the hell out of my way."

"Think about the consequences. Erin will *never* forgive you." I attempt to appeal to his more rational side, but at this point, I doubt he has one.

What the hell have I unleashed?

"She will, in time. If you stay out of my business, everything will be fine."

"Ashton, this is crazy—"

"Stay. The fuck. Out of my business, Jakyra." His hand

releases my chin and finds its home around my throat, applying gradual pressure. I freeze. All I can think about is my sleeping daughter. My eyes shine with tears as I gulp in large swallows of air. "I really don't want to hurt you, but if—"

There's a knock at the back door.

Jason.

I *cannot* be more grateful for Jason than I am at this moment. Ashton releases my throat, swiftly heading toward the front door. He swivels around, pinning me with a dagger piercing stare.

"If you get in my way, I *will* hurt you. That's a promise." As the door shut behind him, I exhale the breath I'd been holding.

On wobbly legs, I rush through the kitchen to the back door. Swinging the door open, I practically leap into Jason's arms.

"What the hell, Kyra? I thought we already discussed boundaries. Do you need a refresher?" I'm not sure if he's serious or not, but as I tremble in his arms, he takes notice. Unraveling me from his body, he pulls back. "What's wrong? Is it Jordyn?" His worried eyes search mine.

I shake my head. "I'm sorry, no, she's fine. I… just needed a hug. That's all." Jason's body instantly relaxes. "Well, next time warn a brotha. I don't need any more surprises. Now where's my princess." Moving past me, he removes his jacket, heading to the living room.

I shut the door, leaning against it. Subconsciously, I rub my throat, still feeling the ghost of Ashton's firm grip.

"I have to do something." I murmur. "I can't let you do this, Ashton."

CHAPTER 31

Erin

He's been brooding all afternoon. I know it has something to do with whatever happened in that damn OR, but he won't talk about it. Right now, he's standing on the balcony staring out over the lake. It's seasonably warm for a mid-April day; almost seventy-six degrees.

I step onto the balcony, with only a shirt and panties on—barefoot in all— and slip behind him. Pressing my body against his, I snake my arms around his midsection. "You've been quiet all day. Do you want to talk about it?"

"Not necessarily, no."

"GQ, I know something happened last month when you were in the OR with Jakyra. Why won't you tell me?"

"Because it's not a big deal."

"Apparently it *is*, if you're still bothered by it after an entire month." We're silent for a moment. "Let me in." I feel his chest rise and fall on an exhale, as he entangles his fingers with my own.

"Jakyra and I lost our baby when we lived in Jersey, a daughter. She was eight-months pregnant." Mike's body tenses, but I hold him even closer. "When I saw her bleeding that day at the law firm— I couldn't let her lose another child because of me, Erin."

"What do you mean?" I unravel myself from him, moving to his side. "Talk to me." The waves of turmoil that swirls in his eyes as he turns toward me, has my mind whirling with different scenarios.

"It was *my* fault we lost her." Mike's face twists in anguish, as his jaw clenches tight. "We argued that day. I don't even remember what the damn argument was about. All I know is that she tried to leave the house. It was pouring outside." Mike stops for a brief minute, shaking his head. I reach for his hand, giving it a gentle squeeze.

Releasing a rugged breath, his grip tightens on my hand, as he continues. "I didn't want her to go out in the storm, but she wouldn't listen. I reached for her arm." He bites down on his bottom lip, as his eyes glisten with tears. "She jerked away from me. I tried to catch her before she fell from the porch… I tried to—" A harsh sob escapes his lips. I'm engulfing Mike in my embrace in an instant, as if I were cocooning him with my love. He holds me close; grieving for the daughter that he feels responsible for losing.

"I'm sorry that you've been carrying this guilt for so long, and I'm so sorry for your loss." As Mike burrows his face into my neck, I feel the hot tears fall from his eyes. We stay in each other's arms for, what seems like, hours but is actually a few minutes. He releases a breath, then finally pulls back, twisting away to head inside.

Creasing my brows, I follow behind him. "Mike?" No answer. "Mike, what's wrong?"

He continues without a word until he comes to the sofa, sits down, and places his elbows on his knees. "This shit isn't me."

"What are you talking about?"

"Being vulnerable. I don't do this anymore."

"You mean being human? Someone who's been through hell and trauma throughout his life and has feelings and emotions?" I stop in front of him, tilting his head up to meet my gaze. "You don't *ever* have to hide from me, Mike. I've *seen* the man behind the mask; the scared broken boy, the brave teen. I've seen your tears before and I've wiped every single one of them away." Mike closes his eyes as a tear falls. I kneel in front of him, wiping it away and grazing his stubble bearded face with my knuckles. "I'm sure you've heard it before, but I'm gonna say it anyway." His tired eyes open once more. "That accident was *not* your fault. I can't even imagine what it must feel like to lose a child, but I *can* say that her falling isn't your fault, okay?" He's silent. The pain in his eyes reveals a battle going on within him to believe what I'm saying. This is something he's going to have to come to terms with on his own. Until then, I will be right here to support him.

Mike rakes his fingers through my hair, then tenderly kisses my lips. "Thank you." He whispers, then gives me another peck. "Maybe one day I'll believe it." He exhales a rough breath. "That isn't the only thing that's bothering me though." Standing from my kneeled position, I sit beside him, resting my hand on his thigh, encouraging him to continue. "I've been thinking about… goin' to see Don. I need to confront him, tell him how I feel. Then maybe I can close the door on that part of my life."

"I think that's a great idea. You *need* this."

"I know, but when I think of seeing him face to face, this paralyzing fear overwhelms me. After all these years, it fuckin' kills me that deep down, I'm still afraid of him." He places his hand on top of mine, still avoiding eye contact.

Leaning my head on his arm, I give his thigh a squeeze. "Harmone, he terrorized you for most of your childhood and teen years. You were abused; you *and* your siblings. Lingering fear is to be expected, but don't let it stop you from getting closure. You need to do this for *you*."

He shifts toward me. "I'm glad I talked to you."

"I'm glad you trusted me enough to *tell* me."

"I *trust* you, Erin, but it's hard to talk about that part of my life, when all I want to do is forget it."

"You don't have to explain, I understand."

"Have I told you how much I love you?" Mike gives me a smile that reaches his eyes, and I damn near turn into a puddle on the hardwood floor.

"Yes, but there's always more room for adoration." I giggle.

He lifts me onto his lap so that I'm straddling him. "Brooklyn aka Dimples aka Erin Avery Brooks, I love you."

I wrap my arms around his neck, all playfulness forgotten. "Harmone aka GQ aka Michael Julian Harmon, I love you more." I whisper as I kiss him. He trails his fingers underneath my shirt, unhooking my bra. "You *do* remember that Chris is coming by, don't you?" I point out, between his erotic, open mouthed kisses that have me trembling with need.

"What I wanna do won't take long to get you there." He stands up with me in his arms, then drops me on the sofa. "Take off your panties and lay back." His voice suddenly drops an octave lower, sending a tingling sensation from my spine to my core.

"I don't think we have enough—"

"Now." I practically purr at his command, as I slide them off in a hurry, lying back. My breaths are now coming in short pants. He takes one of my legs and puts it up over his shoulder, trailing light kisses down the inside of my thigh.

I grab his head, directing it towards his prize. He glances up at me smiling, a dirty glint in his eyes. Then I see his award-winning tongue dart out, wetting his lips. I moan, the anticipation killing me. As he sets his eyes back on the finish line, the door buzzer sounds, and I slam my head back into the cushion. "Damn you, Christopher Daniels!" I yell into one of the throw pillows. "You *knew* he would interrupt, you teasing bastard."

Mike chuckles, amusement dancing in his eyes, as he moves away from me, and to the door. "You have about three to five minutes to get decent. You know it doesn't take him long." I rush to put on my bra and underwear, then race to the bedroom to grab a pair of sweatpants.

As I make my way back out to the living room, I see Chris—and his irritating smirk—greet Mike, then he turns toward me.

"Hey Erin. I hear you're not too happy with me right now."

I shoot a death glare at Mike, then Chris. "You heard right." Rolling my eyes, I go into the kitchen to grab a bottle of water from the beverage cooler.

Mike laughs as he and Chris joins me at the kitchen island. "Chris, you do kinda have Thee. Worst. Timing." Mike pats him on the back. "I can't even get mad anymore, but…" Chris glances between myself and Mike, confused. "Oh, you're waiting— Well, I *may* have hacked into your computer the last time I was at your apartment." Chris furrows his brows in anger. I can almost see the steam escaping his nostrils as they flared. "Wait, there's more."

Mike sits on one of the stools as he swipes my water bottle.

Asshole.

"I *may* have come across some emails between you and this mystery woman."

Chris's eyebrows shoot up past his hairline as his mouth opens and closes like a fish out of water. "Mike, what the fuck, bro!"

Mike holds up a finger, exhaling a long breath. "Wait, there's more." He guzzles down half my water, then peers at Chris. "I… *may* have sent an email saying that you just weren't that into her, so you were ending things." Chris shoots out of his seat. Raking his hands through his hair, he strides into the living room.

Nostrils flaring as fierce as a bull, his face twists in red-hot anger that causes me to shudder. Chris stalks back toward us. "Why the fuck would you do that?! Do you know how long it took me to get her to open up?! This shit is wrong on so many levels!" I have *never* seen Chris so irate. His chest is heaving in and out, and his fists clamp shut; all the while, Mike remains planted in his seat, unbothered. I won't be surprised if Chris punched him in the face… it would definitely be justified. "I can't believe you did—"

"Are you finished throwin' a fit?" Mike interrupts, as Chris glares fiery blades at him. If I were Mike, I'd tread carefully. "It was a damn joke, Chris. I don't even know the first thing about hacking. Hell, I can't even crack an email password." Mike laughs, finally standing to move toward his friend, who still hasn't said a word. "Say something."

"Fuck you." Chris swivels on his feet, reaching for his jacket. "That was fucked up, Mike. Not funny."

"Come on, Chris. It was a goddamn joke." Chris continues toward the door. I watch as Mike follows behind him. "Are you seriously leaving?"

"See if you get the fucking message when you see the door close behind me… asshole." At that, Chris storms out the door, slamming it behind him.

Mike turns to me, hands on his hips. I meet him between the entryway and living room. "I think I may have gone a little too far, Dimples."

"*Definitely* too far, GQ."

CHAPTER 32

Mike

Just over two weeks have passed and I'm bringing in the month of May with a fuckin' bang. Erin is on my back about going to see Don. Marlon is giving me hell for not visiting him, Koko, and my niece more often, and Chris? Chris still isn't talking to me. I mean, it's been two damn weeks! How was *I* supposed to know he's *actually* serious about this woman?! A woman he still hasn't told me shit about.

Right now, I'm sitting at my desk, *attempting* to get some work done while trying— and failing— to listen to Nate on speaker phone. As I look out at the overcast sky, it seems to reflect my mood: dark and depressing. The office is usually filled with Chris's laughter and lighthearted nature, but now it's quiet, with tension that's palpable.

It's been awkward around the office between him and I to say the least. He's as professional as a lawyer defending their client, but when the workday is over, Chris is gone as quick as a check going towards bills. I need to talk to him, so he can go back to being the pain in my ass that I'm used to.

Besides the circus that I seem to keep putting on, the Leeman project is moving along quicker than I first thought. We should be wrapping up around August of this year. Speaking of, I still have Nate on the phone as I sit at my desk, hacking away at my laptop. "—Good to hear, Nate. I'm glad you like what we've done so far."

"I *more* than like it, Mike. I *love* it. Adira certainly lives up to its reputation. You can be sure I'll leave a rave review."

"I appreciate that, Nate. It's not every day that we receive the praise of a company of your caliber. I don't take it lightly." I finish up on my laptop, closing it, then stand to stretch my legs from sitting for the past three hours straight. "You know, we should be finished with this project before the original October deadline. I'm predicting August as our completion date."

"So not only is Adira professional, efficient, and thorough; you're prompt as well? We will *definitely* be using your services again in the future." I amble over to the window glancing down. People are out, each hurrying to their destinations.

I hear the click of the door, then footsteps of someone entering. No one comes in unannounced except… Chris. I turn to see him standing at the closed door, waiting until I finish my call, face as hard as granite.

I need to fix this shit, now.

"Again, thank you, Nate. I appreciate the generous compliments, and I look forward to working with you in the future." I take measured steps towards Chris, eyes directly on his cold ones. "I have to finish up some paperwork, but I'll be talking to you soon, Nate." We say our goodbyes and I end the call, standing a couple of feet from my best friend.

I let out a sigh. As I open my mouth to speak, he cuts me off.

"Your two o'clock had to reschedule, the fax from Mr. Giovonni came through and Jakyra is waiting to talk to you." He turns to leave, but I grasp his arm.

"Chris, are we gonna keep doin' this? I'm sorry, okay? It was shitty of me to do that to you. I just *assumed* it was like any other time we joked around with each other."

"Not with *this*… not with *her*."

"I didn't know you were serious about her. What's her name?" I release his arm as he turns fully toward me. His features soften and the tension he carried seemed to melt like heated butter.

"Her name is Lizzy Jamison. I met her on one of those chat sites."

"Have you even seen how she *looks*? You know there's a lot of catfishing goin' on." He saunters over to the chairs in front of my desk and takes a seat. I follow suit.

"Yes, *dad,* I've seen her. We video chat when we both have

the time." He runs his fingers through his dark hair. "She's beautiful, Mike. I didn't believe in love at first sight, but now…" When he peers over at me, I see a reflection of that same kind of love I feel for Erin. My eyes widen at his admission. Chris has *never* kept a girlfriend more than a month, and *that's* being generous.

"*Damn*, Chris. How long have you known her?"

"Almost seven months."

"And you didn't think to divulge this bit of info to me within all that time? Is *this* what we're doin' now? Holdin' out on each other?" He shoots me a look that screams, *you've got to be fuckin' kidding me, right*?!" But I sit there, awaiting an answer, knowing I have no leg to stand on.

"I don't recall *you* spilling *your* guts about Erin in the beginning *or* middle stages of your relationship." He lifts a smug eyebrow. I clear my throat but remain silent. He has me, so there's no need for further argument. "Anyway, Lizzy and I agreed to keep it flirty casual, but the more I get to know her, the more I fall down the rabbit hole. And I don't see myself wanting to escape it."

"Are you in love with her?"

"I don't know. I mean, Lizzy's funny, smart, supportive, and a great listener. She's goddamn amazing, and I wanna take the next step—"

"But you're afraid she doesn't feel the same."

"Yeah." He exhales a long breath, both of us silent for a second. "This isn't something we can really discuss *in-depth* right now. Jakyra's waiting for you, and I'd rather *not* be consumed by her wrath." He rises from his seat, heading for the door.

I call out to him. "Chris, are we good?"

"We were never *not* good, Mike. Sometimes you let your assholism go too far." He smiles— quite smugly, might I add— then opens the door.

"Jerk." I call out.

"Ass." He shoots back before closing the door behind him. I release a breath of relief. Chris and I are good. I feel a weight lift from me, along with a lightening of my mood. The sun is even beginning to peek through the clouds. "One down, two to go."

As I lean back against the edge of my desk, arms folded, Jakyra paces back and forth, biting her lower lip. She runs her fingers through the length of her wavy hair, stopping to peek at me every few seconds.

Okay, this shit has gone on long enough. I need to know what the hell is bothering her. I push from the desk, stepping in her path to stop her from burning a damn hole in my carpet. "Kyra, I don't think this is how two people having a conversation is supposed to go. What the hell has you so nervous?"

She releases a shaky breath as she stares up at me. "Ashton."

That one name has alarm bells sounding off all around me.

My face remains neutral, but my heart is pounding like a jackhammer. "What about him?" I keep my tone as even as possible, but I can't control the tick of my jaw.

"He's… not a good person."

"Tell me something I *don't* know."

"He's obsessed… with Erin."

My body tenses, giving away my concern. "Explain." My tone is as sharp as a razor blade.

Jakyra turns away from me, beginning to pace the floor again. "*Please* don't get mad. This was before things shifted between us; before I realized we *are* toxic together."

"What did you do, Kyra?"

"I produced a plan to break you and Erin up." She pauses for a second. "I reached out to Ashton for help." My brows crease as sparks of anger ignite throughout my body.

Jakyra stills a few feet away from me, eyes going wide. "I changed my mind though, Mike. I just want to move on." The sparks morph into a volcano of fury erupting within me. How the fuck can Jakyra side with that asshole! How can she…

I take slow, deliberate steps towards her. I want to strangle my ex-wife, then realize, she didn't *have* to tell me. Taking a calming breath, I stop in front of her. The volcano waning to a bubbling irritation. Now, my focus is on 101 ways to slowly torture Ashton. "What is he planning?"

"You're not… mad at me?"

"Oh, Kyra, you have no fuckin' clue how pissed I am at you, but my need for that grimy fucker to die a slow death takes precedence over my annoyance with you right now." She visibly eases, but worry is still burning in her eyes as she meets my fiery gaze. "I'm glad you told me. You didn't have to." My body relaxes, and I soften my features. I don't want her to be afraid of me anymore. I put her through enough shit.

"I'm sorry, Mike. I was acting out of jealousy."

"Now isn't the time to discuss your temporary insanity. I need to know what that bitch is planning. Do you know?"

"No, I came here to warn you to stay close to Erin. I don't know *what* Ashton's gonna do. He kept saying that Erin belonged to *him*. I didn't think he was serious until he threatened to hurt me, then I—"

"He what?!" I don't mean to yell, but the fact that this clown is not only trying to sabotage Erin and I, but he threatened Kyra, *too*?! I will end this fuckin' asshole! "When the fuck did *this* happen?!"

"About two weeks ago. He didn't take it too well that I changed my mind. He's *going* to come after me." Kyra's voice is so broken that it has me reaching out to her, enveloping her in a protective hug. "He said if I told you, he would… hurt me." She trembles in my arms, her hands gripping my back tightly.

"He won't lay a *finger* on you."

"He already did."

My heart stops for a long gut-wrenching second. Pulling her from my arms, I search her troubled gaze. "He… put his hands on you."

"Just a little harsh with his grip on my face… and throat. It was a scare tactic, that's all. I'm okay now."

My jaw clenches so hard, I think I hear the crunch of shattering teeth. "No, it's *not* okay. He put his goddamn hands on you?! He had no right—" All the things I did to Jakyra during our marriage flashes before my eyes. I have to take a step back, to distance myself. The harsh reality hitting me like a battering ram. Jakyra is a survivor of physical abuse… at *my* hands. *I* had no right. "I'm… sorry."

Kyra closes the distance between us, her eyes penetrating mine. "Don't go there. You've changed… and you are *nothing* like Ashton."

"Have I though?"

"I see it in the way you are with Erin. It took you a while, but you're not the same man I was married to. Let's just say, if you *hadn't* changed, this wouldn't even be a conversation right now." She reaches for my hand, squeezing.

I sigh, shaking my head. "Still doesn't make what I did to you right, and I won't let Ashton get away with hurtin' you. He won't lay a *finger* on you." I repeat, retribution flowing through my blood.

"You don't know that Mike. You didn't see the *look* in his eyes."

"He won't fuckin' *touch* you, Ky."

Jakyra releases my hand, swiping at the tears that had fallen. "Focus on protecting Erin. I'm leaving the state for a while, until I feel it's safe to come back."

"Where?"

"Doesn't matter. I'll be safe. You just keep Erin close.

"You don't have to worry about that. I will *never* let anything happen to her. Does Jason know you're leaving?" I can't believe those words slipped out of my mouth, but she's talking about leaving with his child. He should at *least* know about it.

"I'll let him know where I am when I get there. I really don't want to involve him in all this shit."

"He's kind of already involved. I mean, you're taking his daughter without his knowledge." The words glide past my lips before I even realize what I said.

Jakyra walks over to the chair that holds her jacket and purse, then heads to the door. "It's none of your business, Mike. Let *me* handle Jason." And she's right. It's none of my goddamn business, but how Kyra is going about this is wrong on so many levels.

"It's his *daughter*, Kyra."

"Leave it, Mike. Focus on protecting Erin. *That* should be your priority right now." My lips seal shut at her words. Erin *should* be my only concern right now.

She turns to me before opening the door. "Please don't let Ashton get wind that it was *me* that told you; because I *know* you'll go after him."

"You *know* I won't." With a nod, she slips out of my office, leaving me with my rage brewing like a coming storm. Ashton, you fucked with the wrong woman.

CHAPTER 33

Erin

Mike has called me every freakin' hour for the past four hours. Apparently, Jakyra fabricated some bullshit story about Ashton being dangerous. He wants to "take back" what belongs to him. I do *not* believe that for a second. Ashton is *not* dangerous, and he is *not* a threat; to me or anyone else. Granted, his actions at Mike's office was… out of line. Me personally? I don't see him as some rampant psychopath. Of course, Mike took Jakyra's accusations and ran with it. Why would Harmone believe anything that she says anyway? I think *I* know Ashton a little better than—

"Erin, are you busy?" Liz calls out before entering, pulling me out of my thoughts.

"No, not really. Just tying up loose ends before the end of my workday. Why?"

She closes the door, then walks up to my desk, a grin plastered on her face. "Is there anything you want to tell me?"

I know what Liz is hinting at, but I want her nosey ass to spell it out for me. "Oh, yes!" I feign excitement. "Mr. Leeman is hosting karaoke at his home for all of the department heads!" The smile disappears from her pale face. "Don't worry, you're a special exception. He told me to invite you personally."

"That's it? You *sure* there's nothing else you would like to share?"

"No? What else would there be?"

She scowls, folding her arms across her artificial sized double D's. "Really, Erin? This is what we're doing?"

"Apparently so." I smirk.

Liz huffs, rolling her eyes. "Fine. What's going on between you and Mr. Harmon? I've more than noticed his presence here for the past several months… particularly in *your office*." She raises a brow.

"Oh, *that's* what you're getting at."

"You knew what I was getting at, hussy."

"Maybe." I laugh, leaning forward against the desk with my elbows.

Liz pulls up a chair, and sits in front of my desk, eyes bright with curiosity. "So…"

"So… *Maybe,* Mike and I are… together."

"I knew it!" She squeals, clapping her hands. "When? How?"

"Slow down, curious George. I'm not going into detail right now." She frowns at that. "But… I will say, we've known one another much longer than you think." Standing, I gather my things.

"Come on, Erin. That's all you're gonna give me? Spill the tea!" Liz scurries behind me.

I grab my purse, heading for the door. "Sorry, you'll have to wait until the next episode of the Brooklyn and Harmone escapades."

"What escapades, and who are Brooklyn and Harmone?"

"Wouldn't *you* like to know."

"Ugh! You really suck balls right now."

I meander out of the door, toward Mr. Leeman's office, feeling the daggers of Liz's glare on my back. "That *may* have happened more than a few times." I hint, turning back to wink at her.

"What?!"

"Lock the door for me, Liz. I really appreciate you!" I call out.

"Do it yourself, witch."

"Thanks, doll!" I know she'll do it, despite her little attitude at the moment.

I knock on the open door before entering. "Hey, Mr. Leeman, I'm done for the day. I'll see you tomorrow." It's been the same routine for us as long as I've known my boss. I'd let him know I was leaving. He'd tell me to enjoy my evening, and to be careful out there, smile, then continue his work.

"Erin, come in and take a seat." Wait, what? "Close the door behind you." The sternness in his voice has my heart hammering in my chest. This doesn't sound promising at all.

I shut the door behind me, then make my way to the front of his desk, sitting in one of the white leather chairs. In fact, everything in his office is black and white, including the artwork on the walls. "What is it that you need, Mr. Leeman?" I attempt to keep my voice neutral, but I know he hears the tremble in my words.

"How is everything going?"

"Oh, well, your business trip to Milan has been confirmed, the Tyler account—"

"No, Erin. You misunderstand me. How are *you* doing?"

Oh.

I scrunch my face in confusion. Not quite sure where he's going with this. "I'm... fine, Mr. Leeman. Everything is going great. Why do you ask?"

"Erin, how many times do I have to tell you? Call me Nate. You've earned that right." His stern tone fades into a fatherly voice.

"Nate." I repeat. "Sorry, it's going to take a little time to adjust." I smile, releasing a breath.

"From now on, I'll correct you every time you call me Mr. Leeman. You've been warned." There's a lighthearted pitch to his tone. I don't know what I was so worried about. "Let me rephrase my question. How is everything between you and *Mike?*" I swear, my heart just stopped beating. *What. The. Hell. Is happening right now*!? The room seems as if it's narrowing. I see dark spots in my vision; my heart pumping in the danger zone of erupting.

A hand touches my shoulder, causing me to jump out of my skin. "Erin. Honey, take deep breaths. Calm down." It's Nate, standing beside me, worry radiating off him like bolts of lightning. He knows about Mike and me! How?! How *long*?! I am *so* going to get fired.

"Mis... Mister Leeman— Nate. I... I—"

"Erin." His firm voice snaps me out of my hysteria.

"Yes... Sir?"

"Calm. Down." Nate speaks the words slowly, until they register in my frazzled brain. "I'm asking because I'm concerned for you, not because you're in any kind of trouble."

"But, how did you even know?"

"Anyone with half a brain can see how you two are with one another. It's obvious how much he cares for you." I glance up at Nate, his smile calming me. "But my concern is *you* right now. I don't want there to be a repeat of... Ashton. I don't want you to get hurt again, Erin." He removes his hand from my shoulder and leans against his desk.

As the initial shock of Nate knowing about my relationship with GQ wears off, my brain slowly begins to connect the dots. My eyes widen at the realization.

"Oh, no, Nate. You have nothing to worry about with Mike."

The frown he's wearing dissolves like baking soda in water. "I don't mean to pry, but I—"

I stand to my feet, placing a hand on his shoulder. "Don't apologize. Given the situation with Ashton, I can see your concern." I give a slight smile. "Thank you for looking out for me, Nate."

"You remind me so much of the daughter I lost. Sometimes I forget…" He pauses, then, "From the day you came into the office and broke down because of what Ashton put you through, I embraced you as a daughter. That urge to keep you safe never diminished."

Wow. I… don't know what to say to that. I had no idea.

The same hand that I placed on Nate's shoulder, is now grasping his hand; his paternal gaze penetrating my heart. "I'm grateful to you for all your support over these past few years. I'm so humbled that you think of me in such a way." My eyes begin to get misty.

Damn it. Don't you dare cry, Erin. Don't. You. Dare… Too

late.

A tear escapes my eye. Then another. And another. Nate pulls me into a bear hug, patting my back, softly. I don't even know why I'm crying. "Thank you for helping me at one of the lowest points in my life, Nate. I appreciate all that you've done for me." I can't stop these damn tears from falling.

"Don't thank me, dear. I will always be here if you need me."

I pull away, wiping the wetness from my face. Great. I'm sure I look like a hot mess. "I know you will." I release a breath, sensing a shift in our boss/employee relationship. "But you can rest assured, Mike and I are good." I grab my purse. "And if he *does* do anything to hurt me, I give you permission to kick his ass."

"Oh, I'll do more than that." Nate makes his way behind his spotless black desk, sitting back down. "My foot will be so far up his ass; it'll be a three-legged race to the hospital."

"Nate!" I laugh so hard; I can barely catch my breath.

"What? I don't play when it comes to my family." I need to get the hell out of here before I start bawling again.

"You're family to me too, but Mike won't hurt me. I promise." Walking over to the door, I pull the handle. "See you tomorrow, work dad."

"Enjoy your evening, daughter, and be careful out there." He smiles, opening his laptop. I leave Nate's office feeling oddly lighter than I did when I first walked in. Knowing I have a second dad, who will look out for me when my real dad can't be here right now, puts me at ease.

Next stop? Marlon and Koko's place. But first, I need to call Mike before he pops a blood vessel.

CHAPTER 34

Mike

"I should go to Leeman Intl' and wait for her in the parking lot." Ever since Kyra told me about Ashton, I've been on edge. Of course, Erin doesn't believe her. I don't understand how she *can't* see the crazy in his ass.

As I watch my niece crawl to the couch and pull up on it, Marlon plops down in the middle of the family room. His legs are flat against the floor, as he leans back against his hands. "First off, don't be a creepy ass stalker. Second, isn't she off work already? It'll take at least twenty minutes to get to where Erin is from here."

"Which is why I should have gone there straight from work." Evie tumbles and falls, then crawls her way over to my brother. The family room had yet another transformation. From game room to Eva's world to Evie's playhouse. The table is removed from the room entirely, the T.V. is on a constant loop of Blue's Clues and her toys are scattered throughout the room. It's a miracle that the sectional didn't get booted off the island.

Marlon gives me the familiar "are you stupid look". "And wait there for three hours? Come on bro, you're being irrational."

"Believe me, you'll see just how *irrational* I can be if she doesn't call in the next five minutes."

"Mike, will you listen to yourself?"

"I'm trying to keep her safe, Marlon." I'm sure he hears the tension in my voice.

Marlon stands to his feet as Koko enters the family room; hair in a high ponytail with sweats and a tee-shirt on. She scoops Evie up, steading my smiling niece on her hip, then turns to me. "If you're worried about Erin, go see her. Don't ignore your instincts."

Marlon rolls his eyes, stopping beside her. "Please don't encourage his ass to do anything stupid."

Koko gives him a backhand into the chest. "It's not stupid if you're concerned about the person you love." Koko glances over to him. "You can't stand here and tell me that if Ashton threatened to hurt me or ruin *our* relationship, you wouldn't stay glued to my side." Marlon stays silent. "Do I need to bring up any incidents?" I watch my younger brother as he tightens his jaw but doesn't say a word. That's right Koko, get in his ass. "You know you'd be so close to me; people would think you were my shadow."

Marlon clears his throat, nodding. "You make a valid point."

His eyes find mine. "I *may* have mistaken your concern for being smothering."

I pull my phone out of my back pocket, unlocking the screen, scrolling until I find Dimple's number. "Thank you for that half-assed apology." Marlon shrugs, dragging Koko— along with their cheery daughter— to the sectional to sit down. I check my watch for the third time in five minutes. "She has a minute and a half before—" My phone buzzes in my hand. Looking at the screen, I see a picture of Dimples and I laying on my bed; both of us holding open candy bars as if we were making a toast. I swipe the answer button. "Dimples, you okay?" The weight on my chest isn't lifting like it did the last four times that I've… inadvertently harassed her today.

"Yes, GQ, I'm fine. I think you're making too big a deal about this." She sounds somewhat winded. She must be walking. "Anyway, May 25th is a special day for me. What are we doing?"

Diversion won't work on me, Dimples.

I loosen the tie around my neck, undoing the top button of my shirt. "How many different ways have you asked me that today?"

"About Five."

"And how many times have I answered?" She doesn't respond. "Exactly. Let me plan your birthday in peace. Believe me, at the end of the night you'll be happy… and sated." She huffs her displeasure but doesn't say anything else about it. "Where are you now?"

"Waiting at the elevators. If this is gonna be a play-by-play, tell me now."

Smartass.

"When you get your ass inside of your car safely, then I'll hang up. Until then, a play-by-play it is." Pulling myself up from the couch, I make my way over to the bay window, which overlooks their huge, fenced backyard. I hear a ding in the background. "The elevator."

"No shit, GQ. I didn't notice the big silver doors opening in front of me."

"No one likes a smartass, Dimples." She chuckles; I roll my eyes.

"I can feel you rolling your eyes at me, ya know. I'm in the elevator, by the way." I can hear the sarcasm in every word that leaves her sassy ass mouth.

"Good. Is there anyone that can walk you to your car?"

"Yeah, the security guard, Rick, but that's not—"

"Dimples, humor me, please?"

"Fine." I can imagine her pouting those plump lips of hers right now. How, last night, those same lips were wrapped around my— Nope, not the time.

I hear the ding of the elevator. "Are you *sure* Ashton doesn't know where you work?"

"No, he doesn't know where I work, so can you stop—" I catch a sudden rustling in the background, then, "We *really* need to stop bumping into each other like this." Who the hell is she talking to? It must be Rick because no one else besides Nate is there. "How did you get in? Rick knows not to open the doors after hours." Not Rick. So, who—

"I can be pretty persuasive when I wanna be, Ren." My blood runs cold at the sound of his voice.

Ashton.

"Dimples! Get the fuck outta there! Erin!" I rush out of the room and toward the front door. At my abrupt exit, Marlon and Koko follow behind me, with a baby in tow.

My brother stops beside me, as I open the door. "What's wrong?"

"Ashton is there with Erin! I need to go!"

"I'm comin' with you." I'm not about to argue with him. Marlon would come whether I want him to or not.

He whispers something inaudible to Koko before kissing her forehead, then we head out the door. We listen for the click of the lock before stepping off the porch.

Marlon dangles my car keys in front of my face. "Koko is calling the police as we speak. They may be able to get to her quicker than we can." My level-headed brother, always thinking ahead. I'm glad he's with me, cause my mind is scrambled right now.

I swipe the keys from his hands, and we head to my SUV. "Thanks." I hear Dimples talking, but when I call out to her, she's not responding. So, either her ear isn't to the phone, or she doesn't want him to know *who* is on the other end of the line.

My cell automatically connects to hands-free phone in my SUV as I peel off in the direction of the freeway. We listen as closely as we can to their conversation. There's a trembling cautiousness in her tone as she speaks.

 I hear deep laughter on the other end of the phone. "And why would I do that?" Ashton's voice seems unhinged. "Who's gonna make me leave? You? Rick?"

Her desperation fills my SUV as she fires back, "Yes, he *will* make you leave. Rick!" Come on, baby, get the hell out of there.

"Oh, you mean, *that* Rick?"

"Oh, my god! What did you do!" I hear scuffling, then silence.

Shit. No!

"Erin! Baby, talk to me!" The call ends abruptly. "Goddamnit!" My heart feels as if it's being ripped from my chest. That bitch has my Brooklyn.

CHAPTER 35

Erin

My head is hammering from temple to temple as I struggle to open my eyes. What happened? All I remember is—

Ashton!

Rick! Oh my god, Rick!

My eyes peel open as I sit upright. Immediately, a bout of dizziness overcomes me. I move to steady myself when it registers that my wrists are immobile. My heart begins to squeeze inside of my chest as if someone were pressing a ten-ton weight down on it. I try to catch my breath, but there's a tightness in my throat that's threatening to close off my air supply.

"Help! Somebody help me!" I shout between gasps. It feels as if my heart is going to burst open. I *have* to calm down and think. Closing my eyes, I breathe in deeply, exhaling the same. An image of Mike flickers through my mind. We're at Hartley's Bar & Grille sitting in the same booth we sat in on Thanksgiving night. He's smiling as he caresses my cheek. I can *smell* his citrusy cologne and *feel* the warmth of his breath against my face as he leans in.

I open my eyes, tears threatening to spill. I have to get out of here. Harmone *must* know I'm missing by now, and I can imagine what's going through his mind.

After a moment, I scan the room I'm in. It's oddly familiar; the coffee-colored walls, huge bay window and the burgundy bench that sits in front of it. My mind is scrambling to remember where I've seen this before. "No, this can't—" I catch a glimpse of the full moon in the dark sky. How long have I been out of it?

The king-sized bed, which I'm currently being held captive on, is covered in a soft burgundy comforter and the two bedside tables each hold shaded lamps. I take a peek over the side of the bed and see dark hardwood floors under an enormous area rug, a cream and burgundy mixture. My heart is in my throat as I peer around the whole room again. The entire décor is the same as…

"How in the hell is this—"

"Possible?" I hear the distinct sound of Ashton's unnervingly calm voice echo in the quiet of the room. I once longed to hear him call out my name, now the very pitch of his tone makes me nauseous.

He strides, purposefully, to the edge of the bed; the dim overhead light casting an eerie shadow over his eyes as he devours me with his lustful gaze. "After you moved out, I could never bring myself to get rid of this place. This is our *home*, Ren." He says it with so much sincerity that I'm sure he believes it, but Ashton has lost his goddamn mind.

Mike was right. How could I have missed this level of craziness that I'm witnessing right before my eyes?! "Ashton, you *have* to know what you're doing is wrong. Let me go, please." I sway my head from side to side, searching the bedside tables. Where the hell is my phone?!

"Looking for this?" And there it is… my cell, dangling from his fingertips. "Don't worry, you won't be needing it anymore."

The hell I don't!

"You belong with *me*, Ren. You *will* be with me. I didn't plan all of this for nothing." Ashton makes his way to the side of the bed and sits down; my eyes glued to the phone he placed on the closest bedside table. "Focus on me, not that damn phone, Ren. Mike can't help you, although the son of a bitch *is* persistent with the calls." He caresses my bare thigh, causing my skin to crawl. "He won't be able to track you. I turned your location and your phone off." I tighten my fists as I pull against my restraints. "He'll never find you. I can *promise* you that."

The blood in my veins freeze at the certainty of his words. "I don't *love* you, Ashton!"

"You'll learn to love me again… in time." His hand creeps further up my thigh. I recoil inwardly. "Mike will be an afterthought when I'm done with you."

"You can *never* make me forget about Mike. He's my soulmate!"

"*I'm* your soulmate!" The thunderous sound of Ashton's voice seems as if it's vibrating off the walls of the dusky room. He squeezes my thigh to the point of pain, causing me to flinch. The warmth that glistened in his eye's mere seconds ago, is now a dark void that seems unending. "*I'm* the love of your life. Say it." I lift my chin in defiance. "Say it!" Ashton's hand travels from my thigh to my face so quickly, I don't have time to blink. His grip is so firm, I cry out in distress. "Say. It." His hard features are inches from my damp face, his breath like live coals against my cheek.

"You're… the love… of my life… Ashton." I force the words out past the bile coming up my throat. I'm gonna be sick.

Releasing his iron-clad grip from my jaw, he smiles, placing a chaste kiss on my dry lips. I want to spit in his fuckin' face. As he stands, I notice the bulge in his jeans. I can't hold it anymore. I vomit all over myself and the bed.

"Damn it, Ren! Why didn't you tell me you weren't feeling well!" I pull against my restraints harder, until my wrists feel raw from the coarseness of the ropes. "Stop it, Ren. Calm down! Let me clean you up."

"Don't touch me!" I'm gasping now. My headache feels as if it can split my skull wide open. Fatigue has taken hold of my body, prompting me to slump over a bit. "No! Don't… touch me!"

"I need to get you out of this shit, now settle the hell down."

Ashton begins to untie one rope, then the other. This is my only chance to get out of here. "Lift your arms so I can get your shirt off."

"I can do it myself." I yank away from him, and he backs away to give me space.

Just as my captor places one foot back on the floor, I twist my body, kicking him with both feet, hard. He takes a brutal tumble onto the floor, and I swipe my phone, scurrying off the monstrous bed and toward freedom. Dizziness causes the room to spin as I turn my cell back on. Stumbling in the direction of the door, I grasp at the wall to keep from falling on my face. I swing the door open, not to the upstairs of the townhome we shared, but to a short hallway, leading into a living room that appears to be nothing like the townhome we lived in.

As I scurry out into the hall, Ashton ambushes me from behind, sending the phone flying from my moist hands; both of us nose-diving onto the carpeted floor. I twist and squirm in his grasp until I'm on my back, then I try my best to gauge his eyes out of their goddamn sockets.

Ashton traps my wrists above me, sitting on my legs so I can't move. "You really wanna make this difficult, don't you? Why can't we have a normal relationship like any other couple?" Here he is, unfazed; physical exhaustion is nonexistent in him, while I'm heaving in enormous amounts of air. My lungs feel as if they're shriveled at this point.

"We're not a fuckin' couple, Ashton! This shit isn't normal! You kidnapped me and refuse to let me go! This isn't love!"

"*You* tell me what it is then, Ren!" His demeanor changes instantly from a state of calm to that of a raging bull. "I put you on a pedestal; worshipped the ground you walked on. I would protect you with my *life…* at *any* cost." His eyes glaze over as if he were a million miles away. "I would kill for you… *have* killed for you."

"What?" I whisper. My heart plunges to the depths of my bowels. "What have you done? Is it Rick? Did you kill him?!"

"He'll live." His hold loosens on my wrist, but not enough to fight free. "Mel, on the other hand." He allows that comment to linger a second or so. "She wasn't gonna stop. Mel had already *ruined* our relationship." He releases a deep sigh, his brow furrowing even more. "I wouldn't let her hurt you anymore. She'd done too much, and I wasn't willing to take the chance of her exposing you to the world. You're for my eyes only!"

"So, you *kill* her!" I shriek, fighting full force now. "It wasn't an accident then?! And what about the video? Were you lying about that too?!"

"Stop fighting me."

"Let me…. go!"

"Ren, stop!" Releasing one of my wrists, he latches onto my throat with one hand and continues his tightening grip with the other. I still, instinctively latching onto the hand that's wrapped around my throat with my free hand. "No, it wasn't, but you don't need to know the details. Mel was a problem… now she's not." Dread creeps up my throat, causing my lungs to seize. I can't breathe! "And I meant what I said under that shed. There *are* no more copies of that video. You destroyed the last one." Ashton loosens his grip around my neck, moving his hand up to my cheek, stroking it. I want to fight back, but terror has paralyzed my body. "I wouldn't do that to you, Ren. I wanted to protect you, and that's the only way I knew *how*." Leaning down, he kisses me, softly. My hands ball into tight fists as his hand travels from my cheek to the outer curve of my breast.

Tears sting the corner of my eyes as I push against him with my free hand. "Ashton, don't. *Please.*" He looks into my horrified eyes and sees tears greeting him.

Ashton frowns. "Why are you crying? After everything I've done for you, you *must* love me, right?"

"You hurt Rick, killed Mel, and took me away from Mike, Ashton! Why would you think—"

"Mike?! You're still hung up over that asshole?! What else do I have to do to prove how much I love you, huh?! That I'm better for you!!

"I didn't ask you to go murder anybody! That was all on you! Mike is who I belong with, not you!" I'm so tired of this shit! He doesn't get to dictate who I should be with! Fuck him and his delusional fantasies!

Ashton stands abruptly, leaving me with legs that are half asleep and arms that feel like noodles. "So, you refuse to let him go? *That's* who you wanna be with?"

I sit up, glaring at him, legs still tingly. "You don't get to tell me who the fuck to be with, Ashton."

"Is that so?" I glower at him as he towers over me; the deadness in his stare, causing me to flinch as he draws closer. "If I can't have you, neither can he." The wicked curl of his lip and steel confidence of his tone has me trembling where I sit, unable to peel myself from the floor. I'm not gonna make it out of here alive.

CHAPTER 36

Mike

Marlon and I are in the waiting area of the police station. The two lanky officers in front of us are about the same in build and height. They're attempting to explain what the hell they have been doing to try and find Erin. The amount of money they spent to renovate this glorified reception area— with the decorative furniture, dimmer lights, and colorful wall paintings— they could have had more people out searching for Dimples. "She's been missing for a full goddamn day! What was the fuckin' point of coming here if you're not gonna do anything!?" I yell my disapproval. We've been at the police station since last night.

These clueless ass cops have done absolutely nothing the past twenty-four hours. I'm sick of sitting around while Erin is out there with that son of a bitch. "Have you at least gotten a lead from the security footage that Nate gave you last night?" Marlon and I got to Erin ten minutes too late. By then, Nate was outside talking to the cops, giving them access to the security cameras. The ambulance had just pulled off with Rick, and from what we heard, the cameras got a glimpse of the car, plates, and Ashton carrying Erin out of the building. It looked as if she was unconscious. "Why the fuck is nobody talkin'!" I lunge forward.

Marlon grabs my arm, yanking me back. "Calm down. Give them a little more time. They're doing the best they can with what they've got."

Pulling away from my brother, I glare at him in protest. "Ashton has my *girlfriend,* and you want me to calm down? These idiots have had a full twenty-four hours to locate them. They have Ashton's license plate number, and you mean to tell me they can't get a goddamn clue and find the son of a bitch?! No! I'll calm down when I'm dead!" I stalk off toward the exit of the police station. I hear Marlon call out to me, but I'm too angry to answer him.

I'm running on pure adrenaline alone. My head has not felt a pillow since Erin's been taken and I don't plan to sleep until she's back in my arms. Everything is a blur to me; I can't focus. Before I realize it, I'm in my SUV with the engine running. I have no clue as to how I even got here. As I sit in my seat in a daze, I notice the sky radiating a warm orangish pink tinge as the setting sun casts long shadows on the ground. It reminds me of Erin's warm personality, her passionate heart, and glowing aura. I release a long sigh, raking a hand down my face. "Where are you, baby?" I've not felt like this since—

My cell blares through my thoughts and I hear the sweet sound of Erin's ringtone. Rushing to grab my phone off the passenger seat, I quickly swipe to answer. "Baby! Are you alright? Where are—"

"Sorry to disappoint." His voice hisses through the other end of the line like a venomous snake.

"Where the fuck is Erin?!

"She's safe… for now."

"I swear to—"

"You want her? Come and get her."

"Where are you?" The line goes silent for a moment. It's so quiet on the other end, I thought the bastard hung up.

"I'm sure you've tried to GPS her phone; in fact, I *know* you have. Try it again. I won't turn it off this time. You have half an hour. After that, I won't be responsible for what happens to her."

"Don't you fuckin' touch—" The line goes dead. My heart is dangerously close to detonating. My mind is racing, and I can't seem to catch my breath, but I put the gear into drive and screech off in a hurry. As I open the Locate My Phone app, uneasiness washes over me like a tidal wave. I know this is a trap, but it's a risk I'm willing to take. I need her to be safe. My phone pings with an area that I'm all too familiar with. I release the breath I'd been holding, speeding in the direction of her location. "What the fuck is he doin' at our childhood home?"

###

I pull into the driveway and cut the engine. I stare at the house that I grew up in; that I was terrorized in. Emotions that I haven't felt in years begin to resurface. I shake my head.

Man the fuck up, Harmon. Don is in prison.

Your girl needs you. Don't let her become another victim.

I steel myself, heart racing like a stallion. As I open the door, Marlon's ringtone echoes in the SUV. Against my better judgement, I answer. "What."

"Where are you? You left without lettin' me know."

"I didn't know I had to tell you everywhere I went. The last time I checked, I'm a grown ass man." I glance up at the house again, my patience running thin.

"Mike, I'm sorry about what I—"

"I don't have time for this shit, Marlon. I have to get Erin away from this bitch."

"Wait, where… are you?"

"At the house we grew up in. That's where he's hidden her." I widen the door and step out.

"How did you even get that information, and why didn't you tell me?!"

"Ashton called me on Erin's phone— Look, I don't have time

to give you a rundown of what happened. I'm goin' to get my girl back."

"No, Mike, wait. He's settin' you up!"

"I know." I end the call, then throw my phone on the car seat.

As I walk up the porch, I see that the entrance is already cracked open.

This is all too familiar.

I widen the door, peeking around the side of it. "Erin!" The house is silent as I make my way across the living room. Nothing's changed since the last time I was here thirteen years ago. Gray furniture, hardwood floors with a gray area rug, eggshell-colored walls with a gray brick backsplash behind the sofa. Everything looks as if it's brand new. "Erin!" My feet lead me to the stairs. "Baby, where are you?!" With one foot on the step, I take one last glance around downstairs. It's too quiet. Maybe they're not—

"Mike!" I jerk my head toward her strained voice, my heart plummeting at the sound of terror in her tone. My feet move before my mind processes what's happening. The next thing I know, I'm at the entrance of my parents' room. The room itself is clean, but the one thing that remains is my mom's dried blood on the carpet where she died; the same area where Ashton is standing beside the bed with his hand wrapped around Erin's throat. I freeze. Her eyes are wide with panic, she's trembling violently as her hands grasp at his wrist. There are visible bruises on her face, arms and most likely her neck from the way he's gripping her. "M-Mike, please don't." I hear her pleas, but all I see is my mom crying for me to run.

"Mike, please don't get involved. Go to your room. I- I can manage your dad."

"Ahhh!! Please, Don! Don't do this in front of our kids!"

"Don! Stop it! You're gonna kill him! He's your son!"

"Oh my god, Mike! Run!"

I hear distant sounds of someone yelling, but my mind is bogged down by memories I'd rather forget. I feel beads of sweat forming on my brow as the thumping of my heart against my chest has me panting. I hear the voice again, clearer than before.

Erin.

"Run, Mike! He's going to kill you! Please, go!" I snap out of the time loop from hell, to see tears staining my beautiful Erin's face, and Ashton with a gun to her head. Dread fills me like sand in an hourglass.

Ashton's lip curls up into a menacing sneer. "Welcome home, *Mike*." I tense at the cold, hard metal of the gun against the back of her skull. "Why so quiet? I thought this is what you wanted?" Erin flinches when he jerks her back against him, repositioning the gun to the side of her temple. I clench my jaw at the action. "Don't you wanna come take her from me?" He snakes his arm around Erin's waist, his hand disappearing under her blouse. I follow his movements with tightened fists. "You want her?" I direct my attention back to the threat. He licks the shell of her ear, causing her to take in a sharp breath. "Come get her."

"Put the damn gun down and come at me like a *real* man."

Ashton gives a humorless chuckle. "You're not in a fuckin' position to be throwin' around demands." I glance at my Brooklyn. Her eyes are puffy from crying; entire body is trembling and I wanna torture this son of a bitch, slowly, bury him in a shallow grave and piss on it.

Ashton continues to caress Erin under her blouse and the thin edge that he's walking on with me snaps like a taut bowstring. "Get your goddamn hands off of her!" I take calculated steps toward them, stilling only when he presses the gun further into her temple. "Let her go and come *at* me, bitch!"

Ashton turns the gun from Erin, yanking her even closer to himself. "You think you get your happy ending?!" He extends the gun at me with ferocious intent. "No, you don't get to take what belongs to me!" His grip loosens on her, and I see a spark in Erin's frightened eyes. I know what she's thinking, and I don't like it.

Don't do it, baby.

Erin elbows Ashton hard enough to release his hold entirely, then bolts toward me. Ashton recovers from the shock of her bold move, then sets his menacing eyes on Erin's retreating back.

He glares icy darts at me, aiming for my Brooklyn. "If *I* can't have her, neither can you." Everything happens so quickly that I just react.

I hear shots fired. I see panicked eyes as she reaches out for me. I grab hold of her, shielding her from the rounds fired. "No!" Is all I have time to say before I feel bullets slice through my shoulder and side. Sensing my body crash to the floor, I hear more gunshots, then commotion in the background, but I can't make out anything through the burning agony shooting through my wounds. The sounds of heavy pants and roars surround me, then I realize those noises are coming from me. I can't see anything! Why can't I see anything?!

"Harmone, please! Open your eyes for me!" Cries of distress echo around me, and I feel pressure applied where the pain is. "Please." That final whispered plea has me struggling to peel my eyes open, and when I do, Brooklyn peers down at me, her hands on my shoulder and another set of hands on my side. Who is that?

I feel the blood soak through my dress shirt as Marlon presses into my side. "What the fuck were you thinking, coming here unprotected?" I see my brother staring down at me, his voice strained and chestnut eyes unsettled. Wait? How is he even here right now? Where is Ashton?!

I take in a deep breath, blinking to better focus. "Where… is Ashton?" My voice sounds gravelly even to my *own* ears.

Erin shushes me, grazing my cheek with a bloody hand. "The cops took him down. They have him in custody now." She seems exhausted, her voice raw from screaming. "An ambulance is seconds away. Everything is gonna be alright. Don't talk anymore." Erin continues to caress my jaw as I hear the footfalls of more people enter the room.

Squeezing my eyes shut for a few seconds, I try to focus on what's going on around me, but my vision is blurry. I see black spots in my line of view; all of a sudden feeling like a weighted blanket is over me. I'm able to make out Marlon rising from the floor, but Erin refuses to move away. "— So much blood... No exit wound..." More words pass between the people in the room, but I can't articulate what's being said. My eyes slowly slide shut and I listen to the soothing sound of Erin's voice as she encourages me to be strong.

"I love you, Harmone." Her words seem to fade into the distance, as a cloak of darkness overtakes me.

I love you too, Brooklyn.

CHAPTER 37

Erin

We sit in the family lounge of the hospital, waiting for Mike to get out of surgery. It's been an hour now and my mind is going into overdrive with worry. The nurse came in about fifteen minutes ago. Apparently, the bullet in his shoulder didn't exit his body, hence the surgery. Thankfully, the shot in his side was just a flesh wound, but we don't know how serious the other one is, which is spiking my anxiety to new heights.

MyIesha is sitting beside me, her belly looking as if it's going to burst on command. She seems tired, as Jason massages her lower back. Marlon and Koko sit off to the side with Eva asleep in her mother's arms. The tension in here is as thick as fog, and I'm going to pass out if I don't calm down.

As I stand, the world blurs together and I stumble back.

Jason reaches out to catch me just before I fall on my ass.

"You alright?" He helps me back to my seat.

"Yeah, sorry. I haven't eaten in almost two days. The dizziness must be from that." I rub my hands over my eyes, inhaling deep. "I'm scared for him." My words are just above a whisper, but his sister hears me loud and clear.

MyIesha's hand clutches mine, squeezing. "Mike's been through worse. He's gonna be okay, Erin." I close my eyes as I allow her words to wash over me like a cooling mist. It's then that I hear footsteps enter the lounge. Snapping my eyes open, expecting the surgeon, I find Chris standing in the doorway looking as if he's lost. It's the first time I've seen him appear so disturbed.

He walks in, meeting Marlon in front of the beverage center, then asks, "Have you heard anything?"

"Not yet. All we know is he's in surgery getting the bullet removed from his shoulder. We don't know the extent of the damage." He hugs Chris, patting him on the back. "I know how you feel, bro. He put his life in danger… and for what?" Marlon glances my way, as he releases Chris, eyes relaying regret for what he just said. "Erin, that's not how I meant it. It's not—"

"My fault?" I leap to my feet; guilt crushing into me so hard, I can barely take in a breath. "If I weren't so goddamn naïve about Ashton, Mike wouldn't be in this situation. So yes, it *is* my fault!"

MyIesha's hand slip from mine as I move away from her. "Erin, no one blames you." Her reassuring tone rang with unwavering sincerity, but guilt is eating at me, devouring me whole.

Tears threaten to fall as I turn back to his sister. "*I* blame me! Those bullets were meant for *me*! If I would have listened to Mike in the first place, this wouldn't be happening." I collapse onto the white floors, my legs feeling like lead. Tears burst forth like a dam; my body trembling as I struggle for air.

Chris kneels beside me, hands on my shoulders. "Take deep breaths, Erin." He's calm, although I see the concern in his eyes. "Breathe with me." I follow his actions, until my breathing returns to normal, then I sob violently. Chris draws me into an embrace, sitting on the floor with me, until my sobs subside. He pulls back. "You okay now?"

Wiping my eyes and nose with the sleeve of my blouse, I nod. "Thank you." I murmur, my throat feeling as if it's been scrubbed with sandpaper. Chris helps me from the floor, sitting me in the nearest seat.

As I peek up, I see everyone surrounding me. Marlon kneels so that he's eye-level. "I don't blame you… nobody does. I said what I said because Mike is reckless sometimes. He acts before he thinks." He's silent for a second, then, "I don't wanna lose him." I hear the tension in his voice as the pain conveyed through his eyes tell a whole other story that I don't think I'm ready to learn. Marlon clears his throat, rising to his feet. "Mike is strong. He'll be alright." It seems as if he's trying to convince himself of that, but

I nod all the same. He *will* be okay. I just got him back, and there's no way in hell I'm going to lose him to a bullet wound to the shoulder.

But he could bleed out though... No. He will be—

We all turn at once at the sound of footfalls coming into the lounge. Mike's surgeon and I'm assuming a nurse, stood at the entrance of the door, their expressions unreadable.

"Family of Mike Harmon?" We all rush toward them, Marlon and MyIesha at the forefront.

"Yes, I'm his brother. How'd everything go?"

"I'm Dr. Holland and this is nurse Bernard." He introduces. He's tall, pale, and lean. That's all I can make out. The rest of him is in scrubs and a scrub cap; the nurse dressed the same. "Mike lost a lot of blood. It could have been dire if he weren't brought in when he was." The short curvy nurse hands him some papers that he glances over before continuing. "The surgery itself was a success. We managed to remove the bullet with little to no complications."

Marlon creases his brow. "What does that mean? Little to no complications." Koko strokes his back, I suppose, as a calming effect.

"The bullet stopped just short of the brachial plexus, so things got a bit tricky." He explains. "If the bullet would have gone a fraction further and hit the nerve there, we could have been talking about a lack of muscle control in the arm, hand, or wrist. Not to mention becoming limp or paralyzed in the arm. Mike is incredibly lucky." Everyone stands there in silence. I see Marlon's jaw clench while MyIesha and Koko throw their hands over their mouths. Chris and Jason's expressions are almost identical; horrified. And me? I'm frozen in place, absorbing all of the information Dr. Holland had just given us. Mike could have lost the use of his arm… because of me.

Tears escape my eyes once more, as I wrap my arms around myself. "But he'll be okay, right?" I'm afraid of the answer, but I need to know desperately.

"Yes, he will make a full recovery. I just needed you to understand the seriousness of this injury."

"What does his recovery time look like?" That's Chris asking, as he steps beside me, placing a hand on my shoulder.

"It depends on the patient, but it usually takes a month, at least. At most, three to six months to heal completely along with physical therapy, of course. But again, that depends on the patient."

"When can we see him?" MyIesha asks, her voice rough from crying.

"He's already been put in a room, so you can go up in about half an hour. Although, he won't be waking any time soon, so you may just want to go home and get some rest, then visit tomorrow." Dr. Holland begins to step away. "The next twenty-four hours for him are important, but I anticipate Mike making a full recovery, so don't worry. Go home, get some rest."

"Thank you, Dr. Holland. We appreciate all that you've done." Koko's voice sweeps through the silent room like a fresh summer breeze; cutting through the tension that occupied the space for the past three hours.

"Glad I could bring you some good news." He nods his head, then takes his leave, Nurse Bernard following behind him.

I release a shaky breath, then turn to the rest of the group. "I'm staying." It's not up for debate. There is no way in hell I'm leaving Harmone. He risked everything for me. I owe him my life.

Marlon nods as he shifts his focus on Koko and Eva. "I figured as much." He takes his sleeping daughter from Koko's arms, resting her head on his shoulder. "I'm gonna get these two home. I'll be back first thing in the morning." He drapes his arm around Koko's shoulder, heading toward the exit.

MyIesha sits in one of the chairs, rubbing her belly. "I'm staying, too." She yawns.

Jason shakes his head in disagreement. "No, you're exhausted, and you need to rest. If anything changes, I'm sure Erin will let us know." She peers over at me, eyes full of apprehension. MyIesha really does look beat. She can barely keep her eyes open.

"Of course, I will. But you heard what the doctor said. Mike is okay, so go home and rest, MyIesha. I'll be right here by his side. I'm not going anywhere, I promise."

"Me neither." That's Chris, as he sidles up next to me. I give him an appreciative look, then refocus my attention back to MyIesha. Her worry seems to lessen the more we reassure her.

She reluctantly nods, another yawn tearing through her. "Okay, I guess I'll head home then. Make sure to call me if anything happens."

"We will." Chris and I assure her. MyIesha signals Jason to help her up, we say our goodbyes, then they're out the door.

Chris glances down at me. "Shall we?" He extends his arm for me to take hold of. My chest aches at the thought of seeing Mike incapacitated, but he needs to know I'm here with him.

"Let's go see our best friend." I take his arm and we head out of the lounge.

CHAPTER 38

We sit in comfortable silence for the first hour; both of us positioned on opposite sides of Mike's bed. The atmosphere is suffocatingly melancholy, and my constant crying isn't helping one bit. Guilt is a greedy bitch; it constantly eats at your conscience until you're consumed in self-loathing. I can't stop blaming myself for what happened to him, and it's shredding me on the inside.

I hold his hand, gently stroking his knuckles. They have Harmone in a private room with a TV, bathroom room and decent sized hospital bed. The moonlight casts a soft glow onto the glossy white floors. The walls are a milky white, as are the bed sheets and blanket that lay over my sleeping prince. The three deep violet chairs are the only thing that brings color to the room.

I glance over at Chris. His elbows rests on his knees, and his brows creased, as if he's deep in thought. I can't stand this debilitating quiet anymore. I'm going to scream if I don't hear some kind of sound, other than these damn machines beeping!

"You okay over there?"

He peeks up at me, sighing. "Just thinking."

"About?"

"About how things could have easily gone sideways." Chris sits back in his chair. "It could have been much worse. What if the bullet—"

"But it didn't, Chris, and Mike is still here with us." I had to stop him from voicing what I've already been thinking. I don't need both of us having toxic thoughts. "He's going to wake up soon, then we can go back to our favorite pastime… annoying the hell out of him." We smile at one another, the mood lightening a little. "We don't know much about each other. Tell me something about yourself." I shift the conversation in a different direction, hoping he'd take the bait.

Chris's brows lift, as if caught off guard by the question. "Like what? I'm sure Mike told you all about our high school years. Let me tell you, we were Class-A dicks back then." He chuckles, shaking his head. "It wasn't our finest moment."

I gasp, in feigned shock. "I can't believe what I'm hearing. Not *my* Mike. And *you*?" I point, pursing my lips. "*Thee* Christopher Daniels, an asshole? The same man that unashamedly got a kick out of Mike and I failing to keep our relationship a secret?"

"What can I say? I'm stuck in my assholish ways." We laugh, then silence falls once more. No, I refuse to let the mood decline again.

I place Mike's hand back on the bed. "Any siblings?"

"Nope, just me, myself, and I. We don't get along all that much."

I raise an eyebrow, as I lean back in my seat. "Should I be worried?" I know he's kidding, but I like messing with him.

"I'm joking, Erin."

"I know you are. The look on your face though."

Chris rolls his eyes, smirking. "I *am* an only child though. How about you?"

"I have two other siblings; an older sister, Anyah, and younger brother, Isaiah; Zeke if he's cool with you." I stand to stretch my legs. I really do need to let Ann know everything is okay with Mike. She's not gonna sleep until I call her. "Since you're an only child, tell me about this mystery woman you've been talking to." His eyes sparkle with something I've only seen in my Harmone's eyes when he looks at *me*. Chris must be serious about this woman.

"Her name is Lizzy. She's amazing, Erin." His entire face lights up as he speaks about her. "I don't know if Mike mentioned anything, but we met on a chat site. The plan was to keep things casual, but the more I get to know her…" Chris rakes his fingers through his hair. "I never thought that I could… fall so hard, so fast." He's silent for a moment, then, "Liz isn't looking for anything serious; I didn't think I was either, but we just…. click, ya know?"

I nod my head, peeking over at the love of my life. "Yeah, I do." I smile, then return my attention to Chris, who looks as if he's at war within himself. "Does *she* know this? She *may* feel the same."

He shakes his head, sighing. "No. I don't wanna fuck up what we already have. She made it clear she's not looking for a relationship. I think it has something to do with her late husband being killed."

I scrunch my eyebrows together. "Oh wow. What happened?" I return to my place, next to my man, taking his hand in mine once more. Now it's Chris's turn to stand.

He walks over to the window, staring out into the clear starry darkness. "She still won't give me the full details; just that he was killed, and it destroyed her inside." He turns to face me. "I wanna be the one to make her whole again, but she refuses to let me in entirely."

"Give her time. It can be hard to open yourself back up after losing someone you love." I think about Anyah and how she had shut everyone out for a long time, not allowing anyone to even bring up Ryan's name in conversation. A piece of her died with him in the fire that day. "How long has it been since the death of her husband? As the words fall from my lips, I feel Mike's fingers jerk, then his grip tightens. "Mike?" My voice is a ghost of a whisper, as I see his eyes struggling to open.

Chris stalks over to the bedside, eyes full of anticipation. "Did he hear you?" He scans Mike's face, as if he's willing him to open his eyes. "Mike, if you don't open your eyes, I revoke your future godfather privileges."

I give Chris a "what the hell" look. "What kind of motivation is that?" He shrugs his shoulders, returning his attention to Mike.

"Asshole." My head snaps back in Mike's direction. His eyes are still closed, but his grip on my hand loosens then tightens again. His voice is deep and raspy, but he's definitely awake now.

"Harmone?!" My breath hitches when he slowly pries his lids open; his beautiful mocha eyes staring back at my teary ones.

Mike clears his throat, scanning my blood-stained clothes. "Are you alright, Dimples?" I sit on the bed, and his other hand finds my face, stroking my cheek. "Where is Ashton?"

"He's most likely in jail now." Chris answers, standing beside me. "And shouldn't you be worried about your own condition right now? *Dimples* is alright. *You* on the other hand…"

"That's not a definitive answer, and my first priority is always, Erin." Mike peels his attention away from me, staring at Chris. "And I'm well aware that I was shot, you attitude-ish jerk."

I need to stop their lover's quarrel before it goes too far. Geez, they're worse than a married couple. "Chris, can you do me a favor?" Chris rolls his eyes, focusing on me. "See if you can find a nurse and let them know that Mike's awake." He glares at Mike before turning on his heel to do what I asked of him.

"Before he leaves the room, he glances back. "Ass."

"I love you too, jerk." Chris stalks out, as Mike turns back to me. "Are you sure…"

"I'm fine, Mike. This is *your* blood on my clothes." Admitting that, even now, has my heart shredding. "The nerves in your arm and hand could have been permanently damaged because of me." A tear escapes my eye and I swipe it away. "And Chris is just worried about you, by the way."

He pushes the control on the bed to lift him up to an almost sitting position, wincing as the bed moves into place. "I know, but assholism is the only language he understands when he's upset or worried." I stare at him like he's lost his damn mind. "Believe me, Dimples, he needed it." GQ licks his dry lips. "Can you get me some water, baby?" Standing, I cross over to his tray, pouring him a cup of water. "I'm the closest thing to a brother that Chris has, so he's in freak out mode right now." I make my way back to his side, holding the cup to his lips, but he grabs the cup with his good arm. "I got it."

"Let *me*."

"Dimples. I *got* it." A sigh escapes my lips, as Chris returns with a short, kinky-haired nurse rolling a cart into the room. His jaw is clamped as tight as a man holding on to his last two dollars; but he remains quiet.

"I'm gonna do a quick assessment on Mr. Harmon. Can you two please step out for a moment. It shouldn't take long." The thin nurse ruffles through a few things on the cart as Chris and I head out the door.

I stop Chris, taking hold of his arm as soon as we set foot in the hall. "You okay?"

"If I was there—"

"You would have been right beside him." He runs a hand down the length of his face. "Mike told me this, now I'm saying it to you… Don't blame yourself. There's nothing you could have done. Ashton is responsible for everything that happened." When he peers down at me, I see a mirror of guilt staring back. I inhale a shaky breath. "Mike is awake now, so don't—" I start at the feel of my phone vibrating. "Sorry, it's probably my sister." Chris nods, then takes out his phone, walking down the corridor.

I immediately answer my cell. "Hey Ann, sorry I didn't call you. I know you were concerned."

"Don't worry about it, Erin. How is he doing? Have the doctors told you anything?" I know this must dredge up old wounds for her. I hear the slight catch in her voice. This is Ryan all over again.

"Anyah, take a breath. Everything is alright. Mike is awake

and the nurse is taking a look at him. We had a whole conversation and everything. Stop worrying." I hear her release a drawn-out breath over the phone.

"That's good to hear. Even though it's been years since I've seen him, he's just as important to me as he is to you, Erin." There's silence for a few seconds, then, "Hey, I'll talk to you tomorrow, well, later today. I have a call on the other end of the line."

"Who's calling you at…" I glance at my cell, then put it back to my ear. "Two in the morning?"

"Mind your business, Erin. Love you, talk soon." Seconds later, I hear the click of the phone. This witch hung up on me. Who the hell could be calling her right now? Maybe Zeke? I don't know, but it must be damn important for her to cut off our conversation.

"Where the hell did Chris go that quick?" I peer down both ends of the corridor, then spot him against one of the walls near a nurse's station, on his phone. Stuffing my cell back into the pocket of my cardigan, I amble toward him.

As I near him, he glances up, eyes wide with concern. "Hold on for a sec, Liz." We meet in the middle of the empty corridor as he mutes his phone. "Did the nurse come out yet? What did she say? Is he alright?" His questions hit me quicker than a flash of lightning.

I put my hands up. "Slow down, Chris." He let out a deep breath. "No, she hasn't come out yet."

"What's taking her so long?

"I don't know, but I'm sure everything is fine. Relax." He closes his eyes, nodding. "So, who do you have on the phone, Chris?" I grin, as he opens his eyes. "Anybody *I* know?"

He shakes his head. "*Funny*, Erin." A grin spreads across his face, as he directs us back toward Mike's room. "It's Lizzy. I was just giving her an update on MJ's condition."

Stopping in front of Mike's door, I turn to Chris. "MJ?"

"Yeah, I called him MJ and he called me Dan in high school." He curls his lip up into a slight smirk. "I've been calling him by his nickname when I talk to Liz. She doesn't exactly *know* Mike's name; just that he's my best friend and he's been hurt. Didn't give her all the details either." Awe, that's sweet. He's trying to protect my Harmone's privacy. I nod in understanding, then a giddy smile creeps on my face. "What's with the smile?"

I giggle like a teenage girl finding out something new about her crush. "What's up with Mike and nicknames?"

"Back then, he said it was better pretending to be someone else." My smile fades as I recall the day we'd met, and he suggested that we make up nicknames for one another. I always thought he was being cute. It never occurred to me that he used it as a way of escape. "I knew his crappy ass dad was giving him hell at home, so I went along with it. I wanted him to have peace any way he could get it." I'm at a loss for words.

I can sense the mood declining, so I instantly change the subject. Pointing in the direction of the phone he currently has in his hand; I raise a brow. "Don't you think you should be getting back to your… *casual* friend?"

With a smile, he unmutes his cell and put it to his ear. "Absolutely." He walks a couple feet away, then, "I'm sorry about that, Liz…."

Leaning against the wall next to Mike's door, I fold my arms, biting my bottom lip. I look down to where Chris has stopped, as he continues his conversation with his chat buddy. "Liz is *definitely* more than just a friend."

CHAPTER 39

Mike

Currently, I'm sitting in a meeting with Nate, Erin, and two of Nate's interns that he brought along to observe. Chris is presenting the modern design layout for the reception area and the final department of Leeman Intl.' It's been a little over a month since I was shot; since Erin was taken.

Ashton's court case has come and gone. He's currently in a mental institution, getting the help he supposedly deserves. I don't believe that shit for a minute. He threatens my ex, kidnaps my girlfriend— terrorizing her— tries to kill me on her fuckin' *birthday*, but he gets a *timeout* for his efforts?!

Bullshit.

He should be behind bars, wasting away like the shitty vermin he is, but the fuckin' incompetent doctors say otherwise. *I* get physical therapy; *Ashton* gets to sit in his room and think about what he's done.

Get the fuck outta here.

The doctor's advised me to take— at minimum— another month off the job to finish physical therapy, but I need to work. I can't sit on my ass while Chris carries the company *I* should be running. He's done enough for me, so I will suck it up, and do my damn job, although this meeting is the furthest thing from my mind right now.

The rays of the sun reflect off the conference table as I lean back in my seat. My elbow is positioned on the arm of the chair, chin resting on my knuckles; attention exclusively on Erin. The cooling system in the building is being replaced, so it's a bit warm. The heat has caused Dimples to remove her blazer, leaving me to gape at the way the top of her thin green blouse is open just enough for me to see her cleavage. Of course, she's avoided eye contact from the moment she sashayed her ass into the conference room. In fact, ever since I got out of the hospital, she hasn't spent one night at my place. We talk, yeah, but not like we used to. I know she's still processing what happened, but Dimples isn't going to let herself forget that I was shot. She feels guilty, so she's withdrawing herself, but I've had enough of this shit. It ends now.

"Meeting's over." Everyone snaps their head in my direction, but my eyes remain on Erin. She peeks up at me, her shimmering bronze irises filled with guilt as she immediately looks away to gather her things.

Fuck this shit.

Chris clears his throat, still standing at the end of the table. "Uh, Mike?"

"Chris." I peel my gaze away from Erin for a second to look at him. Understanding passes between us as Chris nods his head, then begins to close his laptop.

"Gotcha." Chris peers over at Nate, who is eyeing Erin and I attentively. "Mr. Leeman, we can finish this up in the meeting room down the hall, if you don't mind?"

Nate's eyes zero in on me. "Is everything alright?" There's an edge to his voice. I need to tread carefully.

Peeking over at Dimples, who still refuses to look at me. I clench my jaw, then refocus my attention on Nate. "I apologize for disrupting the meeting like this, but an urgent matter has come up that can't wait. Chris is more than capable of running the remainder of the meeting." Like he wasn't already. "He'll direct you to the meeting room." Chris motions toward the door, and everybody stands, following behind him.

Dimples rises up, rushing to gather her things. I push back from the table, loosening my tie. "Not you." Her eyes shoot to mine.

Nate's eyes narrow at me then he glances toward Erin, his features softening. "Erin?" Everyone else has left with Chris, so it's just the three of us.

"Yes, Mr. Leeman?"

"Will you be, okay?" Of course, she will! What the fuck is he insinuating!? "A three-legged race is looking real good right about now." Alright, what the hell am I missing here, and how is that even relevant to this damn conversation?

Dimples coughs to cover her obvious laugh, then nods. "Yes, of course. I'll be fine, Nate." He gives her a stiff nod. Nate's jaw is set tight as he glares fiery pitchforks at me, giving me the "I'm watching you" gesture before leaving the room, shutting the door behind him.

Erin and I stare at one another for a moment before I rise from my seated position. "Lock the door."

"You need to understand—"

"Lock. The door." She sighs, ambling to the glossy, dark-wooded frame to do as I ask. When she turns to face me, I've already removed my vest, rolling up the sleeves of my beige dress shirt. "Why have you been avoiding me, Dimples?"

"I haven't been avoiding—"

"Bullshit. You haven't slept in my bed since I got out of the hospital."

"You needed rest and I didn't want to bother you." She doesn't believe *that* lie herself.

Escaping my penetrating stare, she makes her way over to the large, fixed frame windows that covers the wall opposite the door;

me following her. "You don't understand, Mike."

"Make me understand, then." I snake my right arm around her waist. Erin instantly leans into me, resting her head against my chest.

After a long second or two, she pulls away, turning in my arm, eyes glassy. "If I would have listened to you from the beginning, none of this would have happened." Tears cascade down her face as she exhales a wobbly breath; her hands trembling as she rests them on my chest. "Not me being taken, or you being shot…" Erin swipes at the tears, but they keep coming. My heart constricts inside, knowing how much this is eating at her. "It's *my* fault, Harmone. My pride almost got you killed."

"I'm right *here*, Erin. You're *not* to blame. Ashton is responsible for this shit." I engulf her in a one-armed hug. "You have a good heart, baby. You try to see the good in everybody. It's one of the things I love about you." I move my left arm to bury my fingers in her thick, glossy hair; wincing from the sudden movement. My shoulder is still tender, but my need to calm her overrides any discomfort I'm feeling now.

"I'm so sorry, Mike." She chokes on a sob, burying her face into my chest.

Caressing her back, I place tender kisses on her temple. "There's nothing to apologize for, so stop it. Let's focus on us, okay?" Dimples pulls back, as I wipe the remaining tears from her face.

She stares up at me, her face brightening to the radiant glow that I'm used to seeing. Smiling, she kisses me. "You *do* know that today's June 28th, right?" I shrug. Shit. I could have gone the rest of my life without acknowledging this day. "Happy Birthday, Harmone." I should have known she wouldn't forget.

"I don't celebrate my birthday anymore; not for a long time now." I swallow hard. "Recollections of this shitty day aren't so great." I shove memories of seeing my mom on the floor, lifeless, as Don stood over her, far back into the dark corners of my mind. Bile rises in my throat that I force back down. "This bracelet…" I lift my hand as the silver band that she bought me for my sixteenth birthday, dangles loosely around my wrist. "is the best thing about *any* of this day that's a good memory."

She smiles, studying the engraved initials on the plate of the bracelet, then her heated eyes are back on me. "We'll make new ones." Erin shoves me back until I hit the pale gray wall, almost knocking down one of the many colorful paintings that hang throughout the minimalistic room. "Don't you wanna make new memories with me?" She drops to her knees with the grace of a queen sitting on her throne; bronze eyes blazing with determination as if saying "challenge accepted."

As I gaze down at Brooklyn, she licks her plump lips, undoing my belt, then unzips my slacks. "Careful, Dimples. Don't start something you can't finish." The grin that she gives me promises a dirty time in the filthiest way possible. I can practically feel her hot, moist mouth swallowing me whole. I'd be lying if I said I'm not walking the very thin line of exploding right now, and she hasn't even touched me yet. In my defense, we haven't been intimate in over a month, and I miss her touch; crave it like an addict needing his fix. When she lowers my slacks and underwear, she lightly tugs on my balls. Inhaling a sharp breath, I close my eyes, needing to think about anything other than what she's doing right now before I embarrass myself all over her face.

She tugs again, stroking me slowly with her other torturous hand, then, "Open your eyes, GQ. I want you watching me the entire time." She gives my dick a long, wet lick. My eyes shoot open, as I tighten my hands into fists to keep from yanking her thick silk pressed hair and shove myself deep into her throat. That thought alone has my body blazing with barely restrained desire. My panting is heavy with want, as I tilt my hips forward, hoping she'd get the hint, but no, she goes one step further and licks the underside of my swollen head. With a sinful grin on her beautifully flushed face, she takes me deep into her mouth and holds me there.

My mouth hangs slack; a low, ravenous moan escaping my lips. "Erin, s-slow...." I hiss, as she hums around me, quickly bobbing her head with dedicated precision. My hungry eyes meet her yearning ones. I can't take much more of this shit without losing control. "Baby…" I moan; her tongue stroking me, as she continues her erotic ministrations. My control snaps as I grab her by the hair, pumping deep into that filthy mouth of hers. As I reach the back of her throat, she gags, spit dripping from her lips.

Dimples takes hold of my ass, drawing me closer; her eyes wet with tears, purring like a cat in heat but never looking away for a moment.

It's the sexiest thing I've ever seen.

Shit. I'm not gonna last. I need to change this dynamic, quick. Pulling back, I snatch Erin up from her kneeled position, hiking up her pencil skirt. "Panties off." Erin wastes no time discarding her scraps for underwear, sliding them down her legs in a frenzy. As Dimples approaches me, I see the glistening evidence of her arousal coating the inside of her thighs. I can't help the primal sound that escapes my lips.

Lifting her up with one arm, she coils her legs around my waist, as I press her against the same wall that, not seconds ago, was my support. "Guide me, baby." My tone desperate, as she reaches between us, takes my steel rod of a dick in her hand, directing me to her slick awaiting core.

Erin's mouth goes slack as I slide into her. "Ahhh!" Arching against me, she bites my bottom lip as I pound her into the wall.

Grasping her chin, I run my thumb across her bottom lip. "Open." I growl, bringing my left hand between us, finding the heart of her core; hot, slick. I moan inwardly. The pain in my shoulder is so worth the look of pure ecstasy on my baby's face right now.

Erin sucks my thumb into her mouth with force, swirling her tongue back and forth. "Mmm, so good." She murmurs around my thumb. Her moans are music to my ears.

Ramming into her, I replace my thumb with a wet, searing kiss, drowning out her cries and my moans. Finally coming up for air, I lick her bottom lip, bringing my left hand to the back of her neck. "Make yourself come, baby."

Reaching in between us, she gets exactly where she needs to be, moving in sync with me, as I pump in and out of her with an unhinged desire I've never experienced before. "Mmm, Mike!" It doesn't take her long to reach the point of no return as she clenches around me. "Mike, Ahhh!"

I bury my face in the crook of her neck as a guttural, almost animalistic sound escapes my lips as we come almost simultaneously. "Erin! F-fuck!" Panting and sheened with sweat, both of us stay pressed against one another.

After a minute, I set her back down on shaky legs; mine just as wobbly as I lean my head against the wall. Dimples tucks me back into my briefs, zips and buckles my pants, then makes herself presentable. "Dimples?" She grins, gathering her things, then saunters over to me, leaning in to give me a sloppy, wet, tell-me-who-owns-you kiss. I can't move even if I wanted to.

Before heading to the door, she gives me a sexy wink, licking those fuckable lips of hers. "See ya later, GQ. Happy Birthday." Then, without another word, she opens the door, sashaying down the hall.

Well, shit. That had to be the hottest office sex of my life.

Easily.

Chris meanders into my office seconds later, laptop in hand, closing the door behind him. "How long does it take to— Well, you look freshly fucked."

I exhale a breath, still planted against the wall. Freshly fucked, indeed. "I think I just had an out of body experience." Chris chuckles, opening his laptop, but I'm as serious as a pastor is about his tithes. I smile, finally mustering the strength to scrape myself from the wall.

Maybe my birthday won't be so bad after all.

I peel my eyes open to a dark room. I know the sun is beaming right now, and if it weren't for the blackout curtains, Dimples would be awake at the first sign of daylight. Still, there's a sliver of light peeking through the side of the curtain, but not enough to disturb my sleeping beauty. I'd decided to decorate my bedroom in Erin's favorite color— emerald- green with cream accents. The walls are already an ivory champagne, so it blended well with the décor. The fluffy cream area rug is splayed across the center of the room over dark hardwood. When I showed Dimples my room for the first time, she literally cried. She loved everything about it, and she *showed* her appreciation for my efforts that day. Let's just say, my four-poster king sized bed is her favorite part of the room… it didn't hurt that the bedding was silk emerald-green too. It was a… memorable day. Even as I think about it, I feel tingling on my back in the places she left her marks on me.

I glance over, staring at her naked body gracing its presence in my bed like the pervy creep that I am. Ever since our… *talk,* a little over two weeks ago, Erin and I have been goin' at it like two horny rabbits. I'm more than tempted to spread her open and give her the wake-up call of a lifetime.

I peek over at the alarm clock on my nightstand. Exactly fifteen minutes before I start my workday; more than enough time to eat my breakfast while putting a smile on her face. Speaking of…

Carefully I remove the sheet off the lower half of her body, planting myself at her feet. I hear the faint sound of her exhaling as she shifts position, between her side and back. One of her legs is bent at the knee… exactly the way I want her. Hovering over her lower body, I dip my head down to kiss the inside of her thigh, then higher up until I hear a soft moan.

Dimples shifts again, this time fully on her back, spreading her legs for me like a freshly bloomed flower. "Mmm, didn't you get enough last night?" The hypnotic sound of her morning voice has my dick twitching. She bucks her hips upward; my tongue dipping even further into her soft, hot core, to my absolute satisfaction.

Watching her, I take my mouth away from feasting, with a grin. "Think I can get you there in…" I peek over at my clock. "Five minutes?" I lift one of her legs over my shoulder.

"You can get me there in two… if you really tried."

"Challenge accepted." I lower my head once more, giving her one last lick with my tongue, then thrust a finger into her warm slick core. I add another, giving rhythmic circular pressure to her hardened nub with my thumb. I hear Dimples mesmerizing whimpers as she clenches hard around my fingers. "You close?" I growl, thrusting into her with practiced precision, knowing she is. I eagerly dip my head back down, working her with my fingers and tongue. My own body's wound so tight, I might explode just seeing *her* come apart.

"I'm r-right there, GQ. Don't stop." Her throaty moans spur me on, as I increase my speed. Hooking my fingers upward, I stroke the spot that unleashes my liquid gold. She bucks her hips uncontrollably as she grips my fingers tightly. "Ahhh… that's Ahhh, Mike!" Erin shakes violently as she rides out her orgasm, sending my body into high gear.

I slip my fingers out of her, positioned on my knees. I drag her closer to me, giving myself languid strokes, inches from my favorite place to be, ready to combust at first contact. I can't even lie to myself, I'm not gonna last long…. At. All. Sliding into her drenched core, slow and deep, I still. Hearing her purrs and whimpers while she grips tight around me, isn't helping my stamina. "Baby, you're killin' me. Ease up, or I'm not even gonna last two minutes."

"Don't care. Give me the roughest two minutes of your life."

Grinding against me, she grabs my hand, placing it over her throat. "Fuck me like you hate me."

Pulling almost completely out of her, I plunge in hard, repeating a few times before I place both of her legs on my shoulders, leaning into her until she's almost bent at a thirty-degree angle. I piston in and out of her, my hand finding its way back around her throat, giving the delicate flesh of her neck a steady squeeze. Erin's heartbeat matches my own as I feel it thumping wildly against my fingers.

She gasps, taking hold of my forearm. "So…. Close." I can see the mixture of pleasure and pain in her expression as she closes her eyes, giving in to the sensations. I hear the faint sound of my phone, but I ignore it this time. I couldn't stop now, even if I tried. The telling feel of Dimples squeezing around me as tight as a corset, spirals me into the point of no return. Her body moves in sync with mine, shuttering beneath me.

There's so many things happening at once. My vision blurs and my entire body explodes in a warmness I've never felt before. I'm trembling all over. It feels as if I've lost control of my own body. The phone stops ringing, the alarms goes off and I sense tingling from the base of my spine, shooting straight to my tightened balls and up through my, ready-to-explode-at any second, dick. The phone starts back up again as the alarm continues to blare in the midst of our moans. My mouth falls slack, unable to even produce a sound as I pump into her one last time.

I remove my hand from her throat, leaning down to meet her in an obsessive kiss, swirling my tongue against hers, as I languidly move in and out of her. I think I just had a full body orgasm. My limbs feel like jelly, as I pull out, rolling over to the side of her. We both lay there for a long moment before the alarm becomes too much for either of us to bear. Scooting across the bed, I turn off the noisy siren, reaching for my cell in the process. "That was…"

"The best two-minute warning of my life."

"Three, and I warned you I wasn't gonna—"

"I'm joking, GQ." She scoots over beside me, encasing her arm around my midsection. "I can't complain. I came twice in five minutes." She kisses the right side of my chest. "You gave me what I asked for." Lifting up on her elbow, she twists my nipple, causing me to flinch at the twinge of pain. "Maybe next time, don't try to choke me out."

Slapping her hand away, I rub my chest. "Noted." I glance at my missed calls and see that it's Jason. What the hell does he— MyIesha.

Rising with a jerk, I dial Jason's number. Erin follows suit, sitting beside me. "What's wrong?" She places a warm hand on my back.

"It's MyIesha. Something's wrong with—" Jason answers in a panic. My heart drops into my stomach. "What happened? Is MyIesha—"

"She went into premature labor. We're at the hospital now. I'm freakin' the fuck out, Mike." I let out a relieved breath. Good, there's nothing wrong. She's just in— Shit, she's in labor!

Dimple rises to her knees, brows furrowed. "What?! What's wrong?"

I hop outta bed, scrambling for my clothes, phone still to my ear. "We're on our way." Ending the call, I toss my cell on the bed, reaching for my underwear. "We need to get to the hospital. MyIesha's in labor."

CHAPTER 40

Erin

"One more GQ, then that's it. I promise." I move an inch forward to get a close-up picture, as he cradles his nephew in his arms awkwardly, but securely. Marlon leans against the wall next to his sister, and Jason is sitting on the edge of the hospital bed. Unfortunately, Koko didn't come because she knew the staff wouldn't allow her to bring Eva up to visit. "Look down at your nephew." As I zoom in more with my phone camera, I get a better look at the handsome child. It looks as if MyIesha pushed out a carbon copy of herself in male form. His skin is almost a yellowish-gold hue, although I'm sure it will darken as the weeks go by. His hair though, is onyx black, like his dad's, with a head full of thick curls. I can't catch his eye color because he's asleep, but everything else is all MyIesha... and if he has his mom's attitude to match? I don't even wanna think about it.

By the time we made it to the hospital, MyIesha had already given birth, and Mike is a little grumpy about that. His sister's delivery has to be the quickest birth known to man. No, I take that back. I read somewhere that a woman gave birth in twenty- seven seconds in one push, but still. We thought we had more than a forty-five-minute window, but it seems like the baby just slid right on outta there. "Oh, that's a perfect shot! Don't move." Mike is staring down at little Makai, his tiny hand wrapped around his uncle's pinky finger. It's a sight that has my heart fluttering and ovaries about to burst.

He'll be a great dad to our kids.

Where the hell did that just come from?

Okay, settle down, Brooks. You're getting ahead of yourself.

"If I stay in this position any longer, I'm gonna turn into a damn statue." GQ lifts his eyes to me for a second, then back down at Makai.

"Sorry, geez." Just before the camera on my phone flashes, Marlon jumps behind his brother with a huge Kool-Aid smile on his face. "Marlon! That was a frame-worthy shot!" I huff, putting a hand on my hip.

Marlon pats Mike on the back, chuckling, then goes back to sit in the chair next to MyIesha, who's giggling herself. "Believe me, his ass would've done the same."

GQ stands, passing the baby to Jason. "Damn right." He leans down to give his sister a kiss on the forehead. "I'll see you soon." He gives his brother the middle finger.

Marlon leans back, shrugging. "Eh, I'm just not that into you, bro." Mike rolls his eyes.

GQ makes his way over to Jason, and I follow. He's been noticeably quiet. I wonder what that's about? Mike extends his hand. "Congratulations…. Again." Wow, I'm impressed. No jaw clenching. No mean mugging. Mike seems genuinely happy for them… or he's keeping his promise to MyIesha to tolerate him for the sake of Makai. Either way, I'm proud of him. Jason, on the other hand, isn't his usual talkative self.

Jason places his son in his girlfriend's arms, turning back to GQ. "Hey Mike. Can I talk to you for a second?"

"Yeah, sure." GQ takes a quick peek over at his sister, scrunching his brows, as Jason heads toward the door. She shrugs and Mike shakes his head, then follows after him and so do I… because I'm a nosey bitch.

I whip out my phone, holding it to my ear, pretending that I'm taking a call. "Hey Ann,

sorry I missed your call." I shoot past Mike and Jason, far enough away not to seem like I'm trying to listen, but close enough to be within hearing range. With my ear still to the phone, I lean against the wall, glancing at them from the corner of my eye.

Jason has a full-on frown on his face as he paces the glossy floors next to one of the personnel offices. "… I thought maybe she would have, at least, contacted *you*."

Who is he—

"Jakyra's done some fucked up shit Mike, but this… I would never take our daughter *anywhere* without letting her know where I was going. She won't even answer my goddamn calls!" Jason tries a failing attempt at whispering, but the deep timbral of his voice carries in the corridor.

Mike shakes his head. "I can't believe Kyra did that shit. I *told* her she needed to tell you when—"

"Wait, you *knew* she was leaving?!" Jason runs a hand down his face. I can *feel* his anger from where I leaned against the wall a couple feet away.

GQ knew she was leaving? He had an entire conversation with Jakyra, *alone?* He never mentioned this *talk* he had with her… not once. My mind starts to race, thinking of a million reasons why he wouldn't tell me.

Does he have lingering feelings? Of course he does.

Did she tell him not to say anything? It's obvious she did.

Are they making plans to be together? It's a strong possibility.

Is he going to leave me? Shit.

My heart begins to race like I'm in a marathon; my hands

trembling as I take the damp phone from my ear, wiping one clammy palm at a time, on the front of my skinny jeans.

Okay, calm down Erin. You're jumping to conclusions. This doesn't have to mean anything.

The vibration from my cell— that I had pressed against my chest, blatantly gawking and GQ and Jason deep in conversation— makes me jump at the sudden sensation. I hurry to answer my phone, giving up on my spying conquest. "Hey, Ann. What's up?"

"What do you mean, *what's up*. You were supposed to call me—"

"I think Mike still may be into his… Jakyra." I blurt out in hushed tones.

"Why would you think that Erin? What happened?"

I walk further down the corridor, chewing on my thumbnail. "He… he had a conversation with her without telling me about it."

"And?"

"Well… that's it. I mean, he's covering for her." I try to explain, knowing I sound like an insecure brat.

"Don't do that, Erin."

"Don't do what?

"Self-sabotage. Trust me, I know the signs."

I scrunch my face up, as I half-way turn to see if the guys are still talking. "And how would you know the signs, *Ann*? What does that even mean?"

"Nothing." I hear my sister sighing on the other end of the line. "The fact *is*, that you get inside your head and fabricate issues that aren't even there. You create problems for yourself because deep down, you're afraid to be happy." There's silence on the other end for a moment. "You deserve to be happy, Honeybee." I haven't heard that nickname since I was five.

I duck into one of the waiting lounges on the floor, releasing a long breath through my quivering mouth. I don't wanna cry, but how Ann describes every thought that I've had since getting with Mike, is like sensory overload. "Anyah…. I—"

"You deserve to be *happy*."

All of a sudden, my legs feel like lead. My eyes blur with tears as I choke back a sob. Stumbling over to one of the chairs, I plop down, holding my hand to my mouth. I glance around the area; a few people stare in awkward silence, but I don't care. Ann's words opened a whirlwind of worries that I had locked way back into the confines of my mind…. things that I didn't believe would ever see the light of day again.

"Honey bee, are you okay? I didn't mean to—"

"No, I-I'm okay." I sniffle, wiping my face with the arm of my sleeve. "You're right. Mike wouldn't hurt me like that. He's not Ashton." The words spill out of my mouth like an uncontained damn. *He's not Ashton.* A sense of calm fills me, as I wipe the last of the lingering tears that had fallen. "Thank you, Ann. You don't know how much I appreciate you."

"I'm your big sis. I *live* to see you happy…. you *and* Zeke."

"I don't know about baby bro. He's out here livin' his *best* life right now, but *I'm* happy. I really am.

"Good."

Biting my bottom lip, I ponder asking Ann about her non-existent love life, but I know it's too soon, so I improvise… kinda. "What about you? You deserve to be happy again, too." I hear the hitch in her breath over the phone. I know I've hit a nerve that didn't need poking. "It's been so long since

Ry's—"

"Don't, Erin." Her voice is firm, causing me to snap my mouth shut. I pushed a little too hard. "When I'm ready to get out and date again, you'll be the first to know. Until then, we don't speak about my… lack of a love life. Got it?"

"But I'm sure that there's a great guy out there just waiting to treat you the way you deserve to be treated. He's waiting for you, Ann. Why won't you—"

"That's enough. I'll call you tomorrow."

"Ann—" The silence on the other end is deafening. For the second time in my life, my sister hung up on me. I know I went too far, but it's time for Anyah to come out of isolation and live again.

"I've been looking for you." My eyes shoot up to see a pair of mocha brown ones staring back. As he approaches me, his brow furrows. "Have you been crying? What's wrong?" His fingers skim across my cheek as I stand; his eyes full of concern. "Is it because of what you overheard? I *know* you were bein' nosey."

The shock on my face at his damn perceptiveness gives away my guilt. "Um... I... No, I wasn't."

GQ gives me a cheeky grin, wrapping an arm around my shoulder. "You need to up your snooping skills, Dimples." I huff at his words, as he kisses my temple. "I know how your mind works, baby. I didn't tell you about my conversation with Jakyra—"

"You don't have to explain, Mike. I trust you... and your judgement." We meander toward the door. "I... realized some things today. I'm allowed to have happiness and it's okay to embrace it." I smile, feeling as light as tissue paper. "I need you to know that I'm *with* you... I love you."

"I know you are, and I love you too, but there is *no way* in hell I would've gotten caught up spying like you did, Dimples. No. Way."

I playfully elbow him in the side, as we walk out of the waiting lounge. I smile, gripping GQ's waist a little tighter. I'm done being a victim. I deserve to be happy with the love of my life; my soulmate. He took fuckin' bullets that were meant for *me*. I get a second chance at love with the man I've loved for damn near sixteen years. It's time to stop doubting him.... It's time to stop doubting *me*.

My black tank top clings to my body as I give my personal trainer, Nico, a jab to his ribs. I press my elbows to my side and gloves to my face as I get back into defense mode. Sweat drips from the silhouette of my jaw down my neck, heart beating a mile a minute from the rush of sparring. I hear the sound of the bell and we stop our training. Taking my gloves and headgear off, I wipe my face with the towel that one of the other trainers toss at me, then take out my mouthpiece.

Nico takes out his mouthpiece, grinning. "Good job today, Erin. Only a month in and you're boxing like a fucking pro." We bump fists, then he nods in the direction of the locker rooms. "We're done for the day. Go get cleaned up and enjoy your weekend." He goes over to the ropes of the ring, opening them wide enough for me to climb through, and I make my way to the women's showers.

Before entering, I turn toward him again, smirking. "It was the body shot that did you in, right?" I chuckle as he removes the tape from his hands, shaking his head.

Nico has been training and sparring with me for a month. I don't think he has an ounce of fat on his body. He reminds me of Bruce Lee, but taller, a bit bulkier, and with a man bun. He's a sweetheart… don't let GQ hear me say that though. Mr. Lee—Nate paid for me to take boxing lessons and self-defense training.

One of his dearest friends owns the boxing gym I'm currently standing inside of right now. Besides it being hot as hell here, the facility itself is nice; with the sophisticated gym equipment, professional boxing ring and modern décor. I refused Nate's offer at first, but his paternal persuasion had me caving like a crumbling sinkhole.

Mike insisted on me learning how to use a gun and get my CCW. Let's just say, there was no room for discussion. So, not only do I know how to thoroughly defend myself, I'm an efficient amateur boxer who can kick ass and take names, with a CCW.

Step aside. One bad bitch comin' through!

I head inside the women's locker room to take a quick shower. After I shimmy into my olive-green body con dress, coming just above the knee, I step into a pair of green and white chucks. Pulling my hair back into a ponytail, I grab my backpack, heading for the exit of the gym. I wave at the best trainer in the world. "Alright Nico, I'll see you next Wednesday. Remember I need to come in before work because I'll be up to my hairline in meetings, scheduling, and paperwork all week."

"Don't worry, Erin. I'll be here at the ass crack of dawn awaiting her majesty." He takes an ungraceful bow.

Giggling, I walk out of the door and to my car. Today, Harmone and I are celebrating his team finishing the redesign of Leeman Intl' and the finalizing of his divorce back in May. We never got the chance because of everything that's happened in the last three months; although I don't believe Harmone will be up to celebrating after his visit with his father. He's been stressing all week about whether he should go or not. In the end, he decided he needed to do this, and I have to agree. This has been a long time coming.

As I merge into traffic on the freeway, my phone buzzes. I press the answer button on the dashboard. "Hey GQ. I'm on my way home, then we can head out to see your dad." I peer out of the sideview mirror before switching lanes.

"No, Brooklyn, I'm goin' alone."

"But—"

"Baby, I need to do this *alone*." He sighs, and I feel his anxiety through the phone. "What time is the reservation for?" I see what he's doing, but I won't pressure him. I'll let him have this small victory.

I come up on my exit, heading in the direction of my apartment. "Seven. Are you still at home? I'm almost there. I wanna at least see you before you go."

"No, I'm five minutes from the prison. I'll text you when I'm on my way back."

"Harmone—"

"I gotta go. I love you, Brooklyn." The line goes silent.

Pulling into the Foxmoor's parking structure— the high-rise we live in— I blow out a puff of air. I need to let Harmone do this on his own. All I can do is be there for him when he returns. Grabbing my gym bag from the back seat, I stuff my cell into my purse. Quickly, I make my short trek across the lot to the entrance of the Foxmoor and through the glass double doors.

I've been a resident of this nineteen-floor oasis for nearly three years now. The moment I stepped into those double doors for the first time, I knew I'd love it. It has a modernistic vibe with a homey touch. The warm brown, beige, and cream colors throughout has me thinking of my childhood. Sitting around by the fireplace on a starry winter night, drinking hot chocolate and roasting marshmallows. Pendant lights hang above the speckled black reception desk; long and sleek. Vibrant green floor plants are dispersed throughout the lobby and bronze and gold artistry decorate the creamy walls; complimenting the brown leather furniture and glass tables . My favorite part of the lobby though, is the huge fireplace. It sits opposite the reception desk, right in the center of the wall. Several decorative chairs surround it, along with a beverage station and daily snack table. I find myself sitting there, if only for a few moments, to calm me from the stress of the day.

The staff here is friendly, attentive, and protective of their residents. It's like one big happy family at the Foxmoor, and I love it! "Hey, Yvonne! Not working too hard, I hope."

"Girl, no. This is my dream job. I don't have to do anything except sit here and look pretty." She flips her shoulder length kinky twists back in an exaggerated fashion, batting her big henna-colored eyes. She reaches for something on the floor behind the reception desk. "This came for you today." She sings.

In front of me is a full bouquet of red and white, long stem roses set in a beautiful, handcrafted vase. I skim my fingers over the translucent glass, full of exotic shades of greens. "Wow, do you know—"

"Came with a card." Yvonne smirks at me, sliding the card across the counter.

I tear the envelope open, looking at the postcard style note and begin reading:

"These roses represent my undying love for you, baby. Red for the blood I gladly shed for you; white for the purity of our love. You deserve these and so much more. You're my life, my soulmate. I love you. See you soon."

Stuffing the card in my bag, I grin a big, stupid goofy grin, picking up the vase and roses. "Thank you for receiving these for me, Yvonne. This was an unexpected surprise." I feel my phone vibrating in my purse but ignore it.

Yvonne leans against the counter, smiling. "So, do you know who sent them?"

"My boyfriend. He had somewhere to be today and he knew he wasn't going to be able to see me before he left. I guess this is his way of being romantic." I lean in, inhaling the light fragrance of the roses.

"Lucky bitch." She whispers, as she moves away to help a tenant.

Giggling, I make my way over to the elevators and up to my apartment. Once inside, I kick my shoes off by the door, then go to place the vase full of roses on my living room table. As I toss my bag on the couch, my phone vibrates again. Plopping down, I dig inside my gym bag, find my phone, then swipe to answer. "Hey Ann, what's up." I lay down on the couch, with my leg propped up on the cushions.

"Hey Erin, I have Zeke on three-way." I hear ruffling in the background, then, "Sorry, dropped my tampons all over the floor."

Zeke groans in complaint. "I *am* on the phone. Please don't discuss that shit in my presence."

I laugh. He always gets uncomfortable when we talk about "womanly things". It never fails. "Hey bro! I haven't heard from you in like… four months. You *could* call sometimes to at least let us know you're still alive."

"You *do* remember that I'm a grown ass man, right? I didn't know I needed to check in. Besides, I've been busy."

Sitting up, I lean back against the arm of the couch. "Busy doin' what, Zeke? It's not that much fuckin' in the world."

He chuckles. "You'd be surprised." He pauses for a second. "I met someone. It's kinda serious."

Anyah and I both gasp in shock, shouting in unison. "What?!"

I have never known Zeke to be interested in a woman for more than a couple of weeks… and that's being generous.

Anyah screams so loud, I have to remove the phone from my ear. "Are you fuckin' serious?! Not my wild as shit, fuck-a-thon, feelings are for suckers, brother." She laughs.

Zeke huffs. "Yeah alright. Maybe that *was* me, but people can change… if they meet the right person."

Oh, this is new coming from my usually childish brother. I'm impressed. Maybe he *did* grow up. "Stop it, Ann. You're supposed to be the mature one."

Her laughter dies down, and she exhales. "Sorry, Zeke. I really *am* happy for you though. How long have you known her?"

There's silence on Zeke's end for a second, then, "Two and a half months." All three of us are quiet on the line. "Before you say it, I know it's not a long time, but she gets me. I vibe with her so goddamn hard, it's not even funny." The passion in his voice surprises me. My little brother is all grown up.

Lifting from the couch, I go to the kitchen to grab a Gatorade, sitting at the island counter. "If your happy, I'm happy, Zeke. Just don't go knockin' her up. Be responsible." Anyah snickers, Zeke groans. "I'm just sayin'. Now, are you gonna give us a name?"

He chuckles. "*Hell* no. I'll be bringing her to the Thanksgiving get together this year. You'll meet her then."

"Um…" Anyah cuts our conversation off. "I did *not* call to

talk about Zeke's love life. I called to talk about… mine." I'm stunned speechless. Since when did she even have a *guy* to talk about? "We can finish discussing our brother's explorations in our next sibling session. Right now, I need to confess something."

I take a swig of my Gatorade. "Please, do tell. Confession *is* good for the soul." Taking me and my electrolyzed drink, I trek back over to the couch, sitting the drink and myself down.

I hear the shakiness in her breath as she exhales, long and slow. "Well, I met this guy. He's sweet. He's understanding, makes me laugh and is so sexy." Me and Zeke stay silent on the phone, so she continues. "It was supposed to be a little flirting here, a video chat there, but it became something more. What that something *is*, I don't know."

"Hold on. Where did you meet this guy? He could be a damn predator for all we know." Zeke's voice oozes of skepticism.

"I… we met on a chat site almost ten months ago." She pauses a beat. "He's a great guy. He's not like that, Zeke."

"I don't trust that shit. He could be catfishing you!"

"We've video chatted more than once. I'm not naive."

"No, you just trust strange dudes on chat sites that you never fuckin' met in person!"

"Isaiah!"

I listen to my siblings go at it. Meanwhile, my eyes are the size of balloons, as I shoot up out of my seat beginning to pace the floor. No damn way. This has to be a coincidence. "W-What's this guy's name?" I manage to stammer out, interrupting their shouting match. Things quiet down as my question lingers in the air.

"His name is Christopher Daniels. He works with his best friend, MJ." I hear the smile in her voice as she talks about him. "I know this might seem crazy, since I was hellbent on not dating, but his ass is persistent. He's wearing me down."

I stop in place, hand covered over my mouth, silently screaming. I can*not* believe this shit! Chris and my sister?! And they have absolutely no clue that we're all connected. Oh This. Is. Gold. Wait until I tell GQ! I hear my name being called, snapping me out of my overactive thoughts. "Yeah, Ann. Sorry. What were you saying?"

"I was asking, what do you think about all of this. Should I break it off, like Zeke thinks I should?"

"No!" I shout, a little too eagerly. "No, I think you should explore whatever is between you and Chris. This is the first time you've ever talked about another man like this since…" I trail off. I don't want to bring Ryan up right now.

Zeke groans his disapproval. "I can't believe you're encouraging this shit, Erin." He pauses, then, "Y'all can finish this damn conversation without me. I'll talk to y'all later." With that, his line goes silent.

Anyah huffs into the phone. "I can't believe his hypocritical ass. The same person who thinks a two-month relationship is serious." Yeah, I can't disagree with her there. "I… really like Chris, Honey bee."

"Look, screw what Zeke thinks. He doesn't know the first thing about relationships *or* love."

"I didn't say anything about love. Don't get ahead of yourself now."

"All I'm saying is, see where it goes. Stop being afraid of what can go wrong. You've been talking to him for almost a *year*, Ann. I don't know about you, but that seems pretty serious to me." I know her mind is working right now. She's afraid to move on, but it's time. "Allow yourself to be happy. Your happy ending could be staring you right in the face." I hear sniffling on the other end. Oh no, she's crying. "Ann, I'm sorry. I—"

"You're right, Honey bee, but I'm scared to open myself up to someone like that again. I mean, what if this is temporary for him. What if—"

"Believe me, it's *not* a temporary thing." I slap myself upside the head, walking toward the window. "I'm…pretty sure this isn't temporary for him, Ann, or he wouldn't have stuck around for almost a year."

Nice save, Brooks.

"True." She agrees. "Thanks, Erin. You are *definitely* the favorite sibling this month."

"*This* month?! What about all the previous months?!"

"Zeke was always the favorite. I thought you knew that."

"What kinda shit is that?!"

"Talk to you soon. Love you!" The line goes dead.

"Anyah!" I can't believe she hung up on me again! "Ugh!" I amble toward my bedroom, pulling my hair loose from the ponytail it's in. "That's fine. I know something they don't know." I sing-sang, going into my closet to find something to wear for me and Mike's celebration dinner later. I grin. My cheeks hurt from grinning so hard. "When Ann and Chris find out the truth, it's gonna be fuckin' spectacular to witness."

CHAPTER 41

Mike

My mind is flashing with a thousand different scenarios of what can happen today as I wait for the correctional officer to bring my da— Don into the visiting room. I blow out a rugged breath, glancing around the large room. There's a podium with an officer standing behind it and several other officers patrolling the room. The area itself is stark white— floors and walls— with a couple vending machines on opposite ends of the room. The table I'm sitting at is round, brown and looks like imitation wood.

The two chairs are black and cushioned, sitting opposite one another. My back is facing the door, when I hear the sound of it opening, then the officer announcing Don's name. My heart is hammering, and my palms are sweaty as I stand, turning in their direction. When I see him, I freeze. He looks… different. His hair is grayer than it should be at fifty-six years old. He's thinner, but still all muscle as his cold eyes drill holes into me.

I swallow hard. "Hey." It's all I can muster up to say as he draws near. I notice the black eye and healing busted lip as he sits unhurriedly across from me with an orange top, a white t-shirt underneath and bottoms on that resembles medical scrubs.

Don places both palms on the table as he glances over my shoulder then back at me. "What are you doin' here?" His voice is even, but his eyes hold nothing but disdain for me. "I thought you hated me."

"That hasn't changed, but I needed to see you."

"Why? You got what you wanted. I'll be here until the day I die. What else is there to say?" His hands ball into tight fists, as he clenches his jaw.

My hands tremble beneath the table as I stare at him. The words I want to say are lodged in my throat along with the brick sized lump that forms the moment I first set eyes on him. This shit is hard. I don't know if I'll be able to—

"Answer me, boy." I flinch at his sudden command. Don leans forward, clasping his hands together; a demeaning grin splayed across his face. "I see the discipline did absolutely nothing… still weak."

"I'm not a boy, and I'm not fuckin' weak." I growl through gritted teeth. "The one trait that I *did* learn from you nearly ruined me… it ruined my marriage." I manage not to raise my voice. I know if we cause a scene, I won't get the chance to get all of this shit outta me. "Don't you feel the least bit of regret for all of the hell you put us through?"

"The only thing I regret is your mother dying. That…" He hesitates, his eyes hold a haunted look in them. "That wasn't intentional. If I could…"

"But you can't. You killed her… in front of us. Now you wanna feel *guilty* about it?" It's taking all of my restraint not to raise my voice or satisfy my need to reach across this table and choke the shit out of him. "No. You get to drown in your own goddamn misery while I go on with my life and forget about you. I hope—"

"You know what we were arguing about that day?" He eyes the guard as he passes by, then returns his icy glare to me, tightening his fists. "She was tryin' to leave me. Adira wanted to leave me that day… said she couldn't put herself or *you three* through anymore torture." Don usually shows little emotion but his face twists in pain as he recalls that day. Leaning back, he scratches at his beard; something he does when he's upset. "She felt guilty about keeping y'all in that *toxic* environment." He does air quotations as he says the word toxic. "I wasn't gonna allow Adira to leave me. Y'all were *my* property. I *own* you."

I bounce my leg up and down under the table, trying to channel my anger, but I feel it burning in my chest, screaming to be released. They're gonna throw my ass outta here. "You don't own shit." Sitting straighter, I finally rest my elbows on the table, inhaling a deep breath. "Guess what? When I walk outta here today, you'll still be here… wastin' away. I won't even give you a second thought."

"I don't have to be outside of this prison to get to you. I'm in *here*." He gives the side of his head a few taps, smirking. "You'll *never* get rid of me." He pats his chest. "My mark is engraved into your skin. We all know who you belong to, *Mike*."

I swallow hard. I'm done with this shit. I need to get out of here. I said what I needed to say. I don't need to prove myself to him. Leaning forward, I lower my voice. "You're right. You have so much power over me that when I leave this prison, it'll be like you never existed." The guard notices me as I rise to my feet and head toward the exit.

Hearing Don's chair screech back, I turn. "Good luck to the next woman that has the unfortunate opportunity to date you. She just *may* end up like your mother. Lucky your ex-wife got out when she did. Enjoy bouncin' *that* thought around in your head!" He yells from across the room. One of the guards detains him as they put him back in cuffs.

My heart pounds so loud in my ears that I don't hear the officer speak. I feel the stern tug of my arm as I realize the officer is nudging me toward the exit. Following the guard, I leave the visiting room, my mind a destructive mess of Don's taunts.

I mindlessly drive around for a few hours until I find myself at the cemetery, standing in front of my mom's headstone. It's the first time I've come to visit her since she was killed. I already feel stinging at the corners of my eyes from tears forming. I release a shuddering breath. "Sorry it took me so long to come see you." I wipe the debris from the top of her headstone. "I went to see him today. After twenty-one years, he still intimidates me." I shake my head. "He thinks I'm gonna turn out to be just like him…." I trail off, my chest tightening at the thought. "What if Don's right, Ma? What if it's just who I am?" Lowering myself onto the grass, I sit beside her headstone, leaning my head against it. As I release a shaky breath, I feel hot tears roll down my face. "Why did you leave me to deal with this by myself? I'm not as strong as you were. Even out here he's fuckin' with my mind. I can't…" Violent sobs escape my mouth. The sound is so foreign to my ears. I've always had to be strong, keep my shit together, but right now it's just me and my mom in the quiet of the evening.

After a few minutes, my sobs quiet and I wipe the tears away with the bottom of my t-shirt. "I miss you, Ma. I don't know what to do." A rugged sigh escaped my lips as I close my eyes. "I don't know who I am anymore." I hear a gust of wind rustling through the trees, then a constant gentle breeze. Barely audible at first, I swear I hear my mom's voice whisper into my ear as I feel the faintest ghost of a touch to my cheek. I don't dare open my eyes, but her voice is as clear as day:

You know who you are. You're Michael Julian Harmon, my

son. You are the epitome of strength. You are not, nor will you ever be like Don. Of course, you've made mistakes, but you're trying to correct them. Don't allow your father to destroy the life you're building for yourself. He doesn't control you. You control your own destiny; your own joy. And your happiness is waiting for you at home. I'm proud of you, Mike. Now move forward and don't look back.

A peace pours over me like summer rain on a hot day. Opening my eyes, I glance around. Nothing. Standing to my feet, I wipe the lingering grass and dirt off the back of my jeans. I shake my head. "I *know* I'm not going crazy." Peering over to look at her headstone, I give her a hint of a smile. "I love you, Ma. Thank you." With that, I leave the cemetery. It feels as if a ton of weight has lifted from me and a true peace that I haven't felt in a long time, replaced it. I glance at the clock on my dashboard. "Damn it, I'm late." Increasing my speed, I head toward the freeway. "This shit is like repeating history all over again."

CHAPTER 42

Erin

8:30 p.m.

I'm starting to worry. Mike always calls me if he's gonna be late. If he doesn't call in the next few minutes, I'll get in touch with Marlon. This shit is nerve-wracking. I move to get up from the sofa when I hear the door to my apartment open and close. As I'm sprinting toward the door, I practically collide with him as he was seemingly rushing to where I was.

GQ holds his hands up, brows raised. "I'm so sorry I'm late, Erin. Time got away from me and I—"

"It's fine, Mike. Is everything alright?" I caress his cheek; his body draining of all tension as he closes his eyes. "What happened?"

His eyes peel open, scanning my body. "Why aren't you dressed? We can call the restaurant—"

"I cancelled an hour after I got home; figured you wouldn't be up to going out to celebrate after seeing your… Don. Tell me what's goin' on?" He exhales a deep breath, gripping my hand to lead us into the living room. After taking a seat on the sofa, I peek over at him, waiting for him to speak.

After a second, Mike lays across the remainder of the couch, resting his head on my lap. "I went to see my mom after the shit show with Don. That's why I was late."

"Harmone, I don't *care* about you being late. How did the visit with your mom go?" I lightly brush against the trimmed hair on his face.

"Peaceful. It's the first time I've been to see her since…" He trails off, sighing. "I swear she was right there with me. I heard her voice as clear as day." I watch his body relax on the sofa as he describes his experience; peace illuminating from him like billows of sunlight across the morning sky.

"Maybe you were just—"

"No. She was *right* there. I felt her fingers brushing my cheek; her comforting voice in my ear." He peers over at me, shaking his head. "Maybe I'm going crazy Brooklyn, but I can tell you what she whispered to me… word for word."

"I believe you, Harmone. You know what you heard… what you felt. Hold on to that. Never forget it."

Mike's brows crease and body tenses as he swallows hard. "It was the total opposite of going to see Don. I don't know what I was expecting though. It was as fucked up as I thought it would be." He shut his eyes as I comb my fingers through his short hair. "Same shit. Him being manipulative, blaming me for putting him in prison, claiming that I'm just like him. You know, the usual. The thing is, I believed him for a minute." He opens his eyes, sitting up. "One thing he said that scared the shit outta me." His

brows furrow deep; concerned mocha irises staring back at me. "He… basically said that you'd end up like my mom if you stuck around."

Twisting my body toward him, I shake my head. "Harmone, don't. Don't you *dare* let him win." He drops his head, but I lift it again, turning him back to face me. "He's a goddamn bully, you know that. He's miserable, so he doesn't want to see you happy either. Don't give him that power."

"I know, but—"

"No buts. I don't want you—"

"Brooklyn, you don't know what I've done." His voice is barely above a whisper. "I *killed* a man! I—"

"You've also taken bullets that were meant for *me*! You aren't your past, Harmone." I caress his bearded jaw. "You wanna know what *I* see?" He releases a ragged breath as I feel his jaw tighten underneath my hand. "I see the sixteen-year-old who promised he would marry me when we were old enough." Mike pulls my hand from his face, interlocking our fingers. He stares down at the emerald promise ring— that I haven't taken off since he placed it back on my finger— smiling before bringing my hand to his lips. "I see the successful owner of an interior design company that he started *solely* to honor his mother's memory. I see a man who kept he and his siblings together despite the odds against him. A man who took two bullets for the woman he loves." Tears sprinkle my cheeks as Mike gazes into my eyes with a passion that sends shivers through my body. "Don't think of who you *were*." He leans his forehead against my own, stroking my cheek. "Remember who you *are*, Harmone."

Mike brushes his lips against mine and I literally melt against him. "Thank you for reminding me."

Oh, I know that look in his eyes. It's almost feral. I squeeze my thighs together as I imagine the filthy thoughts that I *know* he's thinking. "You're welcome to show me your gratitude." He can probably hear the '*come-fuck-me*' in my husky tone as I lick my lips. Leaning back against the sofa, I spread my legs in invitation.

He stands, removing his shirt in one fluent move. As he begins unbuckling his belt, he pauses. "Run." He says like we're in casual conversation.

Sitting up, I laugh. "What?"

He peers down at me, his mocha irises a molten fire of desire. "*Run.*"

My core tightens and panties dampen as I hop up, dashing past him and down the hall toward my bedroom. I slide in my socks as

I turn the corner, hearing his footfalls close behind me. As I reach for the handle of my door, I feel Mike's arm snake around my waist, then his body pressing me against the wall; his erection rock hard and begging to be sucked. He bucks into me and like a hungry bitch in heat, I push back into him.

Mike's breath tickles my skin as he licks the shell of my ear, slowly grinding into me. "You want gratitude?" The arm that's snaked around my waist moves down until he cups my soaked core, rubbing me through the thin leggings I'm wearing.

Twisting my head so I can get a glimpse of his beautiful eyes, I push my ass back into him again; a groan escaping his lips. "I want whatever you give me."

"Good answer." Without breaking eye contact, I feel the warmth of his hand leave me, then I hear the click of my bedroom door. Backing away, he unzips his jeans. "Go inside and strip naked."

"How do you want me?" I pant, already removing my blouse and bra.

"I want you in every way… in every *position* possible." He shoves his pants down, allowing me to gawk at the bulging treat before me.

"Good answer." I throw his words back at him, as I hurry into the room. By the time I make it to my bed, I'm naked and kneeling on the carpeted floor. I want him to remember this image of me for the rest of his life… that, and I'm dying to suck him dry. When

Harmone comes into the room, he stills for a moment to take me in. I'm practically salivating at the sight of his thick, veiny erection jutting toward me as if it knows what I want.

"Brooklyn." That's the only thing he says before coming to me. As he towers above me, the fiery lust that his eyes held seconds ago is replaced with a warm admiration as he cups my cheek. "Get up."

I grin before taking him in my mouth, holding him deep. He keeps my head in place for a second, his dick jerking in my mouth, as he gazes down at me biting his bottom lip. Relaxing my throat, I take him deeper and he pulls away from me. I wipe my mouth with the back of my hand, scrunching my brows in confusion. "Why did you stop me?"

"That's not what I want from you…. Not tonight." He reaches out for me. "Get up."

Taking his extended hand, I rise from my position. Before I even have a chance to say anything, his mouth claims mine and I open to him in response. He scoops me from my feet, bridal style, then places me on the bed. I spread my legs as he hovers above me, stroking my cheek with a tenderness that has me tearing up. "Mike, what's—" he leans down, gently pressing his lip against mine. I can feel stinging in my eyes from the tears threatening to spill. "What's wrong?"

"Nothing." His captivating mocha irises scan my face, then my eyes as if he's searching for something. "I wanna give you every part of me. The broken…" He kisses my nose. "The shameful…" Then my forehead. "The unseen…" And my lips. "The fearful…" He caresses my cheek, exhaling. "Everything. I'm giving you everything, Brooklyn."

Tears fall as my fingers skim over his pebbled skin. "If you're brave enough to do this, I will too." I find his hand, interlocking our fingers. "I'll let all of my walls down for you. Only for you, Harmone."

"I love you." He whispers, brushing his lips against mine as he enters me slowly, deeply. So deep.

The moan that escapes my lips is almost a whimper as he grinds into me. I tighten my legs around him as he pulls out and repeats, finding a languid rhythm that seems endless as the pressure of release builds ridiculously fast. The feel of him inside of me, filling me, making us one, has me on the verge of orgasm already. "Harmone, I'm gonna—" I clench around him as I buck my hips wildly. My mouth parts and eyes shut tight. "Mmm, Ah!" The sensation makes my entire body tingle causing a burst of white light behind my eyelids. It seems like my orgasm is never going to end. When I open my eyes, Mike is gazing down at me, the heated lust back in his eyes.

Thrusting hard a few times, he grips one of my legs, hiking it up more. "You have no idea how sexy you look when you come for me." His voice is a growl as he thrust one more time before grinding into me again. "Baby… Ah, Brooklyn." He pounds me into the mattress like a man possessed; his face buried in the crook of my neck.

My grip around our entwined hands tightened as I reach for his toned ass, squeezing. "Oh… yes!" The unexpected orgasm tears through me like a tornado. I barely hear Mike yelling my name as I feel the telling jerk of him inside me as we come almost simultaneously. We're tangled in each other's arms for a long moment, then he slides out of me, rolling onto his side, taking me along with him.

Kissing the top of my head, we lay in comfortable silence. No fear. No walls. Just us.

A few hours after coming down from our orgasmic bliss, Mike and I sit on the bed finishing off leftover roast and potatoes from the other night. We reluctantly put on clothes; me, one of his t-shirts, and pajama bottoms for him. I reach for my glass of peach tea, taking a sip. "Guess what I found out today?" I grin, excited to share this particular secret with him.

He removes both of our plates, placing them on one of the bedside tables, then leans back against the headboard with a sexy smirk on his face. "That you can't form complete sentences when you come?"

I purse my lips, slapping him on his thigh. "That makes *two* of us." I smack his thigh again, harder.

"Alright! Sorry." He scoots closer, pulling me onto his lap. "What's the big secret, Dimples?"

"You know the woman Chris has been talking to? The one he's practically in love with?"

"He's not in *love* with her."

"Oh, his ass is in love with her. He literally admitted it when you were in the hospital."

"Wait. He *told* you that?"

I shrug. "Basically. Stop distracting me. The point I'm trying to make here, is I know who she is."

"Impossible. How?"

"I talked to her today."

GQ's eyebrows creases, piquing his curiosity. "Well, are you gonna tell me or am I supposed to use my imagination?"

"No one likes a smartass, GQ."

"I beg to differ. You *love* this smart ass."

"True, but— stop it, GQ! Let me finish!" I pout, smacking his arm.

He chuckles, kissing my pursed lips with a quick peck. "I'm sorry, go ahead. I won't interrupt again, Dimples."

"Thank you." I shift on his lap so that I'm facing him completely and hear a low moan escape Mike's lips, his sudden erection poking me in the crease of my ass. "No. Secret gossip first, dirty deeds later." He rolls his eyes but says nothing. "This mystery woman Chris has been pining over… is my *sister*."

"I'm sorry, what?" Mike twists his face in confusion, opening and closing his mouth like a fish out of water. "Your sister? As in…. Anyah, your sister?"

"Yes."

"How. The fuck. Did that happen?" He shakes his head, just as stunned as I was.

"I know right? Me, Ann, and Zeke were on a three-way call and she confessed it then. I started getting suspicious when she said she met the guy on a chat site, so I asked what his name was." I grin, playfully tapping Mike on his chest in excitement. "She literally said 'Christopher Daniels.'"

GQ still looks baffled, as he leans back on his elbows. "So, she made an alias on the chat site?"

"No, her middle name is Elizabeth… Lizzy, and she still uses her married name."

"She was *married*? You didn't tell me that."

"Yes, I did."

"No, you *didn't*.

Biting my lip, I try to run through our conversations to see if Anyah's marriage ever came up in discussion. My eyes widen as I realize…. Shit, I hadn't told him. "Well… I'm telling you now." He rolls his eyes in mild annoyance, but I ignore him. "Anyway, yes, she was married. Ryan, her late husband, died in a house fire. I don't wanna go into any details right now. The point is….Chris and my *sister*, GQ!"

Mike's expression is blank, until a broad smile spreads across his face. "Do they know?" His words sound as mischievous as the thoughts bumbling around in my head.

"They don't have a goddamn clue."

His laughter radiates through the glint in his beautiful eyes. "This shit is gonna be spectacular to watch."

"My thoughts exactly." I give him a quick peck on the lips. "You up for foolery and fun at Chris and Ann's expense?"

In one fluent move, Mike has me pinned underneath him, grinding into my core. A soft moan escapes me as I wet my lips. His hooded eyes track every movement of my tongue before he returns his gaze to my face, saying, "I'm up for some foolery and fun at *your* expense." He grips both sides of my ass, pressing into my soaked core with deep, slow strokes, causing my body to tremble and breath to catch. There's a sweltering need for me to have GQ inside of me, like molten lava. Chris and my sister can take a backseat because this blaze needs to be quenched, and this man's talented dick is the fire extinguisher.

CHAPTER 43

Mike

As Marlon and Chris wait at the counter for their orders before we head back to work, I sit at one of the few empty tables at Zelle's Café, staring down at the engagement ring that I bought on impulse thirty minutes ago. Marlon met me and Chris at the office on our lunch breaks, then we headed to the jewelry store. It was my intention to only browse around to get an idea of what type of ring I wanted to give her, but when I saw the custom designed emerald ring with encrusted diamonds around it, I knew that was the one. Now, here I am, with an engagement ring in my clammy hands feeling like a damn teenager all over again. Don't get me wrong, I absolutely intend on marrying Brooklyn, but not until I can plan it the way I want. I blow out a nervous breath.

As I close the velvety black box, placing it back into the inside pocket of my suit jacket, my brother and Chris return to the table.

Marlon watches me closely for a second, then puts a hand on my shoulder. "Stop overthinking it. She'll definitely say yes."

I stand as he removes his hand. "Sometimes I really do think you can read my mind." I shake my head as we move toward the exit and out of the door. "I *know* she'll say yes, that's not the issue." We hop into Chris's Durango. "There's a nagging feeling in the back of my mind that something's gonna go wrong."

Chris gives a quick look at me before heading into traffic and back to the office. "Nothing's going to go wrong. Stop thinking about it. You've got the ring, now you have to come up with a plan of action. Do you have one?"

Chris doesn't see me when I shake my head, but Marlon does. "Bro, you can't be last minute about everything. Get your shit together."

I roll my eyes. "It's not like I'm proposing tomorrow. I have time. Don't worry about me. In fact, let's talk about something else." I peek over at Chris, a mischievous grin spreading across my face. "So Chris—"

"Oh! Jakyra finally got in touch with Jason." Marlon blurts out, interrupting my 'fuck with Chris' moment. "He said she was coming back soon, but still didn't tell him exactly where she was."

I shake my head. "That's fucked up. Me and Jason aren't particularly tight anymore, but he doesn't deserve this shit. That *is* his daughter too.. He has every right to know where she is." The words spilling from my mouth sound foreign to my ears. If someone would have told me ten months ago I would be defending Jason, I probably would have beat their ass.

Chris glances into the rearview mirror, looking at Marlon, then back at the road. "I'm not surprised though. Her track record doesn't vouch for her." He shakes his head. "Just when I thought she was turning over a new leaf."

I check my phone, seeing a text from Dimples. "If Kyra thinks she's right about something, then to her, she's *right*. But she's Jason's problem now so…." I trail off, glancing over to Chris again. "How have you and Liz been doin'?" I type a quick reply back to Dimples, then put my phone away so that I can give my full attention to fuckin' with Chris. "Did she change her mind about being in a relationship? The last time we talked, you said she wasn't with it."

"Things have…. gotten better. She's opening up about her late husband now." Chris whips into his designated parking spot, putting the gear into park. "He died in a house fire that she blames herself for."

My brows damn near shoot up to my hairline. I didn't expect Anyah to tell him about that yet. I wonder if Dimples know that her sister blames herself. "So, I guess y'all getting serious if she told you about that." Chris kills the engine, and all of us get out of the SUV simultaneously.

As I round the car to meet Chris and Marlon, he rakes his fingers through his hair, blowing out a puff of air. "I think I'm in love with her. Is that serious enough for you?"

"*Shit.*" Both Marlon and I say in unison. We stare at one another, then back at Chris. Marlon pats him on the back." Welcome to the club, you poor heart-eyed bastard." He glances over to me, walking backwards in the direction of his car. "You got this, right? I need to get my ass back to work."

I nod slowly, as Marlon retreats without another word. We watch as he pulls out of the lot, then I refocus on the man before me. "That's a big step, Chris. You're goin' from 'hit it and quit it; what happens in Vegas, stays in Vegas' type shit to instant love and ever-afters."

"It wasn't *instant* love, asshole. It's been over a year." He rolls his eyes as we head into the building and to the elevators.

"You said you *think* you're in love with her. Do you think or *are* you?"

"I am."

"You *sure*?"

"Goddamn it, Mike. *Yes*, I'm sure I'm in love with her!"

I grin as we enter the elevator and Chris jabs the number to our floor with a little too much force. I love fuckin' with him. "*Alright*, I'm sorry, but I needed you to hear *yourself* say it." I peek over at him. He's glaring at me for only a second, before his features soften and he sighs. "Makes it real, doesn't it?"

"You have no fucking clue." He shakes his head. "We either

talk, text or video chat every day when we have the time. We *have* to say goodnight to each other before bed…. *religiously*." He leans against the wall of the elevator. "I've already decided how many kids we're having, what we'll name them, and I may or may *not* have prematurely decided on a house that I've been eyeing for the past three months." The elevator pings, opening the door to our floor. "Fuck, I have it bad, don't I?"

"There's no coming back from where you're at, Chris. You fell *deep* into the rabbit hole. The question is, are you lookin' for a way out?" We walk over to his office.

Shaking his head in a slow, steady motion, he grins his signature cocky ass grin. "Abso-fuckin-

lutely not."

"Then, welcome to the club you, poor heart-eyed bastard."

CHAPTER 44

Erin

I giggle after reading Harmone's response to my message. He texted me four words… *'don't play with me'*. He's definitely gonna be thinking about plugs and lube for the rest of the day. I glance over to see Koko eyeing me. "What?" I continue to rummage through a rack of clothes at Macy's inside of the mall. I'd decided to update my wardrobe for the upcoming fall and winter months. It's only mid-September, but the weather is seasonably chilly and that's never a good sign of what's to come.

"What the hell are you so giddy about?" Koko smirks, my happiness rubbing off on her. She rolls her eyes, after I give her a cheeky grin but no answer. She got a short reprieve today. MyIesha and Jason volunteered to babysit her and Marlon's one year old– ball of never-ending energy – daughter, so she could hang out with me for a few hours on one of my rare days off. "Seeing that you're not going to give me an answer with damn words, do you wanna stop and get a corned beef sandwich on the way back to Jason and Iesha's house?”

Giving her a quick side glance, I scrunch up my nose in mild distaste. “Ugh, no. I don’t have a taste for corned beef at the moment.”

“I thought consuming corned beef was your favorite pastime.”

“I’m not feelin’ it right now.” She gives me a strange look. “What?”

“Nothing.” Without another word, she tugs my arm, pulling me toward the exit of Macy’s.

“Wait, I wasn’t done—”

“You weren’t even gonna buy anything. We’ve been window shopping for the past three hours. Plus, I was supposed to be back half an hour ago.”

As we approach my car, I spot red and white roses on the windshield. I do a quick scan of the area, then pull out my phone, dialing GQ’s number. “Hey Harmone, did you happen to search for my car while I was inside the mall and place roses on my windshield?” I know it’s a stretch, but I need to confirm that it wasn’t him.

“Unless I have a twin out here somewhere doin’ romantic shit for me, no, I didn’t.” Although GQ hasn’t raised his voice, I can hear the gruffness in it.

Koko hands me the small note that's attached to the roses as I search the parking lot again. "How about the roses that were sent to the high-rise last month. Was *that* you?" I swallow hard, opening the sealed note.

"Somebody sent you *roses* last month? I thought *you* bought those. What the fuck is goin' on, Brooklyn?"

"I'm gonna head over to your office right now, okay?" I end the call, staring down at the message on the card.

Koko touches my shoulder, causing me to almost jump out of my own skin. "So, did Mike send them?"

"No… they…"I trail off, staring at the four words on the note along with the signature behind it; my heart thumping in my ears.

'You belong with me.'

Ashton

I crumble the note, hightailing it to the car, Koko on my trail. "They were from Ashton. The roses on the windshield, the ones sent to the high-rise. I thought they were from Harmone, but they weren't." It feels as if my throat is closing up as an impending panic attack claws its way through my body. "How did he even get out? How did he—"

"Breathe, Erin." Koko turns me toward her, snatching me into an embrace. My entire body trembles as Koko guides me through breathing exercises. "You're fine. Mike is expecting you at his office, right?" I nod, instinctively. "Then let's go, okay?"

As she releases me, her body jerks back and away from me. The next thing I know, she's on the ground and the one person I thought I'd never see again is towering over me. I didn't even see him approach us. "We need to talk, Ren." He steps closer as I take several steps back, then reaches for me.

"Don't put your fucking hands on me, Ashton." He tries again and I maneuver his hand away. My heart is knocking against my chest so hard; it feels like it might split me open, but I refuse to let him intimidate me. "This is my last time warning you. Keep your goddamn hands to yourself."

"Do you think you have any fuckin' choice in the matter?! You're mine, Ren and you're coming with *me*." He tugs me toward him, clutching my hair. "We can do this the easy way or the hard way. Your choice."

After dragging herself from the ground, Koko starts to approach us, but I hold up a hand for her to stay away. I don't need anyone else getting hurt because of me. I briefly see her take out her cell before focusing back on my attacker. Slipping both arms through the small space between us, I quickly break the hold he has on me, then kick him in the balls. As he hunches over in pain, I give him a swift knee to the face, a jab to his side, then his jaw. "Don't ever underestimate me again, asshole!" I kick him backward with everything I have, sending him hurling to the ground in agony. Hurrying back to my car, I go into my glove compartment and pull out my gun, then make a short dash to where

Ashton still lay, curled up in a ball. I cock my weapon, aiming at the back of his head.

"You… bitch." He grunts around his swelling jaw. I move around so that I'm standing in front of him now. He spits the blood out of his mouth, an unsettling laugh slipping through his bloodied lips, causing uneasiness to course inside me. "You'll never get rid—" I aim at his legs, shooting both, then aim back at his face. "Ahhh! Bitch!!"

I lift my eyes when I hear sirens, then see Koko hurry over to me, lowering my arm so that I wouldn't shoot Ashton again. Only when I see the blue and red-light flashes drawing near do I exhale. My entire body feels as if it's bogged down with lead as I put the safety back on my gun. "I wasn't gonna allow him to hurt me again, Koko. I wasn't—"

"I know. You did what you had to do." She nods, offering me a small smile. "The cops will ask questions, but you have me and a lot of other people who witnessed what happened." She gestures to all the others, who I hadn't noticed, standing around. "I already called Mike. He's on his way, okay. It's over."

"Thank you." I breathe, my body finally relaxing. She strokes my back in soothing circles as the police approach us. "I guess I should get this over with." I lower my weapon to the ground and lean against the car. The spike of adrenaline rapidly drains from my body; nausea causing my stomach to churn. Peeking over at Koko, she gives me a quick nod, mouthing, *'it's okay'*, before I

turn back to the officer nearing me. Closing my eyes, I exhale. I'm
shaken to my goddamn core, but I will *never* be anyone's victim
again.

CHAPTER 45

November

Time flies when you feel like shit. Here it is, almost two months later and I feel no better than I did back in September. I've become an expert in these short couple of months at having a poker face because I *know* if Harmone realizes what was going on, he will make a big fuss over nothing. I thought it was a little bug at first, but the headaches, fatigue and my sudden dislike of certain foods have gotten worse. It *could* be my hectic work schedule. Maybe I need to catch up on sleep… yeah that's it. As far as my distaste for certain foods? I'm-I'm sure there's a logical explanation because there's no *way* I can be pregnant. I mean, I still get my periods like a damn regularly scheduled program. Either way, they'll figure out what's got my body going haywire at my doctor's appointment next week.

Ashton is finally in prison where he belongs. It didn't take long for the judge to sentence him… especially when he didn't even put up a fight. Not only did he plead guilty, he confessed to murdering Melanie as if it were just another task he had to complete. When he peered over at me for sentencing the following week— even though it was only for a few seconds— his eyes held an emotion I couldn't quite place. I would even go so far to say… regret? Whether it was remorse for what he did to me or disappointment that he got caught, I have no idea. Maybe it's wishful thinking on my part, but when I heard the judge announce twenty-five years to life in prison, I noticed the sharp intake of Ashton's breath before he closed his eyes.

As they carried him away, he lowered his head, not even able to look at me. I thought there would be some sort of sadness, some kind of sympathy for the man I once loved, but there was only… relief. I strolled out of that courtroom with Mike that day, free and ready to live my life in peace with the man that captured my sixteen-year-old heart… my best friend… my soulmate.

I mix together lemon yogurt and sour cream into a bowl at the table in Jason and MyIesha's large eat-in kitchen, then lick the spoon full of sour cream residue. I'm surprised I have the energy to be up this early on a Saturday. Eleven o'clock in the morning is early for me these days, so when Koko calls me at nine, telling me to meet her over to Jason's house, I get out of bed without hesitation. No lying down for a few more minutes, no yawning.

I'm energetic for the first time in the past few months and it feels great.

Mike left my apartment just as the sun was rising this morning; said he had some things to take care of today before heading into work. In fact, he's been doing this for the past couple of months. Secretive, vague… Is he… no, Mike is 1000 percent with me. I will *not* go down that path again. I trust him.

Digging into the mixture, I lift the spoon to my mouth, nearly moaning in delight as MyIesha and Koko give one another a weird look before refocusing on me. "What?" When they don't say anything, I add more sour cream to my bowl, glancing up at them as I stir. They're gawking at me like I've committed a heinous crime, then round the table, both sitting on either side of me. "What's with these damn looks you keep giving me?"

Koko puts the lid back onto the sour cream, peering down at my bowl before curious eyes land back on me. "You *do* realize what's happening here, don't you?"

"Yes. I'm having a light breakfast because I didn't get a chance to eat before leaving my apartment."

MyIesha shakes her head, rubbing small circles on my back. "Erin." She whispers, as I continue to devour my yogurt. "You're pregnant, bitch."

My head swings in her direction, then Koko's; my spoon frozen in place mid-scoop. "No, I'm not. I still get my periods."

"That means absolutely shit, hun. My pregnancy was the same with Eva." Koko chimes in, a small smile gracing her face. "Are your periods normally how they *would* be?" She rises to her feet, ambling over to the refrigerator to put the sour cream back inside.

I think about her question, swallowing hard. Now that I think about it… "It's been lighter than usual… and shorter." My eyes widen. "I *can't* be." I gape at the mixture in my bowl. "I don't usually eat like this." I rise to my feet, taking in a huge breath; everything I've experienced over the last several weeks coming into apparent view. The fatigue, my tender breasts, weird food cravings, the sudden dislike for my beloved corned beef. How oblivious could I be! "I'm…. *pregnant!*"

An hour later, both Koko and MyIesha close in around me clapping their hands, grinning from ear to ear. I'm sitting on the leather sofa staring down at a blue plus sign on the pregnancy test Koko rushed out to buy. My mind is scrambled; running a mile a second with questions that I'm terrified to answer.

Will GQ be happy?

How will this affect my career?

Is Harmone up for this after going through so much in this past year?

Will I be a good mother?

Do I want to be a mom?

As I sit here silently freaking out, I notice Iesha and Koko sidle up next to me; both of them sitting on either side. Koko pats my thigh. "So now that you know for sure, what's next?" She stares at me expectantly, but I'm unable to produce a single word from my mouth.

MyIesha unfurls my fingers from the pregnancy test, then grasps my hand. "You *are* gonna tell my brother, aren't you? You can't keep this—"

"Of *course* I am. I would never keep something like this from him. I'm just…" I trail off, exhaling a cleansing breath, as I feel my heart rate finally begin to decrease. "He's been through so much. I don't want to burden him with—"

MyIesha lifts her hand to stop me from finishing my thoughts. "Burden him? Erin, he's *crazy* about you. Mike will do anything for you. You're having his baby. Do you *really* think he would see this as a burden? This?" She takes the test from my hand, waving it in front of me. "Is going to heal him in ways you can't even imagine." She blinks several times, shaking her head. I know she's trying to hold back tears, which makes me begin to tear up. "This is a gift for Mike… the best gift that you could give him."

I wipe the splashes of tears that sprinkle across my cheeks, a small smile emerging from my dissipating worry. "This is gonna change everything though." Both of the encouraging women scrunch their brows in confusion. "Not our relationship. I know *nothing* can change that. How am I going to juggle a career and a baby? My job consumes so much of my time and I'm afraid that

I'll… "I swallow hard, a lump forming in my throat. "That I'll fail. What if—"

"Stop overthinking, Erin." Koko interrupts, grasping my other hand. "Don't worry about '*what ifs.*' Be happy. You're family now and we will always take care of each other. For now, enjoy the moment and deal with the rest as it comes." She opens her mouth to say something else but sounds of her daughter's whines on the baby monitor has her jumping up to see about her. "I'll check on Makai while I'm in there, Iesha. I'm sure Eva woke him up." She chuckles as she ambles toward the nursery.

My gaze lands on MyIesha; a genuine smile spreads across my face. "I'm having a baby!" I whisper-yell, hands flying over my mouth as it finally starts to sink in.

"That's it! Get excited about this shit. It's something to celebrate!" She shoots up, pulling me along with her, and dances around me. I laugh, joining in on her hip shaking dance.

Koko strolls into the living room, a fussy Makai in one arm and a chipper Eva running ahead of her. "Sorry, looks like the party's over." She giggles, placing Iesha's son into her arms and scurries off to stop Eva from going into the kitchen. "This girl doesn't know the meaning of slow down. She's on ten from sunup to sundown." Eva squirms in her arms as Koko plops into one of the recliners. "So, when are you going to tell him?"

"He already rented out Hartley's for Thanksgiving. Our family and friends will be there, so I'm thinking about telling him then. I'm mean, it's only three weeks away. What do y'all think?" I glance between the two, searching for any sign of disagreement, but I'm met with nodding and smiles.

"Yes, I think that's a great idea! He's gonna be speechless." Koko agrees, finally settling her daughter in her lap.

MyIesha grins, nodding again as she rocks Makai gently. "You're trying to make my brother shed tears, huh."

"No, no. I just thought—"

"Erin, I'm joking. Seriously though, this is gonna be a day that neither one of you forgets." Iesha smiles again, then pulls herself up, heading toward the kitchen.

As this new reality sinks deeper into my heart, I realize that I *want* this. I want to have Harmone's baby. Never in a million years did I think I would see him again. I always hoped, never fully allowing myself to entertain it. Now, here I am with the man that captured my heart fifteen years ago, about to have his baby. Even after we both moved on, we managed to find our way back to each other. I can't wait to share this news with my Harmone. I can't wait to gaze into his beautiful mocha irises and reveal to him that we created a tiny human out of our infinite love for one other. I won't worry about what's ahead because what's happening right now, in this moment, is enough to make me believe that there is such a thing as fate and I will embrace our baby as it is… a gift handcrafted just for us.

CHAPTER 46

Thanksgiving

Mike

I check my phone for the third time as I slide into one of the high back leather stools at Hartley's. Brooklyn should be here any minute. Smooth R&B fills my ears as I glance around, taking in the transformation of the lounge. Round festive fall-themed lanterns hang from the ceiling, along with soft white stringed lights making the entire lounge feel homey. Fall wreaths decorate the soft taupe walls. Ornamental Indian corn and small round pumpkins sit in bunches around the circular glass bar. Happy Thanksgiving banners hang above the karaoke stage; small bales of hay on either side of the steps.

I nod my head in satisfaction as I watch the event planners gather their things and head for the door. As I scan the tables, they're all strategically placed, adorned in burnt orange and creamy beige tablecloths with beautiful deep orange- and wheat-colored papas in shimmering bronze glass vases. They're placed perfectly in the center of each table along with soft glowing flameless tea candles surrounding the centerpieces.

Everything is just as I envisioned it would be. All that's missing is— I smell the familiar scent of coconut and cucumber melon, then a light tap on my shoulder. I swivel in the bar stool and I'm stunned speechless. Erin always looks damn good in anything she wears but today she is fuckin' edible in her emerald-green plaid shirt, and don't get me started with the sweater she's wearing.

God. Damn.

I wet my suddenly dry lips, giving her another once over. "You *really* want me to drag you into one of these storage rooms and give you the D, don't you?" Taking her hand, I lift her arm up, twirling her around to get a full view. That damn green mid-bareback, form fitting sweater makes her breast seem fuller…. no, they're fuckin' huge. Why didn't I notice this shit before?

Erin beams at me, tucking a loc of wavy raven hair behind her ear; her deep-set dimple making its presence known . "Like what you see?" She winks at me, strutting as if she's on a runway; her green suede knee-high boots clicking as she peers back at me, a hand on her hip. "Well?"

"I *love* what I see. Why don't you come back over here so I can show you."

"Sorry GQ, we have company." She blows me a kiss. "Maybe later. I have a surprise for you anyway. I think you're gonna love it."

"You goddamn *right*, later." I bite my lower lip to keep from moaning. "I'm lookin' *forward* to this surprise of yours." I unashamedly ogle her as she sashays away from me to greet my brother, Koko and their overactive daughter already making a beeline toward the bales of hay. I chuckle as Marlon takes off after her, then I turn back in my seat where I'm met with Tony the tenacious bartender.

Tony smiles as he takes a notepad out. "Happy Thanksgiving, Mike! What can I get for ya?"

"Happy Thanksgiving, Tony. Just a sprite for me."

"No problem!" He smiles again. "I see everything worked itself out." He nods over at Brooklyn.

I smirk, leaning my elbows against the bar as he sets a napkin in front of me, then a tall glass of sprite with ice. "You would be correct…." *Enthusiastic bartender Tony.* It's right on the tip of my tongue, but I stop myself at the last second. "Everything changed for me that night." I take a sip of my sprite. "I know I'm a year late but thank you. I was an ass to you and—"

"No worries. Believe me, I've dealt with worse." He gives me a pat on the shoulder, then repositions the Indian corn and pumpkins. "So, I take it you guys are pretty serious." He points to my suit. "I mean, matching outfits is as serious as it gets, right?"

I unbutton my three-piece dark green suit, giving him a view of the inside. "Right down to the green paid interior and handkerchief." I chuckle, then reach inside my suit jacket, pulling out the velvet box, opening it. "How's *this* for serious?"

He gives a low whistle. "That's pretty major. Nervous?"

"Scared shitless, but she's my forever." I release a nervous breath before closing the box.

"Heads up." He gives a quick nod and I jerk my head in the direction he nodded to see Brooklyn meandering my way.

I instantly stuff the box back into place, then spin around to greet her. "Can't stay away I see." I stand, gripping her by the waist.

"Don't flatter yourself, GQ. My parents are here and they wanna say hi." She gives me a quick peck on the lips. "Oh, Ann will be here in another half hour and *who knows* what time Zeke will be here. He says he's gonna be a little late. That's a first for *him*." She rolls her eyes. "When is Chris coming?"

"About forty-five minutes."

"Oh, I can't *wait* to see the look on their faces." She intertwines her fingers with mine and we head over to her parents.

They're seated at one of the tables near the karaoke stage. Erin doesn't know that I already spoke with her parents weeks ago, clueing them in on what I had planned and asked for their blessing. They were ecstatic; said they wanted a ring side seat for the occasion. It's why they specifically chose to sit near the stage. I grin as we approach the table. I can't wait to make my promise to Brooklyn a reality tonight.

###

Leave it to Chris to be over three hours late. I get it though. His parents sprung a surprise visit on him this year, so that's where he's been. Dinner has already been served, light music fills the large space and laughter mingled with conversation soaks up the atmosphere. Leaning against the far back wall near the karaoke stage, I have a full view of the lounge. Everyone I need to be here is here: Mr. Leeman and Erin's coworker, Liz the gossip. Marlon and his family, Iesha and hers, Erin's parents', and sister Anyah. I even wanted *Jermaine* here. I didn't think George would make it in time because he's been on a mission to find his brother, but he flew in yesterday, surprising the hell out of me when he showed up at my penthouse with Marlon. The only ones missing are Chris and Zeke, and Chris should be here soon. I'm still not sure what time Erin's brother will be here but he promised he'd show.

I check the time on my watch before pulling out my cellphone to call Chris. He answers on the first ring. "I'm ten minutes away. I had to drop my parents off at their hotel."

"You know you could've brought them with you, right? I would've loved to see them."

"Yeah, it was the first thing I asked them but they'd gone through all of the trouble of pre-planning dinner reservations. I didn't want to ruin anything. Besides, they were pretty worn out from the long plane ride. They *do* wanna see you before they leave Sunday, though."

"Lookin' forward to it." I'm silent for a minute, freakin' out over the fact that my mind has drawn a complete blank of what I was planning to say to Erin before I proposed. "I had an entire speech prepared, Chris. I knew the shit like I know the color of my skin. Now, it's like a vacuum sucked the entire fuckin' speech from my memory. I can't—"

"Breathe, Mike. Look into her eyes and speak from your heart. You'll find the words."

I allow Chris's statement to saturate my thoughts as I take a deep breath in. I glance over at my Brooklyn as she laughs with her sister, Iesha and Koko. She's glowing, her infectious laughter filtering through the room causing a peace to fill me. "Thank you."

"No need to thank me. Everything will go as planned, okay?"

"I know." I smile. "See you soon." I end the call, my heart pounding. Not because of any fear that something will go wrong, but because Erin is gonna finally become my wife.

Damn. Anyah is just as obsessed with taking pictures as her sister. We've been doin' a photo shoot for the past five minutes and she doesn't show signs of stopping. Just as Anyah moves me into position next to George and Koko for another photo op, I see Chris stride into the lounge, already out of his coat. His dark hair is an organized mess, and his tanned skin is tinged with pink from the harshness of the wind as he makes his way toward us. As he rakes his fingers through his hair, I wave over to Erin to get her attention. "Dimples, incoming!" She turns in the direction I'm staring and a toothy grin breaks out on her face as she makes a mad dash over to me, interrupting her sister's picture.

Anyah frowns. "What the hell, Erin? That was the perfect shot!"

"Sorry Ann, what I need to tell GQ can't wait." Erin encloses her arms around my waist as Chris stops just off to the side of Anyah.

Anyah rolls her eyes. "It's doesn't look like that to—"

"Liz? What are you doing here?" Chris's eyes widen in shock, unable to move from his position as he gawks at her.

Anyah twists toward him so fast, she almost drops her phone. "C-Chris…." Her eyes scan his confused face as he scrunches his brows. "How did you… know—"

"Surprise!" Dimples and I yell with big Kool-Aid smiles on our faces. Dimples moves toward the two, clapping her hands. "Chris, this is my sister, Anyah."

"Wait, what?" He glances between them both, mouth parted. Then he turns fully toward Anyah. "You said your name was Liz. Why did you lie?"

"Technically, I didn't lie." She releases a deep breath. "My middle name is Elizabeth, so I used Liz for short. I didn't know you back then and I didn't wanna use my real name."

"Did you know who I was the entire—"

She shakes her head, creasing her brows. "No! I had no idea you guys knew each other. You believe me, don't you?"

He rakes a hand down the length of his low trimmed beard. "Okay, I can understand not wanting to tell me your real name in the beginning, but when things started getting serious between us, did you, at any point in time, think about telling me the truth?"

She reaches out to touch his arm. "I… Chris, can we *not* do this right—"

"Don't." He shakes his head. "I have my answer." He turns on his heel, heading toward my brother on the farther side of the lounge.

"Chris!" She glances over at me and Erin, then sighs. "What the hell was *that*?" She peers over at Chris for a second, then returns her focus on us. "How long is he gonna be mad at me?"

Taking a few steps forward, I stand beside Dimples. "Believe me, he won't be mad for long. He lo—"

"— *Likes* to distract himself when he's upset. He'll calm down soon, Ann. Don't worry." She gives me a threatening side eye.

I clear my throat. I need to shut the fuck up. "Why don't you get yourself a drink and relax. I'll talk to him." I check my watch. *It's time.* "A little later. I promise."

Anyah gives us a small nod before heading over to the bar. As soon as she's out of ear shot, Erin punches me in the arm. "I'm sure Chris would like to tell my sister he's in love with her *himself*, GQ." She whisper-yells, jabbing me again.

"Point taken, Dimples." I grab her wrist before she can sneak another shot at me. "That did *not* go like I thought it would."

"Tell me about it. We're gonna have to do damage control. Got any ide—"

"Let's do karaoke." I take her hand, leading us to the stage. "You remember this song, don't you?"

She listens for a second. "Of course I do. We sang this together last Thanksgiving." She halts at the steps. "How did we go from helping my sister and Chris to singing." She shakes her head, grinning. "So random, Harmone."

"I love to do random things. I love *you*, don't I?" I stop center stage, handing her a mic, then take one for myself.

"No one likes a smartass, GQ."

I shrug as the melody continues. My heart feels as if it's going to explode out of my chest, its beating so hard. I put the mic to my mouth and begin to sing the opening lines of Always by Atlantic Starr. "Girl you are to me, all that a woman should be, and I dedicate my life, to you, always…."

"— A love like yours is rare…" She starts. "It must have been sent from up above, and I know, you'll stay this way, for always…" She smiles, taking my hand in hers before we both sing together.

As we go into the second verse, my few short lines breeze by. I release her hand, watching her as she turns toward our family and friends to sing her lines. So carefree; her infectious energy swallowing the entire lounge as they start singing along with her.

Taking the velvet box out of my suit jacket, I assume my position on one knee. As the part comes where we harmonize together, Erin notices I'm not singing along and pivots on her feet toward me. The song fades into the background as I gaze into her surprised eyes and smile. The words that eluded me a few hours ago come pouring out of me before I can even take in a calming breath. "I had an entire speech prepared for today, but the words that I practiced don't do this moment justice."

I take in a breath, suddenly overcome with an influx of emotion. Erin's quivering hands land on her belly, her eyes already beginning to gleam with unshed tears. "Twenty years ago, I met a fiery little girl with sandy brown hair, glasses, and a butterfly birthmark. Throughout our childhood and teen years, she was my safe haven. I promised her I would marry her when we were older." I reach for her hand, kissing each fingertip, before peering into her teary eyes again. "Even though we got separated, we found our way back to each other, and I fell in love with her all over again." I grin, recalling the first time we saw one another at Hartley's a year ago. "Before I even realized it was *you*… my Brooklyn." I swallow down the thick lump in my throat; as I feel my eyes beginning to glisten. "You're the reason why I smile, Dimples. You've seen me at my lowest… when I was your broken Harmone, and you still loved me. You believed in me when I didn't even believe in myself. You're my home, Brooklyn… my forever." I lower my head, closing my eyes as I swallow several times, trying to fight back tears, but it's no use. When I return my gaze to the love of my life, her cheeks are already wet. "A lifetime isn't long enough to shower you with everything you've poured into me, but I promise to spend the rest of my life trying." Taking the emerald green and diamond ring from its case, I brush my lips against her knuckles, then find her gleaming bronze eyes. "Erin Avery Brooks… my life…. my soulmate. Will you marry me?"

CHAPTER 47

Erin

Words can't express what I'm feeling right now as I stare down into Harmone's gleaming eyes, holding a gorgeous ring in his hand that not only represents his promise to me, but finality. He's offering me his heart, his love, his devotion. "Oh my god." I whisper; more tears falling as he awaits an answer expectantly…. Oh! I haven't given him an answer! "I have absolutely no doubt that I want to spend the rest of my life with you, Harmone." I spread my fingers open. "Yes, I will marry you." He barely has time to stand and place the ring on my finger before I leap into his arms, bringing his lips to mine. I hear cheering and clapping in the background, but all I care about is this perfectly imperfect man that has me in his embrace right now.

Mike holds my face in his hands, kissing me gently as I melt into his soothing caress. "I love you." He turns us to our cheering family and friends; his smile reaching his eyes. "She said yes!" Interlacing his fingers with mine, he begins to lead us down the stairs, but I stop him. "What's wrong?"

"Nothing's wrong, Harmone. Everything's *right*." I pull his hand so that he is just a step below me, then I place it on my belly. "This is my gift to *you*." His brows crease as he fixes his eyes on me.

"You're…." He trails off as I see him visibly swallow. "Please don't play with me, Dimples."

"I'm *not*, GQ. You're gonna be a wonderful father to our child." I stroke his cheek with my knuckles. The chatter and excitement of our friends and family evaporate into silence as I focus on this wonderfully vulnerable man before me. "I found out a few weeks ago but decided to wait until now to tell you. I wanted your memories of this day to be unforgettable." Harmone flexes his fingers on my stomach as he drops to his knees, and I feel several flutters in my belly causing me to take an audible breath in. "This is something no one can take away from you."

Mike takes a shuddering breath in as I fall to my knees as well. "I didn't think I deserved something as precious as this, Erin. Not after what I've done—"

"Stop. You can't change what happened in the past. You can only learn from it… grow from it, and you *have*." I take hold of his face with my hands. "I'm ecstatic to be carrying your child. I thought you would be *too*."

"I *am*, Erin." A smile graces his handsome face that illuminates his eyes as he kisses me several times. "I *am*. I'm gonna be somebody's father." He whispers, lifting up off the stairs of the karaoke stage, pulling me up with him, then turns to face everyone else. "I'm gonna be somebody's goddamn dad!" Everyone erupts into cheers once more as we step down from the stage.

After about a half hour of congratulations and hugs, Mike and I sit at one of the booths, with two full champagne glasses of sparkling grape juice in hand, clinking the glasses together. I admire the stunning ring on my finger, then swipe my tongue across my top lip in the most provocative way that I can. I *know* he's watching and when I peek up at him, his dark eyes are laser focused on my lips. I chuckle. "It looks like you got something on your mind, GQ." I take a sip of my sparkling grape juice, then place my glass on the table. With the pad of my thumb, I delicately wipe off the wetness from my bottom lip.

"I can think of a few ways I can put that damn tongue to good use." He leans back, palming himself, a panty dampening promise in his heated gaze.

"*Definitely* later." I squeeze my thighs together to ease the building pressure between my legs at the very *thought* of me on my knees in front of GQ.

Desperate for a distraction, I scan the room and notice Nate sitting at the table with my parents in cheerful conversation. My heart warms knowing that my parents and my boss— who's *like* a father— get along so well. Smiling, my eyes travel to the bar where George and Liz, the cougar, are talking; more like Liz is practically throwing herself at the man. I should have known she would try to snatch Koko's brother up. I shake my head, as my eyes finally land on my sister. "How are we gonna help *their* situation?" I nod in the direction of Ann and Chris, who are off in the distance in deep conversation.

"Absolutely nothing. Let them work it out, Dimples. I *know* Chris. When he loves, he loves *hard*. He'll cave." He glances over to them, then back at me, leaning forward. "What happened to your brother?"

"I have no idea. He promised he'd be here." I pout, knowing I look like a whiny brat, but he missed two important events today. "He could have at least called. I'm so pissed at him right now."

"You ready for fatherhood?" Marlon slaps GQ on the back as Koko slides in beside me with a sleeping Eva.

"Do you even have to *ask*? I didn't think it was *possible* to be this happy." He swings his arm around my shoulder, kissing my temple.

Marlon grins, leaning against the booth. "Happiness looks good on you, bro." He draws his attention to me. "So, how far along are you?'

"Five months." I peek over at Mike, as he twists his body to scan me from head to toe. "I had *no* idea I was pregnant. Koko and

Iesha literally had to *tell* me I was."

Mike put his hand over my belly. "You can't be five months. You're not even showing yet." He rubs my stomach through my shirt gently. "How?"

"It's possible. I didn't start showing until I was almost six months. I thought there was something wrong at first, but after I talked to my Ob-Gyn, she said it's normal for first time mothers." Koko touches my hand, offering a small smile and I give her one in return.

Searching the lounge, I spot MyIesha and Jason headed our way. "Here comes my future sister-in-law!" I beam at her as she hands off Makai to her boyfriend, giving me an exaggerated wave. I snicker as I turn my attention to the sound of an opening door.

Everyone turns as Zeke enters. He looks around until he spots me, then holds his hands up. "I'm so sorry we're late. We missed our afternoon flight and had to get the next available one."

"Lies." I roll my eyes. My brother is *never* late. If he missed his flight, it's because of his… *lady friend.* I bet she's the reason—" My jaw damn near hits the table as he holds open the door and Jakyra saunters in with her daughter. There's total silence as she studies every shocked expression among those who know her. I see a hint of nervousness as she shifts on her feet.

Before I have a chance to react, Jason hands little Makai over to Marlon before stalking over to Jakyra, Iesha hot on his trail. He takes his fussing daughter from her mother.

Without warning, MyIesha's fist connects with Kyra's face causing her to stumble back. Her arms flail around as she takes an ungraceful plunge to the glossy surface. Iesha's voice echoes through the shocked room as she glares daggers at the stunned woman on the floor of the lounge. "Welcome home, bitch."

There are audible gasps and shouting as Mike shoots out of his seat. Chris rushes over to grab Iesha as the group glances around at one another. Like a finely tuned instrument, together our voices ring out. "Oh. *Shit*."

THANK YOU FOR READING!

Enjoyed Broken Harmone?

Please consider taking a

second to leave a review!

JOIN M. MARIE WALKER

M.Marie.com

Want To Follow M. Marie

on Social Media?

Facebook

Instagram

 TikTok

 Goodreads

Bookbub

 Twitter

ALSO BY M. MARIE WALKER

My House (The My House Series)

The Basement: Dark Past

ACKNOWLEDGMENTS

To two of the most supportive, talented authors & friends I know and appreciate. Carol Denise Mitchell & Kat Kinney. Your knowledge, advice and feedback has been invaluable to me. I have learned so much from the two of you and appreciate every single thing you have done for me on my literary journey. I am an admirer of your work and will forever be your biggest fan. Thank you so much!

To all the amazing readers who take the time to give indie authors, like myself, an opportunity to share my work. I am deeply appreciative of all the support and love I have been shown thus far and I will continue to create multi-genre worlds just for you.

ABOUT THE AUTHOR

M. Marie Walker is a multi-genre author who loves cats and dogs equally. She's an avid reader and huge Marvel fanatic. M. Marie is also the author of two books: My House Series, book 1 & The Basement: Dark Past.

When she's not writing, she's reading (of course) her fill of all things romance. Whether steamy, dark, contemporary; she's got her nose in it. M. Marie enjoys a good nature walk, the smell of fresh flowers and family-filled outdoor BBQs.

M. Marie Walker adores the multi-genre worlds she creates. Her imagination is never-ending and as long as she has breath in her body, she'll continue to do what she loves for the readers who love it.

* 9 7 9 8 8 6 9 3 1 2 3 9 6 *